THE
EVOLUTIONARY
EMPATH

"'You are not crazy . . . but you're not normal either,' the words that open chapter 1 of *The Evolutionary Empath*, capture the theme of this wonderful book. Rev. Stephanie Red Feather grew up with the vulnerabilities and trials of one who is exceedingly sensitive and attuned to other dimensions. The wisdom and guidance she offers is hard-won and will help illuminate the paths of many who are similarly challenged as well as gifted."

DONNA EDEN, AUTHOR OF *ENERGY MEDICINE*

"All sentience is deeply empathic in nature. . . . In the shamanic traditions of Peru—into which Stephanie Red Feather was first initiated in 2005—the virtue of empathy and the ability to love unconditionally are inextricably connected. This lived experience of embodied empathy sustained by selfless love for all our relations has been given brilliant expression throughout the wisely crafted pages of *The Evolutionary Empath*. Aside from poignantly addressing the species-wide evolutionary imperative behind humankind's current process of spiritual ascension, Red Feather offers readers an extremely practical and long overdue empathy-based methodology capable of transforming all separation into wholeness, uniting the personal with the transpersonal, and consciously choosing love over fear. I highly recommend it!"

DON OSCAR MIRO-QUESADA, ORIGINATOR OF
PACHAKUTI MESA TRADITION CROSS-CULTURAL SHAMANISM
AND FOUNDER OF THE HEART OF THE HEALER (THOTH)

"Rev. Stephanie Red Feather's *The Evolutionary Empath* is a gift of true medicine to us all. There are a great many of us who have never felt normal but have also felt like we are part of a greater paradigm shift of consciousness currently in play. At last we have a guidebook that not only provides conceptual insight into the empathic spirit but also outlines practical steps for managing energy, establishing healthy boundaries, and using one's own inherent gifts to uncover the true self. Rev. Red Feather's book is both smart and warm-hearted, erudite and clear. *The Evolutionary Empath* is a navigation tool that, if utilized by anyone interested in evolving consciousness, brings hope to a humanity in desperate need of guidance. Having been in ceremony with Rev. Red Feather myself, I can truly say her actions match her words with a tranquil integrity."

DANIEL MOLER, AUTHOR OF *SHAMANIC QABALAH: A MYSTICAL PATH TO UNITING THE TREE OF LIFE & THE GREAT WORK* AND SANCTIONED TEACHER OF THE PACHAKUTI MESA TRADITION

"In the past we empaths were on our own, sorting through our wild and weird experiences, feelings, and knowings and carefully avoiding being locked up or labeled 'crazy.' Today, we have Rev. Stephanie Red Feather's excellent guidebook, *The Evolutionary Empath*. She covers the full spectrum of things you need to know to survive and thrive as a highly sensitive empath. This includes the important topics of energetic hygiene, healthy boundary setting, good self-care, and grounding. A practical guide for you or for the empaths in your life."

LION GOODMAN, PCC, CREATOR OF THE CLEAR BELIEFS METHOD AND COAUTHOR OF *CREATING ON PURPOSE*

THE EVOLUTIONARY EMPATH

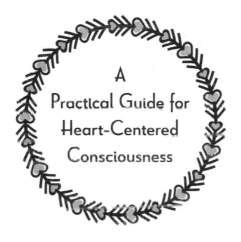

A
Practical Guide for
Heart-Centered
Consciousness

Rev. **Stephanie Red Feather**, Ph.D.

Bear & Company
Rochester, Vermont

Bear & Company
One Park Street
Rochester, Vermont 05767
www.BearandCompanyBooks.com

Text stock is SFI certified

Bear & Company is a division of Inner Traditions International

Cataloging-in-Publication Data for this title is available from the Library of Congress

ISBN 978-1-59143-350-7 (print)
ISBN 978-1-59143-351-4 (ebook)

Printed and bound in the United States by Lake Book Manufacturing, Inc. The text stock is SFI certified. The Sustainable Forestry Initiative® program promotes sustainable forest management.

10 9 8 7 6 5 4 3 2 1

Text design by Virginia Scott Bowman and layout by Debbie Glogover
This book was typeset in Garamond Premier Pro with Gill Sans MT Pro, Futura Std, and Le Havre as display fonts

To send correspondence to the author of this book, mail a first-class letter to the author c/o Inner Traditions • Bear & Company, One Park Street, Rochester, VT 05767, and we will forward the communication, or contact the author directly at **www.bluestartemple.org**.

*To my eight-year-old self
and empaths everywhere*

Contents

PART 2

THE EVOLUTIONARY EMPATH TOOL KIT
The Practice of Being Human and Divine

Foreword

Linda Star Wolf, Ph.D.

If you've picked up this book, then perhaps you are a sensitive human being. While people from all cultures and all walks of life are capable of sensitivity, some of us have an additional dose of extrasensory energies. You may find yourself being highly sensitive or hyperaware of the world around you. You may experience sounds, sights, smells, tastes, and physical touch from a heightened and more concentrated perspective. Perhaps you are able to "pick up on" or "feel into" these different energies surrounding you—especially those of other people and their emotions. As one who was described as an overly sensitive child, I came to realize later on in life that my ultrasensitive nature was indeed not a mishap or curse bestowed upon me, but rather, these extrasensory abilities were my superpowers—special gifts entrusted to me so that I could use them to help change the world and raise consciousness.

As a shamanic teacher seeking to bridge the ancient form of spirituality with the modern world of consciousness, I've had the golden opportunity to meet and support many highly sensitive and/or extrasensory individuals, or empaths, on their healing and transformational journeys to greater embodiment. Through my own personal journey, and through my work as an addictions counselor, shamanic teacher, and psychospiritual guide, I've come to realize that being "sensitive," or empathic, is completely natural. By "sensitive" we mean "in tune with the shared connection to the world around us." From my perspective, having this connection and being able to access it regularly does not just make us sensitive; it makes us shamanic!

I believe that all animals, including human beings, are born with this sensitive and shamanic connection to the world. We are born in tune with our environment, the forces of nature, the other members of our tribe, and all of life around us. This connection—these extra-sensory and shamanic abilities—is our birthright as beings indigenous to the Earth. Through the socialization process of infancy, childhood, and adolescence, we learn and may even be encouraged to suppress and repress these innate abilities. As we continue to grow and develop, we may find ourselves using alcohol, drugs, or other substances to help us numb out and turn down the volume of the world around us. In my field of addictions recovery, I find that a lot of active addicts are really highly sensitive empaths doing their best to survive in a highly stimulating world congested with emotional turmoil and active trauma.

Which brings me to why it is an absolute honor and privilege to write the foreword to this extraordinary, timely, and transformative book. In *The Evolutionary Empath,* Stephanie Red Feather gives voice to the way of the empath. Imparting wisdom from her own personal experience as a sensitive being, Stephanie explains how being an empath is a "choice made at a soul level to support the evolution of humanity." Within these pages, you will find not only a new framework for living life as an empath but also grounded applications, daily practices, and practical skills that will aid in your day-to-day journey as an empath.

When I first met Stephanie, it was evident that she was a divine feminine change agent committed to self-discovery and personal transformation and to sharing her gifts with other kindred spirits. Stephanie's life journey, including achieving a degree in applied mathematics, becoming a respected Air Force officer, and, over the past fourteen years, throwing herself fully into experiential healing practices, has gifted her with a unique perspective that allows her to engage with the world in a versatile and integrated way—bridging both the left and right hemispheres of the brain.

In 2015, when Stephanie began her studies with me and my shamanic psychospiritual organization, Venus Rising Association for Transformation, she was a highly developed and intuitive student, with a natural gift for soaking up the teachings like a sponge. It was a true pleasure to witness her growth and watch her integrate these shamanic teachings into her vast wealth of knowledge and understanding. As she progressed through our university—Venus Rising University for Shamanic Psychospiritual Studies—she quickly budded into her sacred purpose and bloomed into an integrative and embodied empath dedicated to planetary service, evolution, and change.

As one of her mentors and guides throughout her doctorate program, I witnessed Stephanie emerge fully into her sacred purpose as she began working with private clients, facilitating workshops, and developing concrete material that became supportive not only to herself but also to those she worked and engaged with. I encouraged Stephanie to merge these materials—these powerful tools and techniques—with her dissertation and turn this fusion into a book, sharing the integrative and evolutionary wisdom she obtained through her own trials, joys, and tribulations as an empath dedicated to raising consciousness. Even at her manuscript's earliest stages, I could see how her work and the information weaved throughout would be a guiding light and provide validation to the scores of individuals worldwide who walk the empath road.

The material you hold in your hands is rich in personal life experience and detailed with researched and accredited information, and through these pages you will learn practical daily exercises that will support you on your personal life journey. As you travel forward, I encourage you to read this book with an open mind and an open heart and to know that on some level we are all born sensitive and empathic. Some of us have been fortunate enough to hold on to these qualities amidst all the forces that seek to repress and suppress our sensitive superpowers.

In my own work of seeking to awaken people's inner shamans, I find that the majority of the individuals who have retained their empathic abilities or reclaimed them through processes such as the Shamanic Breathwork process, soul return work, and other shamanic psychospiritual practices are the ones who are able to greatly influence and change the world. I believe this to be true because empaths are sensitive shamanic souls who know the power of emotional intelligence and intuition and, most importantly, understand the vital importance of living life from one's heart. In a world filled with mass populations disassociated from the violence and daily traumatic turbulence on our planet, we need people and practices that guide us back to our heart, remind us of our innate sensitive nature, and shine light on humanity's shared connection with one another.

I truly believe that humanity is on the brink of reaching a new octave of being, and empaths and shamans are on the leading edge, accelerating us forward into this new paradigm of consciousness. As I conclude, I leave you with the same thought I opened with: if you've picked up this book, then perhaps you too are a sensitive human being. If you find that this thought resonates deep within you, then perhaps you chose to come to Earth at this time with a mission—an energetic blueprint for change and transformation. Perhaps your sensitivity is a superpower for you to use to complete your mission and enrich the lives of those around you. Perhaps you are here to awaken and evolve humanity to its next octave of consciousness, where we all remember our heart and embody its soulful wisdom in our everyday lives. Perhaps this is your mission. Do you choose to accept it?

LINDA STAR WOLF, PH.D., shaman, author, and creator of the Shamanic Breathwork process, is president and founder of the Venus Rising Association for Transformation and the Venus Rising University for Shamanic Psychospiritual Studies and cofounder of the Shamanic Mystery Tours. For more information, visit www.shamanicbreathwork.org.

Acknowledgments

To my beloved, Joseph, words cannot convey my gratitude. You have been my rock, my unwavering support, my grounding rod. This book would not have been possible without the space you created and the belief you held in who I am and what I am here to do. Your attention to the practical allowed me to purposefully journey through the multiple dimensions and realms of spirit where I could collect the experience, inspiration, and understanding necessary to coalesce into this book. You are a "closet empath" and I love you for your sensitivities and nurturing. My heart is at home in your loving care and tender devotion. I am rich because of you. I love you.

To Linda Star Wolf, my mentor and friend, thank you for your vision and your fire. Through your university, I was able to attain both of my advanced degrees, and this book became a reality as my doctoral project. Because of your belief in me and my sacred work, you introduced me to Inner Traditions • Bear & Company, which was the key to this book becoming a published reality. The day I received word of its acceptance for publication was a trajectory-changing moment in my life. It is a rare gift when you know your life has metamorphosed the moment it happens. I heard the cogs of the Universe moving into place. Thank you for your Aquarian spirit and your genuine desire to lift others up and let them shine.

To my sister Leslie, thanks for being the epitome of my foundation. Through every aspect of my life you have been there, looking out for me and cheering me on. You have been the consistent voice of reason, love, compassion, and acceptance. Your presence in my life provides my "home anchor." No matter where I adventure off to (physically or astrophysically!), you are the unfaltering family rock. I cherish your presence and support in my life.

To my most influential mentors—Carol Rydell, Gary Langston, Oscar Miro-Quesada—and all of those who were teachers and guides, thank you. I could not have moved through so much transformation with any modicum of grace without each of you.

To my family of origin—Mom, Dad, and all of those alive and in spirit—thank you for being my soul family, my co-journeyers. Everything that has happened to me has made me who I am, and you have each had a role to play in my making. Mom, I especially know how challenging it was raising an empath while being one yourself. Our souls have been on a very special journey this lifetime, and this book would not be possible without your belief in my free spirit. I will forever be your "Black-Eyed Susan."

To all of my clients, students, friends, and peers, I send you my deepest gratitude for the ways in which you have contributed to my growth and created the experiences and foundation for this important work.

And last but not least, I thank my soul. Thank you for your guidance, wisdom, perspective, and encouragement, and for the magic you connect me to every single day.

A Wish, a Mission, and a Hundred Monkeys

I am an empath. But for the first thirty years of my life, I didn't know it, and I *certainly* didn't know how to cope in the world as an empath.

At my lowest points I was in total despair, with no clue of who I was, what value I had to offer the world, or how to improve my circumstances. I endured over three decades thinking that everything I felt was mine. I withstood being labeled emotional, fragile, unstable, or too sensitive. I was internally tormented, wondering why everything affected me so strongly. I thought I was too weak or unfit to handle the "real world."

When I wasn't conscious of the fact I was an empath, I simply believed what everyone told me. That's Stephanie. She's just emotional. Or dramatic. Or moody. Or weird. Once I became aware of the concept of being an empath, it helped . . . a little. But at the same time it opened up an entirely new world with which I was completely unfamiliar. Yes, there was a name for "this thing I was," but now what? I still had to figure out the daily task of living life.

When my awakening began, there was very little information available to help me navigate life as an empath. It was an agonizing, confounding, and oftentimes lonely quest. I had an arduous road ahead of me that included learning to reclaim and maintain my identity in relationship, meticulously tend to my energy field, restore my personal sovereignty, fully inhabit my own body, and live from my center. Heck, I didn't even know what—let alone where—my center was when this journey began. But the outcome was worth every scar and every scream.

MY WISH

My wish is that you don't spend as much time bumping into walls, cussing at God, and wallowing in doubt as I did. It is time for empaths to stop *enduring* life and start embracing our role as wayshowers. We deserve joy! And we have a purpose far more extensive and compelling than being the canary in the coal mine of our lives. More than anything, I want you to know you're not crazy. Quite the opposite in fact . . . you are incredibly brave to come onto the planet at this point in our evolution! You have a tribe and you have a purpose.

I see myself as your navigator. You're the pilot, and you are in charge of all the choices in your life. Yet I do have a map, and this is territory I've explored for many years now. I have identified the tricky spots that cause your altimeter to spin backward and your stomach to do a loop-the-loop. I've become adept at troubleshooting problems and getting back on course. And, best of all, I've uncovered that all along we haven't just been wandering aimlessly . . . we were given a special mission!

Life as an empath is not easy. I know it. It is my hope that the lessons, tools, practices, mind-sets, and epiphanies I have gained from my travails will make your journey easier, less painful, and possibly even inspiring. And certainly without all the gnashing of teeth. There is a place for you in the cosmos, and you are here for a noble purpose.

Shall we start the engines?

WHO THIS BOOK IS FOR—
THE MICROCOSM

This book is for empaths, whether you know yourself by this name or not. It is written for all of you who have been called too sensitive or emotional. Who have abilities of perception that others don't possess and who were probably even ridiculed for them. It's for those of you who know you're "different" but can't find your tribe or figure out where you fit in. It's for those of you who wonder if you'll ever be able to fully function in the world. Or, if you've figured out how to be functional, you wonder if and how you can truly thrive and step unreservedly into your dreams.

It's for the nurses, massage therapists, shamans, intuitives, artists, health care workers, energy healers, mediums, coaches, therapists, counselors, psychics, and change agents. And it's for the scientists, engineers, pharmacists, computer programmers, military members, factory workers, financial advisors, lawyers, teachers, politicians, waiters, and bankers.

While most conscious empaths fall into the former group, there are plenty of closet empaths in every walk of life, profession, and corner of the world. The latter group tends to contain the empaths who have forgotten they are empaths. Since empathic qualities don't usually jibe so well with more conservative, left-brain-type environments, these are often people who were forced to shove their "special" qualities so far down in the cellar that they no longer remember their true nature. Yet buried or not, they are still plagued by difficulties and challenges as a result of their empathic nature.

What kinds of qualities am I talking about? The following lists will give you an idea. I have provided a more comprehensive list in chapter 4 that you can use as a checklist to see which qualities you identify with.

Empaths often struggle with the following challenges:
- Drawing boundaries
- Experiencing codependent relationships
- Feeling overwhelmed
- Taking on everyone else's emotions
- Standing up for themselves or saying no
- Addiction to alcohol, drugs, food, sex, or patterns of behavior
- Feeling extreme sensitivity to any amount of disharmony in their environment (people or things)
- Becoming overstimulated from noise, light, scents, too much information, or too many people
- Achieving adequate self-care and energy hygiene practices

Empaths may also have the following qualities:
- Strong intuition or psychic abilities
- An ability to perceive subtle energies or the unseen realms or see angels, apparitions, or the dead
- A predisposition toward paranormal experiences
- An uncanny ability to tune in to other people's emotions and feelings
- Clairvoyance (clear seeing), clairaudience (clear hearing), clairsentience (clear feeling), or claircognizance (clear knowing)
- Ease in astral traveling, shamanic journeying, or accessing altered states of consciousness
- Communication with animals, plants, rocks, or trees
- A strong desire to serve, support, or heal others
- An innate connection to the natural world, God, spirits, nature, or animals
- A sensitivity to the energy of everything in their environment, causing them to often adjust knickknacks, furniture, color, light, sound, et cetera

While there is no magic number of qualities that definitively make you an empath, even finding a few that resonate with you makes them worth noting and investigating. I believe empathic expression lies on a continuum, expressing to an extreme degree in some while barely registering consciously in others. This is due, in part, to the fact that so many empaths have completely buried their empathic abilities. Why? Because for most of us, our special sensitivities were not met with acceptance, understanding, encouragement, or mentoring during childhood, so we learned to shove them underground. If that's you, then I encourage you to not put so much emphasis on how many qualities "fit" you but to listen to that part of you that drew you to this book. You picked it up for a reason.

And more important than how many qualities do or don't resonate is this question: What is your relationship to the characteristics you noted in the lists above? Are you fully conscious of your empathic qualities? Do you embody them, appreciate them, love them, and allow them to shine? Have you pursued your inner work and learned the skills to healthily manage your sensitivities, personal energy field, and relationships?

Or do you hide, deny, or suppress your talents? Do you question your own sanity, mental stability, or ability to function "normally" in the world? Have you resigned yourself to getting your energetic butt kicked every time you go out in public, follow your passion, or engage in meaningful relationships? Have you reluctantly adapted to being constantly misunderstood, judged, or ridiculed?

Or maybe you've kept a lid on this aspect of yourself for so long that you can't recognize how much of your own life-force energy lies trapped as a result. Instead, you have grown accustomed to a certain level of resignation, apathy, daily anxiety, and containment. You know you have passions, desires, and dreams, but you've decided that it's just too hard to follow them and there's too much to overcome.

Wherever you fall on the spectrum of acceptance and awareness, you are not alone. No matter how many empathic qualities you have or to what degree they express or are suppressed, this book is designed to help you embrace your empathic self and relate to your unique qualities as an asset and not a liability. And it is intended to help you unleash your trapped life-force energy so that you have more vitality and passion to apply to the pursuit of your goals and dreams! On a human level, this book will give you the skills, mind-sets, and practices to understand and accept your nature, to thrive as an empath, and to live your life with confidence and authenticity.

But that's not all there is to it. There's a much bigger reason you are here.

WHO THIS BOOK IS FOR— THE MACROCOSM

This book is for those of you who wish to embrace and manage your sensitive natures, but even more profoundly, it is for those who are *seeking an entirely new paradigm*—one that illuminates your place in the cosmos and gives you a sense of belonging and purpose. It is for all of you who chose—at a soul level—to incarnate on this planet right now to help humanity evolve into a higher consciousness.

On some level, you've known in your gut there was a *reason* you were born with this special set of qualities. Maybe you've considered them a burden. Maybe you've turned your gifts into a thriving business. Or maybe you've shoved them deep underground and picked up this book with great skepticism. No matter where you are on the continuum, or whether you've known you were an empath for a long time or are just now discovering the term, at an intuitive level you know you came here . . . to this planet . . . right now . . . for a reason.

And that's because you did. You are the new human blueprint.

"I'm the *what?*" you ask.

You are the new human blueprint.

I believe we as empaths chose—at a soul level—to help humanity move into heart-centered consciousness. The emergence of so many empaths in recent decades isn't a random occurrence. It is the next level in our human evolution—what I call the "empathic big bang." Those of us present on the planet right now are here to help anchor the new human blueprint as we ascend into higher consciousness. Many ancient civilizations believed in (and documented) a grand cycle of time called the Great Year, a 24,000-year cycle with equal periods of ascending and descending consciousness. We are currently about 1,500 years into the ascending cycle. (I will go into the Great Year in much more detail in chapter 2.) As empaths, we *chose* to incarnate right now with our special collection of qualities because, quite simply, it is time. And, as such, we are uniquely qualified for this mission as wayshowers.

Presently it may seem like we are an anomaly (and at times it may certainly feel like we are premature). But truly, we are the new norm! Trendsetters aren't known to be rule followers. They are rule breakers. They do things, see things, know things, and believe things before they are popular or accepted. Your life experiences have prepared you for this unique role. Have you been the black sheep? The weirdo? The one cast out, judged, misunderstood, or ridiculed by your family? Maybe, just maybe, instead of them being here to teach you, you are here to teach them. Instead of your family, friends, workplace, and society trying to get you to fit into their mold, is it possible that you are really here to break the mold altogether?

Being an empath is an honor. And it is the way forward. Instead of walking through life hiding your exquisite brilliance, can you instead walk in full brightness believing—*knowing*—that you are the prototype for the next phase of human evolution? Can you embrace the risk of being different? Can your human consciousness retrieve the memory of your soul's commitment to this work? Can you accept, with humility and confidence, your mission—however small or large—to contribute a higher vibration to the collective?

THE MORPHIC FIELD OF
THE EVOLUTIONARY EMPATH

I wrote this material with the intention of not only informing my readers, but *activating* them. I see this book as a transmission tool, channeling signals directly from a higher source to awaken your inner knowing so that you may remember who you are and why you chose to incarnate right now.

With this body of work I am consciously engaging a morphic field—the field of the evolutionary empath! A morphic field (also known as a morphogenetic field) is *a field that influences the pattern or form of things.* Everything in the universe has consciousness. A morphic field is a type of consciousness that shapes form, pattern, and organization.

Morphic fields were originally postulated by Rupert Sheldrake as he was exploring how organisms develop and investigating what factors influence or shape individual development. To explain how a form comes into being, he suggests that you must have a cause of that form, implying that something tells the form what to become. In biology, more form comes from less form, meaning life starts as something tiny, such as a seed or an egg, and then becomes a tree or a cheetah or a shark. Sheldrake's observations and thought process led him to conclude that something aside from genes and chemicals gives an organism its shape.

To illustrate this more clearly, think of the process of constructing a building. You can't even begin to erect the foundation without knowing what's going to go where, how much of a particular material should be used, and in what order the building tasks should be done. The same fundamental elements—concrete, brick, mortar, steel, wood, glass, paint—can produce endless possible outcomes for the building's final appearance. So you must first start with the architect's plan, or blueprint. This blueprint dictates the order of construction, the amount of materials, and the shape, size, and purpose of the building. It is the vision that creates the final product where all the materials are assembled in harmony with one another and the entire structure as a whole has integrity and cohesion.

Morphic fields are like invisible architect's blueprints that shape an organism as it develops. In the case of this book, the "organism" is the empath, at both an individual and an archetypal level. The evolution of a morphic field can be likened to a habit where a specific energy or frequency is reinforced by doing the same thing over and over. As more empaths incarnate, the energetic field of the empath is forming and gaining strength and resonance. Resonance can be created from similar thoughts, behaviors, cultures, or collectives in which these things vibrate in sympathy with each other. This sympathetic resonance increases the intensity of that vibration, so the more empaths who connect into this field, the stronger and more developed the field becomes.[1]

This phenomenon is similar to the hundredth monkey effect, whereby a new behavior or idea spreads rapidly by unexplained means from one group to all related groups once a critical number of members (critical mass) exhibit the new behavior or acknowledge the new idea. This experience essentially points to the existence of a global atmosphere of consciousness. In *Power vs. Force,* David R. Hawkins speaks of a database of consciousness, or a communal form of consciousness, to which all beings are connected (whether they are consciously aware of the connection or not). Once enough members access the field, a common frequency of consciousness is established.

What does all of this mean? In short, it means that learning something new becomes easier once others have learned it because the accumulated resonance creates a morphic field, which is strengthened through repetition. Further, with the addition of others having similar resonance (more and more empaths arriving on the planet), new information and variety within the field can be generated and integrated. This makes it easier to access the consciousness, knowledge, and intelligence that exist within the field.

In layman's terms, the morphic field of the evolutionary empath has been established. Yet at the same time it is still developing, maturing, and gaining strength and momentum. You are not alone! There is an energetic field—an intelligence—available for you to connect with and benefit from. By actively stepping into this field, you have access to the wisdom and consciousness of those who came before you. And by deliberately choosing to accept your role in the evolution of humanity, you can contribute your experience to the field, thereby making it easier for the ones coming after you to understand their place, use their tools to thrive, and fulfill their mission.

HOW THIS BOOK IS ORGANIZED

This book is designed to give you practical tools you can apply in your daily life as well as a big-picture context to help you understand your place and purpose in the evolution of human consciousness.

In part 1, "Making Peace with Yourself: Understanding Your Nature," I start by providing a higher-level, bird's-eye view so you can identify the larger framework and begin to locate yourself inside the bigger picture and connect to the morphic field of the evolutionary empath. I think of chapter 1 as the welcome-home hug you get from your favorite grandmother whom you haven't seen in years. It is a reassurance that you are not crazy and that being an empath is, in fact, a real thing.

In the rest of the chapters in part 1, I set the foundation, from locating ourselves inside the current cycle of ascension to providing a definition of the term *empath* that includes a comprehensive list of qualities, titled "Characteristics of the Five Empath Qualities," which you can use as a checklist if you like. In this bigger-picture context, I explain the Great Year, delve into our evolution as empaths, and offer explanation as to why we are such an anomaly.

In part 2, "The Evolutionary Empath Tool Kit: The Practice of Being Human and Divine," you'll get practical, rubber-meets-the-road explanations, skills, mind-sets, exercises, and practices to help you thrive in the world as an empath. Accompanying this will be a healthy dose of ideas, such as radical self-care and the release of unhealthy patriarchal and religious influences that challenge the current paradigm. While difficult to choose a single most-important place to start, I believe knowledge of our energy field, creating healthy energy hygiene practices, and understanding the nature of boundaries and practicing them are the most critical competencies to establish. I address these in detail in chapters 7 through 9 and include plenty of exercises and examples.

Because part of our mission is to help humanity move into fourth chakra or heart consciousness, we cannot deny or ignore the influence of the divine feminine. (Originating from ancient Indian culture, a *chakra*—Sanskrit for "wheel"—is an energy center in the body. There are generally considered to be seven major chakras, each with its own focus, purpose, and influence on consciousness and life-force energy.) Heart consciousness is feminine, while intellect consciousness is masculine, and there is a dire need to reestablish a healthy balance—a conscious equal partnership—between the two energies. I explore these concepts in great detail in chapter 10, examining and distinguishing masculine from feminine and *divine* masculine from *divine* feminine, since it is important to understand and develop a personal relationship with both equally if we are to adeptly hold heart-centered consciousness for humanity.

Chapter 11 deeply explores the influence of the patriarchy and religion on our concept of what it means to be a good person. This concept almost always includes some version of sacrifice and putting others first, which implies putting ourselves last. I was surprised and yet not really surprised at how insidious these influences are and how far down the rabbit hole they took me. It is also important to shift our definition of service to recognize that service does not equal sacrifice. Through the exploration of some common archetypes, such as the monk/nun, martyr, and servant, we can begin to deconstruct the influences that have kept us in a place of deficit and sacrifice for millennia.

My exploration of the patriarchal "good person" concept became so robust that it naturally led me to the topic of chapter 12: radical self-care. Self-care is a necessary and indispensable practice for empaths, not a luxury. This flies in the face of the programming that implies that the more we sacrifice, the more we are revered and valued. Radical self-care requires nothing short of a total paradigm shift.

Embodiment is a pillar of my sacred work in the world, and we can't talk about holding the frequency of heart-centered consciousness if we aren't in our bodies to do it! There is a disembodiment epidemic on the planet, and spiritual bypass is rampant in many spiritual communities. In my view, you cannot be grounded and present in your body if you only focus on living in the upper, more spiritual chakras. Of course, it's a lot easier and certainly more pleasant to live from there, but it's an incomplete and half-lived existence. Embodiment requires the difficult and dense labor of working on your shadow and your inner child, healing unresolved issues and/or sexual trauma, and working through fears and whatever else is hiding out in your lower chakras that is keeping you from being present and fully in your body. Chapter 13 explores the idea of embodiment—what it means and why it's important—and provides practical lists and exercises to assist you in learning to inhabit yourself and recognize when you leave your body.

Chapter 14 is the logical outcome to all the previous chapters as it helps you reclaim your identity by living from your own center. By this last chapter you will have hopefully located yourself inside the larger framework of the evolutionary empath and the morphic field and will be ready to use your skills and knowledge to shift into a life practice of self-definition and self-validation.

To some this might feel like an impossible task because we have lived for so long defining ourselves and constructing our identity through other people. Learning to live in your center requires that you have a center to begin with, which means, to some degree, that you have to know yourself! There has to be something "solid" you can locate so that you have something to return to when you are knocked off balance. This can be a massive challenge for empaths because we so naturally absorb the qualities, values, and habits of other people, thus losing ourselves in the process. In this chapter, I offer a variety of exercises and practices that will help you regain your sense of self and define your human identity so that you have a center to come home to.

Throughout the book, there will be references to additional exercises, meditations, and activities that you can find either on the Inner Traditions • Bear & Company website or available for free download on my website.

HOW TO GET THE MOST OUT OF THIS BOOK

History has shown repeatedly that mystics and seers knew and understood esoteric, far-reaching concepts long before science was able to prove them. The chakra system, Ayurvedic medicine, and Traditional Chinese Medicine are all examples of systems whose tenets were believed and practiced before there were instruments to measure and prove what the ancient cultures already knew.

This book is not written from the point of view of science, though I do refer to scientific principles here and there, especially when explaining the Great Year. And although I have a degree in applied mathematics and can get my geek on when I want to, I am also a mystic, shaman, priestess, energy healer, artist, star seed, and traveler of the unseen realms. What I share with you is from my experience as well as from what I have been shown by Spirit, the natural world, and observation of my clients and students. It is supported at times by other works related to this field and yes, where appropriate, science, too.

I am grateful for the ability to speak both left-brain and right-brain languages, and I write from both perspectives. This book is part logic, part personal experience and observation, and part "conscious channeling," with time spent in the practical and esoteric realms. I encourage you to engage with this material from both sides of your brain, as there will be tasty nuggets for each.

At the same time, give yourself permission to take in this information through all of your senses and understand that we receive information through more than just our brains. Don't limit yourself by thinking of this as merely an academic or intellectual activity as per our Western training. Know that your entire system is taking in the information: Your body has its own intelligence. Your cells have consciousness. You are more than just your human body. This book is a portal, an invitation, an *activation*. If you choose, you can receive so much more than content. You can experience an epiphany, a shift in perception, a new awareness, a soul retrieval, a reclamation of life-force energy, a game changer.

Allow yourself to recognize and savor divine inspiration and "aha" moments when they occur. These are moments made possible, not because of me, but because *you* have cultivated a space of receptivity. My experience from numerous workshops, classes, and intensives is that, when you show up, slow down, become present, and open your channels of receiving, the messages and guidance that Spirit has been trying to give you can finally register in consciousness. I laughingly refer to this as the paratrooper moment, where I imagine Spirit saying, "Okay, she's open and receptive. Download epiphanies now, now, now!"

Our lives are so busy, output driven, overcommitted, and productivity focused that it is challenging for us to take the time to just be. I invite you to slow down your biorhythms, let go of "doingness," and be in a space of presence and receptivity as you read this material. Cultivating this state in yourself will create the opportunity for illumination on more levels than you could possibly imagine. So take your time. Make notes. Highlight. Circle. Dog-ear. I want you to get—in your bones—that you belong, that you are not alone, and that you are here on purpose.

PART 1

Making Peace with Yourself

Understanding
Your Nature

In the world of personal transformation, nothing happens without a conscious acknowledgment of what is. You cannot change a behavior, belief, quality, or pattern without first being aware of its existence. A familiar example would be an alcoholic. Until the alcoholic can recognize and admit that she is an alcoholic, there will be no healing or transformation, and she will have a continued experience of powerlessness.

When we are unaware of what drives our reactions, motivations, and decisions, it can feel like we are a victim—powerless—like someone else is at the helm of our ship. However, once a pattern, belief, or behavior is in the realm of conscious awareness, it is no longer operating from the shadows. You can identify, acknowledge, and begin to examine it. Bringing it out of the subconscious and into the light of consciousness restores the power of choice!

This represents a critical turning point, because once you are aware of a particular quality and how it drives your life experiences and decisions, you can then recognize when it is at work in your psyche and make a choice in each moment about how you want to respond. Whereas before, you wouldn't have even been aware of the effect it was having on you, let alone that you had a choice in the matter. This initial awareness gives you a starting point for transformation and opens the door to an entirely new perspective and relationship with that quality.

The first half of this book is about bringing into conscious awareness the *who, what, why, when,* and *where* so that you may come into conscious relationship with what it is to be an empath—nay, an *evolutionary* empath—and why your life unfolded the way it did. This is the moment of empowerment where you can give "this thing you've been" a name! When you are able to understand, make peace with, and accept your empathic self, you can begin to heal the split between who you really are and who you've been pretending to be. A demarcation point is created and, along with it, a chance to step newly into authentic purpose and reclaim the power of choice.

You Are Not Crazy (but You're Not "Normal" Either)

When I was a young girl—maybe eight or nine—I was home alone for a short spell, and for reasons I did not understand at the time, I grabbed a knife and started running through the house screaming in a frenzied rage. At some point I put the knife down and started digging my fingernails into my palms, whimpering, as uncontrollable emotions overtook me. I was staring out the window and shifting my weight back and forth like Raymond in the movie *Rain Man*.

Other than bruising my palms, I didn't damage myself or anything in the house, but the episode terrified me. Sans knife, I have had many similar episodes of exploding unpredictably with rage or hysteria or grief throughout my life and especially before I understood that I am an empath. I would find myself sobbing hysterically, stumbling through the house panicked and lost, writhing on the floor in uncontainable grief, or screaming at the top of my lungs to the point where I had no voice for days afterward. Digging my nails into my palms was also a method of choice when my circumstances didn't allow me to scream, cry, or otherwise overtly express my emotions.

These episodes were usually short-lived—a few hours at most—and when the energies ran their course, I returned to "normal." In my earlier years, I didn't have the self-awareness or understanding of energy that I do now—and I certainly didn't know I was an empath—so I was rarely able to predict when one of these intense "attacks" was about to occur. I had no idea that the outbursts were releasing a buildup of emotions that I had taken on from everyone around me. I only prayed that it wouldn't be witnessed. The events were exhausting and incapacitating and left me feeling completely out of control.

Well into adulthood I was scared that there was something really wrong with me. There is a history of mental illness on both sides of my family, and I thought I got a double dose of defectiveness. Through many years of practicing critical awareness, making a lot of lifestyle changes, and engaging in radical self-care (which I'll expand on in later chapters), I have since learned that I am not crazy or mentally deranged.

Yet, to be completely honest, even now there are still times when I get waylaid by strong emotions or overwhelmed by external stimulus. Knowing you're an empath doesn't necessarily make day-to-day life any easier. Being an empath—and remaining functional on a daily basis—takes constant vigilance, deliberate choices (which often run counter to social norms), and a massive toolbox.

I have worked with many fellow empath students and clients who have had experiences and fears similar to mine. Their questions echoed my own: "What is wrong with me?" "Why is dealing with emotions so much easier for other people?" "Am I the only one who feels this way?" "Does anyone else cry as much as I do?" "Why am I so different?" "Am I socially stunted?" "Why am I so sensitive to every little thing?" "Am I crazy?"

It is commonplace to think that whenever you are in the minority, you are the aberration. For our families who didn't understand or know how to assist us, all the messages of our upbringing most likely supported the idea that there was something wrong with us. For example, if you are the only one in your family who communicates with spirits, the rest of the family usually makes it very clear that "that isn't normal," and you should stop it. From messaging like this we conclude that there is something very wrong with us, and if we want to fit in, gain acceptance, have the same opportunities as everyone else, look like we are normal, and be successful, we have to deny or hide our "abnormal" qualities.

Dorian's Story

Dorian's prime memories from childhood are of dark malicious beings showing up in his life and taunting him, often at night. Though he would be on the second or third floor of his house, he would see horrific faces in the window, banging on the glass, laughing at his terror. Most of the time he was the only one who saw these apparitions, but during one occurrence, shadowy beings were banging on all the windows of the house so he ran into his mother's room for comfort. He was the only one who could see the beings, but everyone else heard them and knew something was going on. On a physical level, when these types of energies showed up, Dorian would feel a suffocating pressure on his chest. He would lose his breath and almost become paralyzed.

Even though other household members experienced enough of the same "dark entity" events to render them undeniable, Dorian was often dismissed and ostracized. He was put down by his father and brother for being different and odd, and he was even submitted to psychiatric evaluation by his father. They would often focus on logic, saying, "That wouldn't logically happen." His mother tended to compartmentalize the events, saying, "God will take care of it," and removed herself from the reality of it. Dorian never received validation, comfort, guidance, or acceptance for what he saw and how it affected him. It kept him isolated, separated, and, for a long time, bitter.

Because most people aren't consciously empathic like us and don't understand the origin of our acute sensitivities, we are often dismissed as being thin-skinned, emotionally erratic, living in a dream world, or even mentally unstable. This is often accompanied by the ever popular notion that our entire existence would be vastly improved if we would just grow up or grow a pair. Dorian's story is typical in terms of his family's reaction. If only the solution were as simple as what other people think we should "just" be able to do.

FROM AUTHENTICITY TO COMPLICITY

For most empaths, suppression becomes our modus operandi. In order to cope in our families, societies, and the world at large, we take our precious uniqueness and banish it. Because we had no guides to help us whenever we expressed our empathic nature, it almost always got us into some kind of trouble. So we made an unconscious decision that it is safer to tuck it away and pretend we are someone else.

Here's how that suppression unfolded for me.

I was a very creative and intuitive child. I drew and painted and made all kinds of crafty projects. I went to a performing arts school where I participated in singing competitions, had works displayed in school art shows, performed in dance recitals, plays, and musicals, and wrote for various school publications, and I was also a member of my city dance company.

I was highly sensitive and could tell when other people didn't feel good or were upset. Even as a small child, Mom said I intuitively knew when someone was depressed, was upset, or had had a bad day, and I would go up to them with some form of acknowledgment, such as hugging them or crawling into their lap. (This behavior still exists today, minus the lap part.) In unconscious ways, I would take on the energies of others who were troubled in an instinctive effort to relieve them of their pain. Friends always came to me with their problems.

I was a little medicine woman before I even knew what that was. I even had my special collection of magical items that I kept in a crocheted drawstring bag. Of course, they were just rocks, sticks, costume jewelry, and bits of this and that, but to me they had special meaning and powers.

At age eight, my world blew apart when my parents divorced. I lived with my mom through the eighth grade, visiting Dad during the summer and at Christmas. Life as the child of a single, poor mother was difficult, and I continued to process a lot of grief and anger over the divorce through acting out and being defiant. I know I was a handful for my mother, so the messages started getting confusing. She encouraged me to continue my creative outlets and artistic expressions, but implications such as don't be too big, too much, too loud, or too extreme started creeping into the subtext. I was a big energy for sure, and the collective programming about women and power that lay in my mother's subconscious played out in the messages that shaped me as I moved into young ladyhood.

My mother is also an empath but was completely unaware of it at that time in her life. So I also observed and absorbed her erratic attempts at managing her sensitive nervous system as well as the anger and other repressed emotions seething just below the surface. This added to the conflicting and confusing messages: Bottle up. Smile. Deny. Pretend everything is okay. Medicate. Rationalize. Project. Please others. Hide. Escape into addiction. I couldn't help but be influenced by—and take on—her unresolved issues.

During eighth grade, in the infinite wisdom of a thirteen-year-old, I decided I wanted to go live with my dad and stepmom, and Mom agreed. I naively assumed I would be able to continue my creative and artistic pursuits, but I was dead wrong. My dad and stepmom wouldn't allow it. They didn't value these activities and had no idea how important they were to my mental and spiritual health. I stopped dancing, I stopped singing, and I stopped performing. I was allowed one elective in high school, so I chose to take art for four years. The once gregarious and expressive young lady began the switch to introversion and suppression. Additionally, my stepmother Betty and I had an adversarial relationship, and we fought regularly.

As my high school years progressed, I started to hide deeper inside myself. Stripped of my creative outlets and plagued by Betty's constant harassment, I spent a lot of time alone, outdoors whenever I could, playing in the woods or sneaking into the pasture up the road to visit the horses. I kept to myself. My arguments with Betty became less defiant and turned into me sitting in the chair with my arms crossed, tight-lipped, staring at the floor while she ranted at me. I rarely said a word.

I spent less and less time expressing my authentic self and more time grudgingly morphing into the "good girl" Betty wanted me to be. It constantly annoyed her when I wanted to be by myself, and she falsely assumed I was secretive or hiding something. Clearly I was not a person who was valuable or precious or worth investing in—or understanding—as I was. My wants and needs were of no great concern.

My father left the child-rearing up to Betty and never realized how much damage he contributed by his silence. He rarely stood up for me, stopped her rants, or supported me emotionally. My empathic nature felt entirely exposed and unsafe. My natural sensitivities, gifts, passions, and expressions were slowly being expunged and replaced by directives of hard work, productivity, logic, responsibility, and practical and mental skills.

During my junior year it became time to start thinking about the future. In a moment of reflection, I remember wondering what would happen if I somehow dusted off my performing arts skills and pursued a career as an artist, actor, or performer. But by that time, practicality and logic had taken a firm hold, and I quickly pooh-poohed the idea, as it was not a *sensible* choice. After much deliberation that involved only my head (my heart had long been banished from the decision-making table), I chose to go into the Air Force. I accepted a four-year scholarship in applied mathematics to the Missouri University of Science and

Technology, where I received my commission as a second lieutenant in the United States Air Force upon graduation.

If you're doing a double take about now, wondering if you somehow jumped to another person's story, you're not alone . . . and let me assure you, you're in the same story. The confusion of how a creative, intuitive child who lived in the performing arts world got a math degree and went into the Air Force defined my adolescence and plagued my early adulthood.

In my formative teenage years I had been taught *not* to trust my heart or listen to my intuition, and that much of what naturally wanted to be expressed inside of me was wrong and not valued or desired by the world. My sensitivities were misunderstood and disregarded. They were misattributed to the effects of being melodramatic, the angst of being a product of divorce, or the hormonal swings of an adolescent girl. And added to this misunderstanding was the unintended yet equally potent transmission from my mother about staying small and minding my place as a woman. By the time I left for college, my internal dialogue had begun to mimic and regurgitate the same messages of disdain, rejection, and contempt that I experienced growing up, and they continued to do so for fifteen more years. I became the perpetrator I railed so hard against.

THE SHADOW COMES FIRST: LIVING FROM THE UNHEALTHY ASPECTS OF OUR EMPATHIC QUALITIES

My story is similar to that of many empaths. And, of course, the censoring we experience inevitably destines us to live from the unhealthy aspects of our empathic nature. Why? Because anything that we disown becomes banished to the realm of the shadow.

In simple terms, our shadow is composed of the unloved, disowned parts of ourselves. Because our empathic nature was forced underground, we, in short, abandoned ourselves. But as anyone who has worked with the shadow knows, anything we banish there doesn't just disappear. These emotions, personality traits, and beliefs are still, and always, seeking expression. Until we welcome these pieces back into conscious relationship with ourselves, they will continue to express sideways, at inappropriate times and in unhealthy ways.

When we engage in life from an unconscious place, we are unaware of what truly motivates us. Therefore we are also unaware of what triggers us or why we're behaving the way we are or making the decisions we're making. It seems to be part of the human construct that we live somewhat "half asleep" for the first portion of our life and then at some point we "wake up." This awakening is a time where we recognize that what we've been doing isn't working anymore. We are no longer willing to settle for our current experiences or the results we've been getting. You've probably heard one of my favorite definitions of insanity: *doing the same thing over and over again and expecting different results.* Our individual awakening is a trajectory-changing moment where we suddenly sober up to our insanity. Usually an internal alarm goes off that sounds something like *I can't do this anymore; something has got to change; it's over; this isn't working anymore; I'm going to die if I stay here.*

But up until the point where we have that trajectory-changing epiphany, we're destined to live from the shadow aspect of ourselves. Meaning, we live from a place of low or no consciousness around the choices we're making. We're not living deliberately, we're not making decisions from an adult perspective (because we're often regressed), and we don't understand what motivates us. In living from the shadow, we have old, outdated tapes playing in our head that give us false information. We have unresolved wounds and a neglected inner child. We're slamming up coping mechanisms like we're boarding up the house in a hurricane. The consequence of living from our shadow self is that the unhealthy, unconscious aspects of our personality drive the bus.

In living from the shadow aspects of our empathic nature, experiences like codependence, losing ourselves in relationship, taking on other people's emotions and problems, and struggling with boundaries become our fate. Because we don't know we're an empath and because we've denied this part of ourselves, we move through the world feeling broken and anything but whole.

In examining how living from the shadow shows up for you personally, it is important to understand that no one quality is inherently good or bad. There's a continuum that most behaviors, feelings, and expressions fall along. It's a matter of when and how each characteristic is expressed that determines whether it is operating in the shadow or in consciousness.

For example, being able to merge easily with others and absorb their energetic state is not inherently good or bad. It just is. But if you don't recognize that you merge with every person you come in contact with, you will experience all of the unhealthy consequences that come from unconscious merging. Without being consciously aware that you're doing it, you won't be able to call upon key skills that allow you to balance the merging with appropriate boundaries, grounding activities that help you stay in your center, and vital practices that assist you in clearing energy. You will be compromised and almost certainly end up losing yourself completely. Unfortunately, many of us have spent decades operating this way and haven't been aware of it.

Coping Mechanisms

When we live from the unconscious aspect of our empathic nature, we naturally develop coping strategies to help us survive and manage the elements in our environment. Coping mechanisms (also known as defense mechanisms) are a normal part of our development as humans and no one escapes them. So as empaths, we're not unique in relying on them, and when used for a short period of time, they can be beneficial in helping us deal with and process whatever is happening in the moment. However, when deployed over a long period of time, they become unhealthy avoidance behaviors and sometimes even develop into pathologies or phobias.

Simply put, coping mechanisms are the ways in which we manage internal or external stress. Because of our highly sensitive nervous systems, every day can be a barrage of overstimulation that can quickly lead to overwhelm. From there we can degenerate into a plethora of other unhealthy reactions and behaviors.

Common coping mechanisms include regression, denial, dissociation, passive aggressiveness, projection, overcompensation, suppression, intellectualization (overemphasis on thinking), repression, rationalization, self-harm, and somatization (stress manifesting in the physical body producing symptoms with no discernible cause). There are dozens more. If you desire to understand coping mechanisms at a deeper level, I recommend that you consult a resource on psychology.

Once we reach that critical point of awakening (where our insanity is not working for us anymore), we begin to see the world with new eyes. It is often then that we come face-to-face with our patterns of coping, especially the long-standing, unhealthy ones. And only then, in our newly awakened state of consciousness, do we recognize that these patterns can only hold us back in our effort to grow and thrive.

As empaths, we have had to rely heavily on our coping mechanisms just to manage daily life. Without the tools and conscious mentors to teach us how to clear our energy field, draw boundaries, and identify what is ours from what isn't, our daily interactions, decisions, and stimulus were difficult—if not completely impossible—to navigate.

Different coping mechanisms have predominated through various stages of my life. In my earlier years, regression was a go-to move. I took the regressive pattern of sitting in a chair, arms crossed, staring at the floor while my stepmother ranted at me from my teenage years into my first marriage. For years I couldn't debate or have a challenging conversation with my husband (now ex) because I did not see myself as an equal whose opinions or feelings were valued. I became that silent fourteen-year-old who stared at the floor and wouldn't say anything. It drove him mad, and I understand why. Even now, it takes a lot of effort and consciousness for me to relate to people as an equal when important topics or feelings are being discussed, and especially with someone in a position of authority or whose approval or agreement is important to me.

Coping mechanisms of denial, fantasy, projection, and somatization have all danced in and out of my life as stressors became unmanageable, which of course is when our coping mechanisms are most likely to activate. Times of chaos, stress, trauma, or high pressure illuminate the deficits in our ability to cope or be flexible. Challenging times reveal where our coping strategies are less developed, less mature, or less capable. For many empaths, every day is a day of heightened stress because our sensitive nervous systems process way more than the average human and/or take longer to process and clear than "normal."

Unconscious behavior modification has also been prevalent for me. In the first several decades of my life I was a master at bottling things up. This behavior was also modeled to me by my mother, so it was a particularly tenacious habit to break. I had a tendency to implode instead of explode, so when the energies became too intense, it would result in those frightening episodes of intense emotional eruption, like the incident with the knife I described at the beginning of this chapter.

Rick's Story

Rick is a naturally intuitive, sensitive man who easily tunes in to the unseen realms and perceives energies outside of most people's awareness. Achieving altered states, journeying in the shamanic tradition, and traveling outside his body are all easy for him. He is kindhearted and gentle-natured. Yet you would have to look hard to see those qualities.

Rick's life has been a classic "bad boy" story. He is an addict who has journeyed for years with alcohol and illegal and prescription drugs. He rides a Harley and often dresses in biker garb. He is also a rebellious and defiant rabble-rouser who has been in fist fights and knife fights and has participated in more than one illegal disturbance of the peace.

As with many such boys, his sensitivities were shamed out of him through heavy-handed parenting and poor socioeconomic conditions. He grew up in the school of hard knocks. His needs were too often ignored by parents who were themselves operating from the shadow of their own unresolved issues, and he was made to feel guilty or bad if he didn't exhibit the proper "manly" qualities. He quickly learned a whole host of coping mechanisms just to survive, including shoving down his empathic nature. Approaching his seventh decade of life, he still reveals those sensitive parts of himself only rarely and is continuing to peel off the layers of masks, personas, and coping mechanisms he has draped himself in to survive.

As you begin to consider the coping strategies you have had to employ to keep your empathic nature hidden and safe, I invite you to be gentle with yourself and even grateful. Your psyche is an amazing protector! The mechanisms you deployed to keep you safe, though done subconsciously, served a purpose. But what happens is that long after the threat is gone, the coping mechanisms stay in place. It takes time to recognize and fully comprehend that when something triggers us, it accesses an event that occurred in the past and plops it right in the present moment. Our emotional reaction is therefore actually originating from that point in the past. But because the issue is unresolved, the emotions (and the threat) feel just as real as they did during the original episode years or decades ago.

Add that now to the daily overstimulation we are exposed to and it can seem like an insurmountable task to shift our patterns and believe there is a different, healthier way to conduct our lives. But it can be done. Awareness is always the first, and most crucial, step.

WE'RE ALL EMPATHS
WHEN WE ARE IN SPIRIT FORM

There are many institutions, structures, and belief systems in our society that seem hostile toward our sensitive empathic qualities. We have had to become masters at wearing masks and pretending. And while we might be in the minority in the physical world, it is essential to remember that being an empath is actually our *natural state of being*.

In spirit form, the human constructs of division, separateness, and the need for protection don't exist. We all feel and sense everything in the realm of spirit, although our experience of "feeling" manifests differently in that form. In the spirit world we are highly attuned to the fact that we are all one. Illusions and ignorance are not part of the paradigm. We are grounded in the knowledge that we come from the same source and therefore don't perceive another soul's energy as a threat. We are supremely aware of our connectedness to all things. What we call intuition in this dimension is the way of things in spirit form. The challenges we experience as empaths in human form—being codependent, overwhelmed, or unable to ask for what we need, merging unhealthily with others, being judged, and/or needing to keep our energy field clear—don't exist when we are in spirit form. These are accoutrements of the human experience.

As a collective species and at the level of our souls' consciousness, we have decided that it is time to anchor god consciousness more fully—and *more accurately*—back into the human experience to more wholly embody our spiritual nature. It is time. Human consciousness is expanding as we trek along the current cycle of ascension, and this ascension is waking us up, reminding our souls of ancient knowledge and practices we once had access to. Our vibration is being raised. We are in the upswing, once again moving toward enlightenment and illumination. This time has been predicted by the wisdom teachings and sacred texts of civilizations that span the globe. In the great spiral of life, we have emerged out of the Iron Age and into the Bronze Age. (Here I am referring to the Greek mythological Ages of Man—Iron, Bronze, Silver, and Golden—and not the historical/archaeological Bronze Age or Iron Age that refers to the period when man began using bronze or iron.) While we have many thousands of years to go to reach the next Golden Age, we are most definitely in a time of expansion and remembering, no matter what the "outer world" looks like.

In the construct of this Earth school we make a collective soul agreement to travel the cycles of ascension and descension (explained in more detail in chapter 2). In the lower strata of consciousness we forget the bigger picture and what connects us all, so we experience ourselves as separate and therefore "other." We forget that we are all one. We buy into the illusion that anyone outside of us is different from us, and from there we make a whole bunch of assumptions about the "other": *He comes from a different upbringing and set of values, so I can't trust him. She doesn't look or act like me, so I need to protect myself from her. Clearly I am better than him because I live in a three-bedroom house and have a family and a regular job, and he chooses to live in a commune and rejects the monetary system.* We project and play out these assumptions on each other every day, all over the world.

There is a part of you—a higher-self consciousness—that is totally comfortable with being an empath and understands implicitly that this is your highest nature. What is crucial in this whole equation is how you choose to experience yourself and these qualities in *human* form and how you choose to handle the unique challenges that present themselves in this Earth school. On a deep subconscious level, all of us know and remember our true nature. But what we choose to experience is often a totally different reality. The challenge is to bring the empathic nature that we experience in spirit form into a physical body and interact with the one another at the *human* level. For that endeavor we are still sorely lacking in skills.

You are here to lead by example. To awaken in yourself and our fellow souls the memory that we are all sensitive, loving, heart-centered, compassionate beings. We are ready to embody in the physical world what is entirely natural to us in nonphysical form. As a collective, we are ascending out of the consciousness of the lower chakras and into the consciousness of the heart. We came here to experience our God-selves in physical form. It is time for empaths to accept, love, and embrace who we are and *be that* as an example for our families and communities. Suppressing our true nature only creates a petri dish for dis-ease, lack of fulfillment, and disillusionment. Empaths are not going away, and more of us are embodying every day. Take this as the rallying call from deep within your consciousness. You are different because you are *supposed* to be different. You chose to be different, whether you remember that choice or not. Embrace your gifts. You are not alone.

You are the new human blueprint.

The Great Year and Current Cycle of Ascension

To understand why so many empaths are incarnating now and to appreciate the role we are playing in the expansion of human consciousness, it is crucial to first comprehend the bigger cycle at work driving our collective experience. We cannot look at the entire picture of humanity's evolution without considering the Great Year.

Just as there is a cycle of day and night caused by the Earth spinning on its axis and a cycle of seasons caused by the Earth's orbit around the Sun, there is also a much larger cycle of time based on a celestial motion called the "precession of the equinoxes" that explains the rise and fall of civilizations, as well as the rise and fall of human consciousness. This grand cycle of time was understood by ancient cultures, and while it goes by different names, it is most commonly referred to as the "Great Year," a term coined by Plato.

As I will illustrate, the Great Year is directly related to the current cycle of ascension that we are in. Ascension isn't just a spiritual concept; it is really happening, and an exploration of the Great Year will show us why.

The length of the Great Year cycle is 24,000 years. Many ancient cultures were aware of this larger cycle of time and broke it into four smaller segments. The ancient Indians called these periods "yugas" and named them the Kali Yuga, Dwapara Yuga, Treta Yuga, and Satya Yuga. The Greeks broke the Great Year into ages: the Iron Age, Bronze Age, Silver Age, and Golden Age. (Not incidentally, the yugas and ages align precisely.) Other ancient cultures such as the Egyptians, Babylonians, and Greco-Romans had different names still, yet they all seemed to agree that the length of the cycle is approximately 24,000 years and that the cycle includes equal periods of ascension (moving toward enlightenment) and descension (moving toward ignorance).

It is important to recognize that this contradicts the linear model of the development of human civilization used by many historians, religious scholars, and archaeologists, which postulates that we humans are now as "intelligent" as we have ever been! In this model, ancient artifacts, megalithic structures, and texts that point to highly complex civilizations with advanced technologies are considered anomalies. Traditional historians and archaeologists don't always have an explanation for the existence or purpose of these anomalies because they look at these ancient societies through a lens that does not allow for cyclical development (rise and fall and rise again) or human existence on grander scales of time.

A LITTLE SCIENCE

It's going to require a little bit of science to explain the Great Year in greater detail, so my apologies to those who aren't scientifically inclined. I will do my best to keep this as simple as possible. However, if you desire a full exploration of this subject, I encourage you to read Walter Cruttenden's book *Lost Star of Myth and Time* or to visit the Binary Research Institute's website and/or watch their forty-six-minute documentary called *The Great Year*. It is from these resources that much of my research comes.

So we have this grand 24,000-year cycle, but what causes it? It is almost universally agreed that it is linked to the observable celestial phenomenon I mentioned earlier: the precession of the equinoxes. By "observable" I mean that you can see it and track it, as opposed to it being theoretical or unproven. Let's start our examination there.

Imagine you are standing at any point on the Earth during the spring equinox, at dawn, looking at the sky where the Sun is about to rise. At that point in the sky you would notice a constellation; which constellation would depend on the year. Right now in the northern hemisphere the constellation Pisces is moving out of that location, and the constellation Aquarius is moving into it.

As you probably know, there are twelve zodiacal constellations: Aries, Taurus, Gemini, Cancer, Leo, Virgo, Libra, Scorpio, Sagittarius, Capricorn, Aquarius, and Pisces. (It is worth noting that almost all advanced ancient civilizations named and tracked these twelve major constellations.) It takes approximately 2,000 years to "move" through each constellation. If you were able to stand at that same point on the Earth year after year for 24,000 years, it would appear as though the constellations were moving backward in the sky (tracking right to left from your point of view); hence the term *precession*, as *pre* means "before." After 24,000 years, the constellations would make a complete cycle, and you'd be back to where you started.

While scientists agree that the precession of the equinoxes happens (they can observe it, measure it, track it), what they don't agree on is *why* it happens. Yes, the constellations "trek backward" slowly through the sky, but why? What is causing this to occur? A thorough explanation of this could take an entire book, so I will briefly mention the major, most pertinent points of the matter and leave it to you to explore further if you wish (the resources I noted previously would be a great place to start).

The most widely accepted current theory is called the "lunisolar" theory, which basically says that what you see in the sky changes over time because the Earth wobbles on its axis, like a wobbling top spinning on the floor. More specifically:

Lunisolar theory states that the Earth's changing orientation to the fixed stars (primarily seen as the Precession of the Equinox) is principally due to the gravitational forces of the Moon (luni) and the Sun (solar) tugging on the Earth's bulge (the fat part around the middle). These lunisolar forces are thought to produce enough force or torque to slowly twist the Earth's spin axis in a clockwise motion.[1]

Copernicus first proposed the lunisolar theory in 1543. In the following century, Isaac Newton made some assumptions about the theory, and he, along with subsequent men of science, continued to tweak the formula and keep the theory alive. However, the math doesn't exactly work out elegantly, as the formula to express this motion does not accurately predict the observable phenomenon. As we have seen throughout history, just because it is the prevailing theory doesn't mean it is correct (consider times when we believed the Earth was flat or that the Sun revolved around the Earth). Because the theory was proposed and adopted by such great scientists as Copernicus and Newton, many later scientists didn't doubt it or thoroughly check their assumptions and formulas.

What Walter Cruttenden (and the Binary Research Institute) propose is that precession (the backward movement of the constellations through the sky) actually occurs because our entire solar system is moving through space. And not just randomly, but in a predictable cycle. They say that a Great Year is one orbit of our Sun around its binary center of mass.

In technical terms, the significance of this statement may not be obvious, so let me say it in layman's terms: our Sun has a sister, and these two celestial objects—our Sun and her sister—are orbiting around each other in a 24,000-year cycle.

Whoa.

For me, this realization went straight to the core of my being and activated something deep inside. Though we don't know which celestial body is our binary companion or what kind of celestial body it is (there are theories), I personally don't need to know "who" our sun's sister is to know that this theory lands as truth in my body. Now, is my body an accurate scientific tool of measurement? No, of course not! While I have a degree in mathematics and love science, I am not a scientist. This book focuses on the spiritual, and I trust your judgment to decide what your own truth is.

It's actually not all that uncommon for a system to be in gravitational relationship with one—or more—stars. If we know that the Earth spins on its axis, and moons orbit around planets, and planets orbit around their sun, it doesn't seem like much of a stretch to assume that our Sun (and hence all the bodies in our solar system) are moving through space as a group, too. "When the lunisolar model was put forth in the West, there was little or no knowledge of the extent of binary star systems (two stars in orbit around one another)."[2] "However, it is now estimated that more than 80% of all stars may be part of a binary or multiple-star relationships."[3]

Okay, this is all really cool, but how does this cycle affect human consciousness? What does ascension have to do with it?

This is where it gets interesting.

According to Walter Cruttenden in *Lost Star of Myth and Time*:

As our Sun moves in a vast orbit around its companion star, it carries the Earth in and out of a magnetic or electromagnetic field that impacts the planet and life on a grand scale. Eventually the effect shows outwardly as a positive or negative change in civilization, depending on whether we are getting closer [to] or farther from the source of influence. As the Earth moves into the field, a beneficial change occurs, and as the Earth moves out of the field, a disruptive or deteriorating effect occurs.[4]

Is the electromagnetic (EM) influence coming from our sister sun? Maybe. Is it coming from another star system that our orbit brings us closer to? Maybe. Is it both? Maybe. Again, there are theories, but nothing has been proven.

Yet, even though we can't identify the exact source of the electromagnetic influence, the concept of EM influence on human (and other) life bears out. We are exposed on a daily basis to the EM spectrum of our Sun. If we didn't have these influences—in the exact proportions, amounts, frequencies, and intensities that we receive them—humans and every other life form on this planet would most likely die.

Walter explains it simply:

Every elementary school student knows that as the Earth goes through its daily motion activity on the sunny side accelerates, photosynthesis and growth occur, and man awakens and becomes active. Conversely, when this side of the planet turns away from the Sun, most biological systems start to shut down and become inactive, including man, whose body has adapted to slowly slip off into subconscious sleep to re-energize in sync with this diurnal motion.

The same principle holds true with the Earth's annual orbital motion. During the six months when the northern or southern hemispheres move into a position to receive more light (an increase in photons per square inch as we leave the winter solstice) we see a proportionate increase in the activity and growth in that region— and when the hemispheres receive less light during the opposite six months we see a slowdown and decay. Clearly the action from our closest star has a profound influence on life on Earth.[5]

There have been myriad experiments, observable phenomena, hypotheses, and research regarding the effects of the presence or absence of electromagnetic fields on the Earth, humans, and other life forms. While I'd love to offer you multiple examples, in the interest of brevity, I'll offer one: the Mu Room. Dr. Valerie Hunt, while a professor emeritus of physiological sciences at UCLA, was one of the first to document the relationship between changes in energy fields and human behavior. The Mu Room (also known as a Faraday cage) is designed to allow researchers to adjust the levels of electromagnetic energy, magnetism, and particle charges within its walls as it is able to block external influences of the same.

In one series of experiments, Dr. Hunt placed subjects in the Mu Room, removed the electrical aspect of the atmosphere in the room, and noted that "the auric fields became randomly disorganized, scattered and incoherent. Sensory feedback was so impaired that subjects were totally unaware of the location of their bodies in space."[6] "The subjects burst into tears and sobbed, an experience unlike these people had ever endured. Although they reported that they were not sad, their bodies responded as though they were threatened, as they might be if the electromagnetic environment which nourished them was gone."[7] "When the electrical field of the room was increased beyond the usual level, the auric fields were restored to normalcy. The subjects' thinking because clear and they reported an expansion of their consciousness."[8]

If instead Dr. Hunt kept the electrical aspect of the Mu Room environment normal but decreased the magnetism, "gross incoordination occurred. . . . Subjects could not balance their bodies; they had difficulty touching finger to nose or performing simple coordinated movements. They lost kinesthetic awareness. Contrariwise, when the magnetic field was increased beyond the normal state, subjects could stand easily on one foot, even on tiptoes, or lean to previously impossible angles without falling."[9]

Dr. Hunt summarizes her findings with the Mu Room experiments thus far:

In a normal electromagnetic environment, the human field is nourished; physiological processes are carried out efficiently, and emotional experiences occur with clarity of thought. When the level of electromagnetism reached a critical saturation, there was evidence of improved motor performance, emotional well-being, excitement, and advanced states of consciousness. However, when the critical deficit was reached, motor, sensory and intellectual capabilities diminished with increased levels of anxiety and emotion.[10]

It is undeniable that we are electromagnetic beings. And it is undeniable that EM influences affect us, both positively and negatively. As Cruttenden says, "Electricity is a result of electrons in motion and everything has electrons, so it can be said that everything in the physical universe has electrical properties or 'electricity' to some degree. All rotating bodies have magnetic fields, from the tiniest electron up to the largest star. Our universe is literally awash with subtle electrical and magnetic properties or electro and magnetic waves."[11] It doesn't seem like a stretch to me to believe that our solar system's grand 24,000-year orbit through space around our binary companion brings us into—and out of—periods of amplified EM fields that affect our consciousness.

It also bears noting that when two bodies are gravitationally bound, their attraction (or pull on each other) increases. If you imagine our Sun and its companion orbiting around each other, the closer they get to one another, the faster they each move through space. At the closest point in their orbits (called the "periapsis"), they are at their fastest velocity. As they swing around the other, leave periapsis, and move farther apart, their motion slows down. At the point in the orbit farthest away from one another (called the "apoapsis"), they are at their slowest velocity. These cycles exactly match the cycles of ascending and descending consciousness that the ancients perceived and documented! The point of apoapsis represents the depth or lowest point of the Iron Age. The point of periapsis represents the height of the Golden Age.

This is a tremendous notion and has far-reaching implications, the scope of which could fill another book. In spiritual and New Age circles we have long talked about time speeding up, the quickening, and progress occurring at a rapid rate. Now we have evidence (through mathematical calculations) that shows we are literally moving faster through space!

WHERE WE ARE IN THE
GREAT YEAR CYCLE

References to precession and the rise and fall of the ages are found in over thirty ancient cultures, an observation documented by historians Giorgio de Santillana and Hertha von Dechend in their work *Hamlet's Mill: An Essay Investigating the Origins of Human Knowledge and Its Transmission through Myth.* Yet, as we entered into the last Iron Age, or Kali Yuga, much of our ancient knowledge—including what was known about the Great Year and its influence on humanity—was lost. We have evidence from ancient cultures, but experts (historians, archaeologists, scholars, etc.) are not always sure how to interpret these signs, symbols, texts, structures, and artifacts.

On top of all this, remember that the prevailing belief in the academic community is that our progression as a species has been linear, which implies that ancient civilizations could not have had more advanced technology, more in-depth knowledge, or higher consciousness than we currently demonstrate. Those who espouse the Great Year, a binary star system, and belief in a grand 24,000-year cycle of ascension and descension are considered to be on the fringe of their respective fields.

Trying to assemble a cohesive and explicable picture of life during these ancient civilizations is difficult at best, as we are sorely lacking in clues and the ability to accurately decipher them. It's like trying to determine what image is on a thousand-piece puzzle with only twenty-five pieces. We make assumptions based on contextual clues and create theories about how we think the ancients might have lived, conducted governments, performed medical procedures, or enacted spiritual ceremonies. But remember, we are viewing these clues through a specific paradigm that is still highly skeptical that these ancient humans could possess greater intelligence or more refined consciousness than we currently exhibit.

However, there are ancient documents that have survived, along with a few sages, indigenous wisdom keepers, and holy men and women who are alive now and know how to interpret them.

India has one of the oldest civilizations and longest-surviving cultures in the world. Their sacred texts, called Vedas, have endured through millennia. In this collection of materials are references to the Great Year, which they called the yuga cycle, as well as information that tracks each of the yugas. From these pages (and from teachings passed down through generations), a number of Hindu scholars have placed the low point of the most recent Kali Yuga (Iron Age) at 498 CE.[14] This means that the Bronze Age began in roughly 1699 BCE. By these calculations, we are approximately 1,500 years into the current ascending cycle and just a few hundred years (319 at the time of this writing) into the Bronze Age, or Dwapara Yuga.

If you chose to comprehensively research this topic, you would almost certainly find other sources that would give different dates. What's most important to glean from this discussion is that, while experts may not agree on precisely when the low point of the Iron Age occurred or when the Bronze Age began, it is clear that we are in a cycle of ascension.

To give a bit more context, one needs to understand that the yugas, or ages, are not of equal length, meaning they are not each 3,000 years long. Each age is of a different length in a ratio of 4, 3, 2, and 1, as shown in the list below.

Satya Yuga (Golden Age):   4,800 years
Treta Yuga (Silver Age):   3,600 years
Dwapara Yuga (Bronze Age):   2,400 years
Kali Yuga (Iron Age):   1,200 years

Note that these add up to just one-half of the Great Year cycle, totaling 12,000 years. The sequence occurs in a repeating cycle of ascension and descension. The cycle doesn't just start over by jumping back up to the Golden Age when the Iron Age is complete. In a descending cycle, Golden gives way to Silver, which gives way to Bronze, which gives way to Iron. Then, on the upswing, the ascending cycle begins with an Iron Age, moving into Bronze, then Silver, then Golden. And around and around the cycle goes as we move through space in orbit around our star companion.

So what can we expect in this early Bronze Age of the ascending cycle? It's hard to say precisely. Ancient Hindu sages tell us that each of the four ages or yugas has a correspondence with one of the four powers of *Maya,* a Sanskrit word meaning "the darkness of illusion that hides from man his divine nature." As described by Cruttenden, these powers, from the grossest to the most subtle, are listed as (1) atomic form, (2) space, (3) time, and (4) vibration. Each ascending age brings an opportunity for mankind to control and understand one of these universal powers. In declining ages, man gradually loses this knowledge and control.[13]

Walter Cruttenden summarizes the Bronze Age or Dwapara Yuga as follows:

> The fog of materialism begins to lift and man discovers that he is more than mere flesh and bones; he is an energy form. Men of this Age build great civilizations, more concrete and less spiritual than those of the Golden and Silver Ages, but still superior to any civilization of earlier times. During this Age, man has mastery and control of the "illusion" of space. He understands the finer forces of Creation which are reflected in many new discoveries and inventions. Knowledge of all kinds is accelerated tremendously, transforming all strata of life. The end of our Dwapara Yuga marks the completion of two of the four Ages and the Divine powers inherent in man are developed to half their true extent.

Man begins to expand his horizons and understands that all matter is an expression of energy, vibratory force, and electrical attributes. They begin to comprehend the mystery of matter, harness electrical energy and ultimately conquer space. The ancients referred to this Yuga as the "space annihilator"—a time when man understands the five electricities and when "space" itself no longer separates objects from object, person from person.[14]

It is fair to ask, "Where's the evidence of this?" The world—and outlook for humanity—can look pretty bleak on any given day of the year. A concept that has helped me greatly in trusting the ascension process is to look at what happens when we move from one season to the next. Let's take winter into spring, for example. Temperatures do not rise in a linear fashion. Meaning, when winter moves into spring, each day is not always warmer than the day before. We can experience warm days in winter and cold days in spring. But if you graph the trend, it will always show that—as an average!—the days are getting warmer.

It is the same with the cycles of ascension and descension, from one age into the next. Some days the news bodes extraordinary discoveries in astrophysics or neuroanatomy, or advances in technology or medicine. Other days the news bodes horrific atrocities of war, mass murders, loss of human rights, or famine. Each day is not always going to be "better" than yesterday. But over time, we are definitely trending toward greater consciousness.

THE TURNING OF THE AGE

In addition, we are smack-dab in the middle of the turning of the astrological ages (moving from one constellation at our reference point in the sky to the next). Remember, an astrological age lasts 2,000 years on average. Here I need to recall a small bit of science to explain what age we are actually in. Remember when I talked about standing at any point on the Earth at the spring equinox and looking to the point in the sky where the Sun is about to rise? I also mentioned that right now, in the northern hemisphere, we are moving out of the constellation (Age of) Pisces and into the constellation (Age of) Aquarius.

Things get a little tricky and muddled again when you start doing exhaustive research on this subject. Cruttenden and other scholars suggest that ancient civilizations used the fall equinox as their yearly marker, not the spring equinox. So if you stand at any point on the Earth in the northern hemisphere at the fall equinox and look to the point in the sky where the Sun is about to rise, you will see that we are moving out of the constellation (Age of) Virgo and into the constellation (Age of) Leo. (These are exactly opposite, as they should be, because the fall and spring equinoxes divide a year exactly in half.)

So both the time of year (spring equinox or fall equinox) and hemisphere (northern or southern) matter, as what you see in the sky is going to be different depending on these factors. Most ancient civilizations that tracked the stars (Greeks, Egyptians, Sumerians, etc.) were in the northern hemisphere. As best historians can tell, this reference point was one of the pieces of information that was lost as we descended into the last Iron Age. When we emerged and started "regaining" lost knowledge, many who tracked the stars began using the spring equinox. This is why we speak of the Age of Aquarius.

Once again, what is most important to deduce from this is that whether you use the spring or fall equinox as your reference point and whether you live in the northern or southern hemisphere, we are unquestionably moving out of one age and into the next. Whether you think of it as Pisces to Aquarius or Virgo to Leo, each constellation (age) represents an energy, an archetype. And that archetype (and its relationship to its opposite constellation) will influence the planet.

My friend and astrologer Ruby Falconer, who has been studying this field for forty-five years, says that because we live in a dualistic paradigm, when we talk about one sign, we must always take into consideration the influence of the opposite sign as well. Breaking it down into its simplest and most general terms, she suggests that we consider the following: "What might be the biggest challenge of the Age of Aquarius? Making sure the considerations of the collective (Aquarius) don't override the needs of the individual (Leo). The shadow side of Aquarius is authoritarianism and the shadow side of Leo is megalomania."[15] As we move into the next astrological age (however you choose to define it), these will be the overarching themes that humanity will be working through.

ASCENSION SYMPTOMS

As we have traversed the symbolic death and rebirth of millennia, humans awakening in consciousness have been experiencing what have been labeled *ascension symptoms*. Not just empaths but all humans in general have been experiencing a quickening, an accelerated period of growth where we are undergoing rapid, unprecedented transformation. I have often described the time of my spiritual awakening as living a hundred years in the space of five. The list of potential ascension symptoms is massive, ranging from all manner of physical issues and changes to alterations in perception and development of intuition to spontaneous bliss in experiencing oneness with all things.

I have been familiar with the concept of ascension symptoms as well as the multitude of ways they can show up (having experienced many of them personally) for over twenty years. An internet search pulls up many sites with lists and articles about ascension. The Ascensionsymptoms website does a great job of listing the variety of symptoms one can experience. I imagine many of the items listed there will resonate with you. Here is a sampling that I have organized into physical symptoms and emotional/energetic/intuitional symptoms.[16] These symptoms may come and go and are often unexplained.

Physical Symptoms:
- Stomach and gastrointestinal issues
- Changes in appetite and diet
- New intolerances to foods
- Temperature fluctuations in the body
- Being less tolerant to heat or cold
- Feeling waves of heat or chills through the body
- Random flulike symptoms
- Feverishness
- Headaches
- Cranial pressure
- Third eye and crown chakra sensations
- Increased sensitivity to sight, sound, and smell
- Hearing tones, odd sounds
- Achiness
- Joint Pain
- Clumsiness
- Dizziness
- Increase sensitivity to and dislike for scents and chemicals
- Insomnia or a need for much more sleep
- Sleep pattern disruption
- Fitful sleep
- Heart rhythm changes (heart chakra)
- Tingling and similar sensations
- Skin changes
- Rashes

Emotional/Energetic/Intuitional Symptoms:
- A general feeling and knowledge that a change is happening
- A preference for natural settings and less populated environments
- Synchronicities increase
- Seeing meaningful patterns around you

- Craving time alone
- Grief for your old self and desire to discover your true self
- Emotional sensitivity
- Cycling from one emotional extreme to the other
- Time pressure and urgency
- Changes in experience of time (speeding up and/or slowing down)
- Lack of mental clarity
- Confusion and fogginess
- Forgetfulness
- Psychic and extrasensory abilities increase
- Heightened communication with other beings; telepathy
- Intense dreams and lucid dreaming
- Intuition and insight increase

Quite literally we have been dying while still being alive, undergoing repeated cycles of figurative death and rebirth on a global scale as our systems have been preparing to hold a higher frequency. In shamanic terms we often refer to it as a "dismemberment," where we are metaphorically (yet with real-world discernable symptoms) being dismembered and re-membered.

As empaths, we've been hit with a sort of double whammy, experiencing both ascension symptoms and our normal complement of unusual peculiarities. Because of this, making adjustments to and addressing what is present at the subtle level in your body and energy field is just as important as the steps you take to address the physical body. You are sensitive enough and are wired to be able to detect things long before the evidence shows up on the physical plane. Part of walking the path of the empath is learning to listen to and trust yourself. This coincides directly with developing the consciousness of the heart—listening to and trusting your body, intuition, and feelings. We are choosing to be anchor points for these new frequencies to assist those who are currently in body as well as the ones coming behind us.

It is an understatement to say that this has been a challenging time to be in human form.

THE IMPLICATIONS

These celestial cycles of ascension and descension carry tremendous implications! Time is speeding up. We are experiencing accelerated growth and the feeling of living multiple lifetimes over the course of one lifetime. We are being subjected to rapidly increasing amounts of data and stimulus energetically, psychologically, intellectually, and digitally. For example, we are exposed to the equivalent of 174 newspapers' worth of data a day. A hundred years ago, people were lucky to read the equivalent of fifty books in a lifetime.[17] Our consciousness is awakening and expanding. Our minds are comprehending complex data we couldn't have conceived of even fifty years ago. Our energetic bodies are being recalibrated. The Earth and the very dimension we operate in are undergoing an enormous process of purification and upgrade.

Have you ever stopped to ask yourself, "Why did I choose to incarnate *now?*"

As empaths we are both cause and effect. Because we are in an ascension cycle, our consciousness is elevating. We cannot help but be affected by myriad changes at both the microcosmic and macrocosmic scales. The planet is once again ready for humans with a more refined energy body, highly tuned nervous system, and sensitivities to subtle energies and the unseen realms. We are here because it is time—the cosmic tumblers are in the right position, unlocking the next phase of human development.

And at the same time, empaths incarnating collectively now and in the last century are also wayshowers. In choosing to embrace our unique collection of characteristics, we can help others "remember" and welcome what has been dormant inside all of us, waiting for the next upswing in the Great Year cycle. In *A New Earth: Awakening to Your*

Life's Purpose, Eckhart Tolle says collective human consciousness and life on our planet are intrinsically connected. He declares that "a new heaven" is the emergence of a transformed state of human consciousness, and "a new earth" is its reflection in the physical realm. In this New Earth, the main purpose of human life is to bring the light of consciousness into the world.

In the past several decades we have been downloading the energetic upgrades designed to help us access and live in the higher frequencies that humanity is evolving toward. This time period is an initiation! Empath or not, all humans are initiates of the New Earth mysteries, the New Age mysteries, and the New Great Year mysteries.

Evolution of the Empath

We are groundbreakers.

Even as little as a hundred years ago there was scarcely room in the world for people with our perceptions and sensitivities. Empaths would have been eaten alive. The level of human consciousness and the general energetic frequency of the world at that time would not have supported our existence for very long. As a species we were not evolved enough—had not awakened in consciousness enough yet—for people with our highly tuned physiological and energetic makeup to survive in the world on a larger scale.

EVOLUTION OF CONSCIOUSNESS

As is demonstrated in Abraham Maslow's hierarchy of needs pyramid, our motivation as a species is driven first by our basic needs—the lowest-level of the pyramid. His theory states that one must satisfy lower level deficit needs before progressing on to meet higher-level growth needs. A hundred years ago human consciousness was very self-centered, and poverty and lack were widespread (recognizing poverty and lack still exist today, but they are not as pervasive). Attitudes such as "each man for himself" and "it's okay to climb over others to get what you want" were not only common but expected. Like the plot from so many old Western movies, "It's either me or you, partner."

Anodea Judith, psychotherapist and author of many books on the chakras, brilliantly superimposed the chakra system onto the development stages of a child as a way to characterize and quantify individual human development. In that system, development progresses from the first chakra, which corresponds to time in the womb through our first year of existence, up to the seventh chakra, which equates to early adulthood and beyond.[1] In her book *The Global Heart Awakens,* Anodea extrapolates her mapping of the relationship between chakras and the developmental stages of an individual to the developmental progress of humanity as a whole. She says:

> We're now at the threshold of the global heart, the era of planetary adulthood. We have been slowly emerging into the fourth chakra, with the advent of rational philosophy, human rights, women's rights, democracy and a spiritual revolution that is moving beyond dogma toward compassion, higher wisdom, and personal connection with the divine. I argue, however, that we're now suffering from a syndrome of arrested development in our journey to the heart. Parts of our collective psyche are moving forward, while other aspects remain trapped in the egoic third chakra's love of power.[2]

Taking this perspective, it is obvious that we were still animated by lower chakra consciousness even a century ago, most notably the third chakra. The third chakra is the place of personal will and personal power. In an individual, this consciousness is driven by self-definition and the formation of the ego. It is naturally a self-centered focus as autonomy is sought. In this level of development, individual identity motivates decisions and reactions. Other themes of the third chakra include self-esteem, strength, energy, vitality, focus, discipline, freedom, and purpose. Enlarge and adapt this template now to the whole of humanity and you can see that we have been experimenting with asserting our will and power in all of its forms and expressions for centuries.

While many agree that we are currently in our cultural adolescence, there is also clear evidence of higher chakra development in the realms of communication (fifth chakra), vision (sixth chakra), and spirituality (seventh chakra). Judith says it's important to note that "in both individual and cultural development, the opening of a particular chakra does not mean that its development is completed in that phase. Often higher levels of realization are necessary in order to consolidate a previous chakra phase."[3] This means that as an individual or society progresses or matures through the chakras (which you can also think of as levels of consciousness), progress is neither complete nor linear. We cycle back through these levels of development multiple times in our lives, revisiting aspects that were aborted, damaged, shut down, ignored, overemphasized, stuck, or otherwise unable to develop in a normal and healthy way. It's actually a form of soul retrieval, essentially going back in time and collecting up the processes and parts of ourselves that were incomplete or got left behind so we can move forward in wholeness.

In looking at our collective stuckness in the third chakra, it would be easy to make the ego wrong. But if you look at the larger picture, taking into account the entire chakra system (whether applying it to an individual or society), each level creates a necessary foundation for the next. Lower chakra consciousness is not summarily "bad," and likewise upper chakra consciousness is not summarily "good." This is too simplistic a perspective. Any chakra quality (like the ego) can be taken to an unhealthy extreme. All chakras functioning together in balance and harmony is the ideal. Each stage of development is necessary because the next level of consciousness is only made possible by the establishment of the previous level. Each chakra is integrated as one (or a collective) moves to higher levels of consciousness. Integrated, not vacated.

Just as individuals can be highly mature and developed in one aspect (mental or intellectual, for example) and sorely stunted in another (emotional, for example), societies can be, too. And to complicate matters more, our level of consciousness and maturity changes from moment to moment and day to day. Just as humans can get triggered, regress, project, act out, deny, or go into addiction, so too can societies. But taken as a general average, humanity is at the fourth chakra level of development.

Anodea says that "our collective initiation from the *love of power* [third chakra] to the *power of love* [fourth chakra] is the drama of our time."[4] This is where empaths come in. We are a catalyzing force in humanity's journey toward heart-centered consciousness. Morris Berman, author of *Dark Ages America,* says, "Love is the social equivalent of gravity."[5] The period of ascension we are in now is creating somewhat of a pressure cooker as polarities are amplified, energies are intensifying, and the collective ego is fighting to maintain dominance in the face of the gravity of love. Our arrested development cannot maintain a stasis for much longer. As empaths, we are here to help humanity get unstuck.

EMPATHS COULDN'T HAVE
SURVIVED A HUNDRED YEARS AGO

If you think about what it would be like to have been an empath given the state of the world a hundred years or so ago, it's easy to see how overwhelmingly difficult it would have been just from a physical standpoint alone. The vast majority of people did not have electricity. Penicillin had yet to be discovered. In 1900, every third child died before the age of five (an overall 63.8 percent survival rate).[6] People still struggled to harvest or slaughter enough food to last them through the winter. The practical work of carving out a life, feeding the children, and keeping a roof overhead took every ounce of mental and physical effort. While we entered into relationships because we desired the love, support, and security they provided, we didn't have much time to devote to developing rich connection, understanding each other's needs, or practicing equality. Relationships were conducted mostly out of practicality, with clearly defined roles, and the entirety of life was consumed by meeting basic, lower-level needs.

Naturally, there was very little time in the past century to devote to meaningful or long-lasting spiritual pursuits on a larger societal scale, let alone becoming self-actualized, the pinnacle of Maslow's hierarchy. Intellectual pursuits like higher education were still considered frivolous, impractical, and reserved for the wealthy. Even basic psychological needs such as intimate relationships and feelings of accomplishment, the middle tier of Maslow's pyramid, were rarely a priority. When you're trying to stay warm, feed your family, and keep your children from succumbing to disease, it's difficult to find value in the esoteric or intangible.

In third chakra consciousness, people were trying to individuate and assert their will. This means they hadn't figured out yet how to be in true partnership—to collaborate, compromise, or listen deeply. Anything different or unusual was considered a threat, which created a volatile polarity. On the one hand, we were experimenting with expressing our unique voice and individuality, learning how to wield our power, and discovering how to assert our will. Yet on the other hand, we didn't have the skills to manage the fear we felt when we encountered something unknown or outside the norm, so our natural instinct was to overpower or destroy it.

While developmental progression through the chakras isn't perfectly linear, as discussed in the previous section, humanity has just begun to move into fourth chakra consciousness. The era of the heart is upon us, and it is time to collectively mature out of our adolescence and into responsible adulthood. As empaths, we are the forerunners, coming into this world with huge, open hearts, refined sensitivities, and a strong desire for harmony and cooperation. For many of us, I'm sure it feels like we are centuries premature. Considering the state of affairs in the majority of the world, our minds question whether the world is ready to move into the realm of the heart and increasing levels of consciousness. Yet here we are, our courageous souls imploring us onward.

Even Accepted Empaths Struggled

It makes sense that only a small number of incredibly brave souls would choose to come into the world a century ago sporting a highly sensitive nervous system and an ability to access the unseen realm as well as perceive energetic fields around living beings. Very few like us were incarnating in previous centuries, and if so, it was usually in pockets of indigenous tribes or cultures where those qualities were valued and nurtured. (Yet on a bigger scale, those societies were typically misunderstood and viewed as uncivilized or unsophisticated.)

Early empaths—even into the first half of the twentieth century—were generally tolerated as eccentric at best or outcast at worst. Sadly, to deal with the harshness of reality, they oftentimes ended up self-medicating and falling into addiction to drown out their sensitivities. They were dismissed, chalked up as being crazy, disowned, or relegated to the fringes of society. They were forced to construct a complicated network of coping mechanisms to even make it through daily life. Many created elaborate fantasy worlds to escape into or flirted with deep depression. Early psychology gave these people diagnoses such as melancholic or hysterical. And if they didn't manage or mask their empathic qualities well enough, they ended up in asylums, mental institutions, or jail, or they ended up dead.

At that point in our human and spiritual development there was no room for the idea that we could become self-actualized, or that we could all access the unseen realms, live our lives as conscious co-creators with Spirit, or source from the great All That Is. It was practically sacrilege to think that we could each be our own spiritual authority or that we could communicate with animals or the dead or see into the future.

In some instances, an empath would incarnate as the spiritual leader for a community where his or her "anomalies" were interpreted as preordainment for that role. For the nun, priest, rabbi, shaman, mystic, or spiritual devotee, possessing these "odd" qualities was acceptable, yet still viewed as unattainable for the simple masses. But even for these special empaths, survival outside of the ashram or convent was bleak. Their sensitivities were considered abnormalities, acceptable within certain bounds because they were "in touch with other realms or deities," but ridiculed or feared outside of their accepted societal structure. Sadly, many of them, too, medicated to escape. Or they practiced spiritual bypass, a form of suppressing and ignoring the more basic human needs and desires so they wouldn't have to feel the pain of the physical or emotional world. In this way they could experience greater transcendence and connection to higher consciousness. At that time in our development it was another, almost impossible, matter to bring that consciousness back into the physical world and be fully embodied.

As was pointed out in the movie *Moneyball,* "The first guy through the wall always gets bloody." Empaths were a rarity a century ago, and even fifty years ago they were still highly uncommon. For the first waves of empaths incarnating on this planet, make no mistake, it has been challenging. But at a soul level we chose this as part of our human mission. And more and more of us are dropping in every day. We are a specific segment of the larger collective of souls who came here to anchor the new frequencies of consciousness on planet Earth. Those of us who came first did so in order to pave the way for the newly incoming souls and for the current souls choosing to "wake up." Don't let outer appearances dissuade you. The time of the empath has arrived.

EMPATHS ARE AN ANOMALY IN WESTERN MEDICINE AND PSYCHOLOGY

As a general set, empaths and the characteristics we exhibit are not accepted in mainstream society. (Yet!)

Western psychology and Western medicine don't have much room in their professional cosmovision for empaths. Quite often our everyday experiences and innate sensitivities are trivialized or dismissed as psychosomatic. Or misdiagnosed entirely. I can't tell you how many empaths I have talked to who have been diagnosed with depression, bipolar disorder, agoraphobia, borderline personality disorder, or anxiety. And while some traditional therapies are effective in helping to lessen symptoms related to these conditions, as well as to create new awareness and offer new coping tools, it only solves half the problem. Without an understanding of what it is to be an empath and how that uniquely contributes to one's experience of life, the diagnosed can feel trapped and limited by their diagnosis.

Walker's Story

One particular long-term client, Walker, was so agoraphobic that he rarely left his apartment except to go to work or the grocery store. He shut himself away emotionally, and relationships were difficult. He was so incredibly sensitive to others' energies and emotions that going to social gatherings or being with large groups of people was nearly impossible because of the level of anxiety it created. He told me he felt hemmed in and that no one could ever understand him. This condition rendered him practically asocial.

After coming to me and discovering that he was an empath, he gained an entirely new understanding of his reactions as well as newfound hope and compassion for himself. Over a period of months and years I led him through a variety of techniques and exercises, which have made it possible for him to interact with others and feel more comfortable in large groups and lowered his anxiety level tremendously. He started feeling strong enough to interact with the human race again and began engaging in more of his own self-directed spiritual and healing practices, such as Buddhism and meditation. One of the most powerful tools for him has been getting in touch with his body and tapping into the innate wisdom of his body. In this way, he can determine what exactly is making him anxious and where in his body he is storing it so *that he can address and release it. These are all awarenesses and tools that the mental health profession could not provide.*

Lydia's Story

At different points in her life, Lydia has been diagnosed with bipolar disorder, depression, and borderline personality disorder. She's been on a variety of medications, including lithium and several antidepressants.

One of the main diagnoses that she said put her in a box and didn't give her the "full story" was borderline personality disorder. When she was first introduced to the idea that she was an empath and began developing life skills and doing inner work (including participating in the Priestess Process, which I facilitate), she began to see how her inner voice of intuition was always there, but she either denied it or couldn't hear it. As a child she was labeled "weird" and "a liar" and made to believe something was wrong with her whenever her intuitive empathic nature presented itself. Her shadow and unresolved issues from childhood began to push her into codependent relationships and self-denial so that she could attempt to gain the love and acceptance she didn't receive when she was young. On top of all that, because she was an empath, she was taking on everyone else's personality traits and energies.

If her mental health providers understood that she was an empath, they could have done so much more to empower her instead of relegating her to years of marginally useful traditional therapy. Lydia says about her inner voice of intuition: "That voice was always present beforehand telling me not to do it [enter into destructive relationships], and when I finally started honoring and listening to that voice, those situations stopped occurring." Part of honoring that inner voice was recognizing and embracing that she is an empath. Doing so helped her reframe her multiple diagnoses and all the experiences of her life. She shared the following:

At first it was scary because if I'm not these things, then what the hell is wrong with me? When I realized there wasn't anything wrong with me and that it was all about the ways in which I denied myself, I went through mourning and anger phases for the little girl who was told she was weird and wrong. But then I became able to forgive the individuals who put the thoughts in my head (such as you're weird, there's something wrong with you, you're a liar, a cheat, or fake). They didn't know what they were doing to me.

I freely admit that I am not a traditional mental health professional, but I have seen many clients and students improve their ability to thrive in their relationships, become more functional in daily life, heal unresolved issues, and take back their power after doing nothing other than owning that they are an empath and practicing the tools and concepts I teach.

Physical Peculiarities

As empaths, it is not uncommon to experience all manner of physical symptoms as a result of our sensitivities, overwhelm, or taking on others' emotions. Remember, too, the long list of ascension symptoms from chapter 2 that also affect us. On at least three different occasions I have gone to urgent care with symptoms I knew were a result of overload on my nervous system or from my energy field processing rapid change or intense emotions. One of the most recent visits was a consequence of several weeks of severe anxiety attacks. Well, at least that's what a traditional Western doctor would say I was experiencing. At random intervals I felt like a massive belt was being tightened around my chest. My throat and chest felt constricted, I felt like I had a knife in my back, and I often had difficulty falling asleep because of it. Sometimes my heart would race or my pulse would thump strongly. But I couldn't correlate the "anxiety" to any particular event or stressor in my life.

I was clear that my cells were in an intense period of purging and recalibrating. I referred to the multiweek period as a "shamanic heart attack." My system was being rebooted as I was downloading an upgrade to my energy body. Old patterns were being cleansed and new ones being activated. My system was experiencing the results of this burst of new frequencies. However, since anxiety attacks and heart issues share similar symptoms, I did the pragmatic thing and went to the doctor. Of course, every system they checked was operating perfectly. Blood pressure, pulse, EKG, blood enzymes . . . all of it normal with no indication of even the mildest heart episode. At least, not on the physical dimension.

Over the years I have experienced heart palpitations, difficulty breathing, anxiety symptoms, uncontrolled crying, chest pains, exhaustion, headaches, depression, gastrointestinal distress, neck pain, dizziness, and back pain as a result of processing intense energies, emotions, and stimulus in my world. To be safe I always went to the doctor if the symptoms potentially pointed to something more severe, but I always checked out perfectly on the physical level.

Everything that manifests on the physical level is created first at the etheric level. Diseases and conditions don't just randomly appear. They begin in the energy body as unresolved issues, suppressed emotions, or destructive belief systems. And in addition, sometimes we just get blasted with high-frequency energies from solar flares and other cosmic, planetary, and as-of-yet-unknown sources. Investigating the multiple layers of cause that can lie at the heart of whatever physical symptom you might be experiencing and understanding these "unseen" sources will give you a new framework upon which you can make a more informed decision about your course of action.

So, while I am not advocating that you eschew entirely any form of modern medicine or psychiatry, it is my hope that understanding yourself through the lens of "empath" will allow you to apply a different set of filters and criteria when determining the relevance of your health care professional's diagnosis. Western medicine most definitely has its place, but there are severe deficiencies in modern medicine's scope of knowledge and understanding. Western medicine does not focus on prevention and is so specialized that doctors have lost their ability to think and diagnose holistically. Their frame of reference tends to focus on treating symptoms, not causes. It is critical to recognize that there can be much more going on at a subtle energetic level that traditional modern medicine can't diagnose and doesn't acknowledge exists.

If you choose to pursue modern psychology for emotional support or working through personal issues (and maybe you already have), understand that the model most practitioners subscribe to includes medication. For me personally, depression or anxiety medication is undesired and a last resort. You should know that there is a growing population of nontraditional therapists, energy healers, counselors, shamanic guides, and more—with highly effective tools and techniques—who can help you understand and process issues on the emotional and energetic level without numbing you out or causing more harm than good with the side effects of depression and anxiety medicine. Modern psychology and Western medicine have their value, but they often play in a very small box that doesn't include an understanding of subtle energies or what it means to be an empath.

EMPATHS ARE AN ANOMALY IN WESTERN CULTURE

Similar to Western medicine, Western culture in general doesn't have much tolerance or appreciation for the traits of empaths. Being open-hearted, sensitive, emotional, vulnerable, intuitive, heart-centered, or service-focused is generally considered weak, leaves you open to exploitation or attack, and is devalued. People often say they appreciate and value altruism, cooperation, vulnerability, and people who share their emotions honestly. They nod their head in agreement when they see an astonishing story of intuition or providence. They speak about the need for "more people like that." But their behavior tells the real story.

There are many in our families, communities, churches, work environments, and governing bodies who talk a good game about being tolerant, open-minded, and compassionate. To their credit, they are doing the best they know how, and at a superficial level, they mean what they say. But for many there is still an enormous disconnect between their words and their deep-seated, unconscious beliefs. This is true for all humans at this stage in our evolution, and it is why "just doing x" doesn't always net the promised results. If our core beliefs run contrary to our actions, we either will sabotage what we are trying to create or won't be able to hold on to what we created for very long. Unearthing our conflicting beliefs and bringing them into alignment with our actions is part of the emotional and spiritual maturation process. (It's also called "shadow work.")

At this point, much of what is repressed in our collective psyches is coming forward and playing out on grand public scales. Yet our society is merely reflecting the struggles we experience on an individual scale. The spiritual axiom "as the one, so the circle; as the circle, so the one" applies here. It means that there is a mirroring that occurs between the one and the many. As individuals, we are part of a larger body and that same body is made up of individuals. We are all connected. What affects one affects all. Sometimes it is hard to remember that, on a collective soul level, we all chose to be in this experience together.

We are learning how to bring our subconscious beliefs and motivations into the light of consciousness to heal old wounds and create greater integrity between our beliefs, words, and actions. Like the process of extracting iron from iron ore by heating the iron ore in a blast furnace, we are being cooked in this ascension crucible until the impurities rise to the surface and can be skimmed off. In this way what remains will be pure, authentic, and tested.

So, as empaths, it is often difficult to know in our current society whether we are truly being accepted and honored or merely tolerated and humored. Sometimes we are exploited. The attitude we are met with is usually a reflection of people's deep-seated (and unconscious) beliefs and fears. Even if they are skilled at deluding themselves and pretending they really believe what they are saying, their true nature will eventually reveal itself, usually showing up as a whole slew of judgments: you're weak, fragile, too sensitive, undisciplined, unstable, unpredictable, erratic, eccentric, unrealistic, and on and on. To be fair, this doesn't mean people are evil. We can only operate from the level of consciousness we have achieved.

But one of our gifts as empaths, if we develop it, is bullshit detection. This alone can be of tremendous help in navigating life and relationships. If you know how to listen to yourself, you can determine if someone is saying one thing but motivated otherwise. Our nervous systems are finely tuned receivers, and we can identify the smallest aberration in a person's integrity. It can help keep you safe and make prudent decisions in a world where authentic expression and conscious living are still in their infancy, provided you have retained (or redeveloped) the ability to hear yourself, trust yourself, and act upon your inner knowing.

Discernment in an Inauthentic Culture

Human contact is a basic human need. In spirit form, we don't have to run every relationship through the can-I-trust-this-person filter. In human form it's different, and we certainly can't avoid living among other people. But we can benefit from learning greater discernment and being more discriminating as to when we let our openhearted, sensitive, service-oriented nature lead the dance. We don't want to waste our gifts and talents on people who don't understand or appreciate them or, moreover, would take advantage of them.

One of the most important tools of discernment I have learned is this: if you want to understand what a person's (or society's) values are, look at their *actions*. Words are an important form of communication, but they are not the only form. People's actions will clearly demonstrate if they walk their talk (and are trustworthy) or if they are dealing with some unacknowledged shadow pieces.

From this measure, it is clear that much of society is still centered in and motivated by fear. From my personal and professional observations, the actions of our society, taken in total, still overwhelmingly demonstrate the following values and messages:

- Be strong. (Never show weakness.)
- Suck it up. (Never complain.)
- Work hard. (Never rest or give yourself a break.)
- If you don't know what to do, conquer/destroy/overpower it. (The unknown is to be feared and therefore should be eliminated.)
- If you don't know how, fake it. Never act like you don't know. (Pretending is okay; asking for help isn't.)
- Honesty is dangerous. You must keep your cards close to the vest, be manipulative, and play the game to get what you want. (Don't tell the truth or you'll be taken advantage of.)
- There isn't enough. (We must compete, even if that includes dishonesty or manipulation to get what we want.)
- Never say you're sorry. (Don't admit you're wrong because it's a sign of weakness.)
- Suffering is expected. You have to sacrifice and keep going no matter what. The reward comes at the end. (Sacrifice is exalted. Moderation, rest, and balance are overrated and won't get you ahead.)
- You can't trust anyone. (Everyone is out for themselves and you should be, too.)
- Only physical proof and what you can demonstrate or verify matters. What you feel or sense isn't trustworthy. (Practicality, logic, and action are virtues. Intuition, relativity, and natural timing are unreliable.)

Whether we heard our parents say things like this growing up or digested messages from the media, video games, books, school authorities, churches, or social media, we made an unconscious decision to temper or hide altogether our empathic qualities. We were forced to operate inside a system that was fundamentally at odds with our very nature. So, we donned our cookie-cutter khakis and light-blue button-downs, swallowed hard, and lined up behind the thousands of other lemmings like good little girls and boys.

We began to adopt these highly patriarchal, fear-based maxims as if they were true. We contributed to their perpetuation because we thought we were doing what we were "supposed to"—the "right" thing. After all, this is what we were taught. Yet at some point we recognized the sickening feeling in our gut that tells us we are out of alignment with our truth. A major leap forward in our liberation occurs when we begin to assess what we were taught by our parents and teachers and make our own decisions about what is true for us and what isn't. Only then can we begin to extract our true essence from the soup of deception we were cooked in. Recovering our authenticity is a daunting—but doable!—undertaking.

THE LONE WOLF HAS A NEW PACK

It is hard enough for most of the people in our lives to understand or accept our quirky sensitivities, but many empaths also possess uncanny abilities to connect to the unseen realms, sense subtle energies, and access different dimensions of consciousness. These gifts can show up as seeing and communing with angels or spirits, having premonitions, being psychic, channeling those who have passed, being medically intuitive, seeing people's chakras or auras, having visions, sensing disturbances in another's energy field, being able to astral travel, and much more.

These abilities are usually met with even greater disdain and plenty of judgment by our family and society, so we become masters at censoring and concealing our true nature. We learn to do a lot of pretending. And one of the more insidious consequence of the external messages of rejection we received growing up is that they passed unobserved into the lexicon of our own inner dialogue. We now perpetrate upon ourselves the same messages of rejection and censorship that we received while growing up through our current self-talk.

Another consequence of being rejected, misunderstood, and criticized is that we often feel and live like lone wolves. We are extremely good at adapting, so we create the best illusions we can in our marriages, workplaces, and social groups to make us feel like we are normal and embraced. Yet underneath we cannot deny our true nature. Just like the phrase "alone in a crowd" suggests, we are surrounded by people yet unable to be seen and accepted for who we truly are, causing us to feel painfully isolated.

Many of us have been looking hard for new families—soul families—and communities of like-hearted people who can accept and understand us for who we are. We have had to look high and low for teachers and mentors to help us manage our energy and learn new coping skills because traditional therapists, clergy, and mental health professionals don't know what to do with us. Many of us have found refuge in some of the fringe or growing minority communities and sociospiritual groups like progressive churches, shamanism, divine feminine circles, LGBTQIA communities, drumming circles, and intentional communities who share similar values. These are groups who have already experienced a more-than-average amount of rejection and judgment and who can meet us with more compassion than the average citizen. At the same time, people are still people, and many people, no matter what groups they align themselves with, don't know what it means to be an empath.

Because we are pioneers of the new human blueprint, the existing ways of coping, living, and thriving don't work for us. How could they? We are coded differently. It's like trying to plug a three-prong plug into an old two-prong outlet. In the end, we are forced to throw out the old formula for "living a successful, productive, and fulfilling life" and design a new one that fits our speed and values. Which is no small order, I know! Many of us have a similar life lesson of learning to love ourselves, to believe in our own worth, and to trust our own inner compass, regardless of what the external world says or does. Moving from external validation to internal validation is a foremost opportunity for all humans to experience on this Earth school, but it is exceptionally more challenging for empaths.

You are not crazy, but you must stop the madness of trying to fit into a system that is unwittingly designed to invalidate, suppress, and pervert you. It's not personal, but that makes it no less harmful. You don't have to stay enmeshed in it. Quit justifying yourself to people who don't understand. It is time to fearlessly create a lifestyle and relationships that *support and enrich you*. We are a growing pack, and you don't have to continue living as a lone wolf.

What Is an Empath?

At first, defining what an empath is felt like an intimidating task. I have spent many years working with empathic clients and teaching empath workshops. I mentored myself through the ugly years of realizing I was an empath and having no idea how to be one in a healthy way. Through all of it I have listened to guidance from Spirit, as well as feedback from students. I have trusted my intuition in building tools, mind-sets, and exercises to help people, and myself, navigate this way of life. While I believe I have undeniable experience, creating a formal definition felt like proclaiming a level of authority I wasn't sure I possessed.

The term *empath* has been used casually in spiritual circles for many years, and people who use the term have a general idea of what it means. But as I began the process of writing this book, I felt Spirit telling me that it was important to offer a clear definition to the world to help anchor the energy of the empath into the new consciousness grid. To give the term a clear definition so that everyone—empaths and non-empaths alike—would know exactly what is meant. In this way we can connect to and strengthen the morphic field of the empath for the benefit of all.

As the new human blueprint, these emerging, somewhat intangible, hard-to-define concepts need to be given voice. We talk about "speaking something into existence" because it is true. Words are creative and they structure reality. Naming something gives it form and substance. So, while this chapter might be a little drier than the others and might read a little more like an academic text, it is more than just about creating an academic definition. My belief is that having a definition will help empaths truly understand and claim their nature. When we own something, we can show up powerfully as that. And I want you standing next to me as the powerful empath I know you are, helping me awaken the world to heart-centered living.

To define the term *empath* more precisely, I will address it from several perspectives: what an empath is *not*, the five qualities of an empath, and the empath as a life path. At the end of the chapter I will condense it all into a concise definition.

WHAT AN EMPATH IS NOT

When explaining a concept, it is sometimes beneficial to first describe what it is not. This helps us eliminate misunderstandings, myths, and confusion so we have a clearer foundation to build our understanding and definition upon.

To begin with, being an empath is not just a feeling we experience. Feelings are transient or fleeting. How we feel about something can change, and oftentimes feelings are reactions to something happening in the moment. Feelings are impermanent. We can feel many different emotions and sensations throughout the course of a day, and maybe there are certain ones we feel often or regularly. But as humans, we are not defined by our feelings. They aren't permanent character traits.

Being an empath is not a psychological or emotional state that we access inside ourselves when someone in our world is going through a difficult time. Every human has the ability to feel *empathy*, but that's not the same as being an empath. When we identify with and feel compassion for a person or situation that we see on TV, read about, observe in person, or hear about from a friend, we are experiencing empathy for that person. We can insert ourselves inside his or her circumstances, imagine what it would be like for us, and then, from that bridge, establish an emotional connection with that person. We develop a sympathetic response, a concern for what that person is going through. A common bond, however temporary, is created as we recognize the sameness in a stranger. Every human has the potential capacity to feel empathy, but not every human is an empath.

Being an empath is not a magic act, gimmick, or parlor trick. And it is certainly not a conjuring of "evil" forces. Many people don't understand or believe in paranormal or supernatural phenomena, and some even fear these types of experiences as well as people who demonstrate such abilities. Sadly, depending on a person's religious background, we are often labeled as anything from "woo-woo" to being a witch, being crazy, and even being of the devil. Or we are accused of practicing some form of subversive, dark, or suspicious religion. Being an empath is a real thing and people from all expressions of spiritual and religious traditions can be empaths. I have absolutely nothing against people who practice magic, call themselves witches, use divination, or work with the paranormal. I know many people (and *I* am one of those people) who work in, experience, or can access one or more of these realms, and I know that empaths, because of their heightened sensitivities, often experience or are drawn to the metaphysical or paranormal because they simply see things that other people don't see. They feel things other people don't feel. They sense things other people don't sense. And because of this, empaths often live on the edge of the "real" world, bridging the seen and unseen realms, walking in both worlds simultaneously.

Being an empath is not something you can turn on and off. This is not to say that you don't have control over it or that it can't be developed, cultivated, and managed. But make no mistake, being an empath is not a skill, competence, knack, or proficiency. It is a purpose, if you will . . . something you were either born with or not. And if you were born with it, it is something you live with 24/7. Whether you acknowledge it or not, whether you suppress it or not, it is an undeniable part of who you are. It is a choice you made at the soul level.

Being an empath is not just about being highly sensitive. I love Elaine Aron's book *The Highly Sensitive Person*. I read it back in the late 1990s, and it was the first time I realized I was not alone in my energetic makeup. But although being highly sensitive is a major component of being an empath, there was a bigger context I had yet to discover. So much of what Elaine's book includes and concludes applies to empaths, but being an empath also consists of a few key qualities that Elaine does not include in her book. I think of her work as the precursor to the discourse on being an empath, before the term *empath* became more common.

FIVE DISTINCT QUALITIES OF AN EMPATH

Now that we have eliminated some misconceptions, we are ready to get into the meat of this definition and explore the types of qualities that are common among empaths and set us apart as unique.

Through my encounters with hundreds of clients and students, surveys and interviews I have conducted, and my own direct experience, I developed a list of qualities that I have observed most empaths possessing. Over years of refining that list, listening to guidance from Spirit, and collating data from multiple sources, I have identified five qualities empaths demonstrate that, taken in total, separate us from the rest of the population and are akin to personality traits we were born with:

1. **The ability to merge with and absorb the energy of other beings (people, animals, or anything with life force), which stems from a very open personal energy field.** This is the quality that causes us to unconsciously take on others' emotions and problems and to struggle with boundaries.
2. **A highly sensitive nervous system.** This makes us prone to

overwhelm and overstimulation, which require extra-vigilant self-care.

3. **Great sensitivity to the energies around us and an ability to perceive or access subtle information stored in the energy fields of all types of life-forms.** This makes it easy for us to tune in to the "unseen" realm of spirits, including angels, apparitions, the dead, energy fields of people and things, paranormal experiences, past lives, the Akashic records, people's emotions, and much more. (Akashic records are an etheric library of each soul's human incarnations, including events, thoughts, actions, emotions, karmic patterns, and intent occurring in the past, present, or future.)

4. **The premium we place on peace and harmony in relationships, our environment, and our own energy field.** Given our heightened sensitivities, we will do anything and everything to keep our relationships and environment—and therefore ourselves—as stress-free, calm, and harmonious as possible.

5. **Big, open hearts and a desire to serve others.** This makes us inclined toward careers focused on service as well as overgiving and putting ourselves last on the list.

I understand that this might be the first time anyone has associated these traits under one heading and that you might now be in a process of reframing the experiences of your life. Some of my students have almost cried in relief when they fully digested these qualities as a set and realized that there was an explanation for their behavior, reactions, and choices. At a human level, I know how liberating and highly validating it can be to realize that you are not alone and that you are not crazy.

If you are hungry to find out more about these descriptors, I unpack them all in chapter 5, explaining each of them in greater detail and providing many real-life examples from clients and peers.

Are You an Empath?

I now want to examine the effects of being born with these five qualities. Below is a list of those qualities and the ways they show up in our
lives, including a variety of personality traits, adaptive behaviors, experiences, self-care strategies, and coping mechanisms that develop through
our personal process of maturing and individuating as an empath.
Remember that until we come into conscious relationship with our
empathic nature, we almost certainly experience the unhealthy aspects
of these qualities, so this list consists mostly of what I would consider
to be unhealthy outcomes or behaviors.

I invite you to use this as a checklist to see how many qualities you
identify with

CHARACTERISTICS OF
THE FIVE EMPATH QUALITIES

1. **We were born with the ability to merge with and absorb the
   energy of other beings, which stems from a very open personal
   energy field (or energy container).**

   ☐ We can't figure out where we end and the next person begins.

   ☐ We take on others' characteristics or personality traits, such as
   political views, sleeping habits, favorite TV shows, food choices,
   hobbies, et cetera.

   ☐ We have difficulty drawing and maintaining boundaries.

   ☐ We lose ourselves in relationships.

   ☐ We have difficulty saying no and maintaining consistency, often
   giving in if someone badgers us or asks multiple times.

   ☐ We are highly codependent.

   ☐ We have difficulty standing up for ourselves.

☐ We feel responsible for other people's emotions.

☐ We can have difficulty making decisions because we're unclear on what we really want and can't discern it from what everyone else wants, or wants us to do.

☐ We feel responsible for solving other people's problems.

☐ We think others' emotions are ours; we feel them so strongly that we think they are our own.

☐ We have difficulty separating out what is ours and what isn't—what we feel, think, desire, like, don't like, et cetera.

☐ We struggle with self-identity or defining ourselves, often seeking validation outside of ourselves or relying on others—parents, partners, bosses, et cetera—to define us.

☐ We tend toward addictive behaviors and often fall into addiction(s).

☐ We are overly compassionate and can identify so strongly with others' problems that we will make excuses, rationalize, enable, and stay in relationships way too long.

☐ We struggle with pacing in relationships, often getting too intimate too quickly because we are so sensitive and intuitive and can pick up others' feelings. We have a natural desire and ability to merge and connect on a deep level.

☐ We can seem very moody with drastic mood swings, but this is because we pick up the emotions of others without realizing it and then react to others with those emotions.

☐ We are highly intuitive and can often unnerve our friends and relatives because we know exactly what they are feeling or thinking.

☐ Our ability to blend and merge make us great therapists, counselors, healers, et cetera, yet we have to be careful in determining what is and is not ours, so we don't get overwhelmed and go home with all of our clients' problems and emotions.

2. **We were born with a highly sensitive nervous system.**

☐ We are easily overstimulated by large crowds and public places and prefer smaller groups and intimate settings.

☐ We don't like yelling, loud noises, or grating repetitive sounds.

☐ We are highly sensitive to smells, sounds, taste, and even certain fabrics, textures, and light.

☐ We are sensitive to violence and general chaos.

☐ We are often sensitive to alcohol, medication, or any mind/body-altering substances. Our bodies may even react in ways that are opposite from or counter to what the substance is prescribed to do.

☐ We avoid TV and movies that depict emotional dramas, harsh situations, violence, war, et cetera.

☐ In large crowds we often experience a shift in mood, becoming cranky, irritable, anxious, and agitated or feeling sapped.

☐ We remember (consciously or unconsciously) what it is like in spirit form and often have difficulty parsing and relating to "Earth" reality. This can cause us to seem detached, aloof, or socially awkward.

☐ We are easily overwhelmed, whether it be by information, noise, crowds, emotions, et cetera.

☐ We are highly sensitive to and have difficulty dealing

with cruelty, criminal acts of violence, suffering, torture, et cetera.

☐ When witnessing a traumatic, injurious, or shocking event, we experience a visceral and/or emotional reaction in our own physical and energetic bodies.

☐ We struggle with being fully embodied and often leave our body without knowing it. It is possible to live for many years partially out of our bodies without realizing it.

☐ We can experience difficulty in being "fully ourselves" and relaxing completely when meeting people for the first time or in groups because we are so sensitive to others' energies and get overstimulated. This can manifest as extreme anxiety, social awkwardness, or even what appears as antisocial behavior in an attempt to relieve ourselves of the overstimulation.

☐ We are rejuvenated by nature and require regular time outdoors, preferably alone.

☐ We can struggle with staying focused because we are constantly overstimulated and sensitive to the stimulus all around us.

☐ We often space out, daydream, or sleep to escape intensity, over-stimulation, or overwhelm.

☐ It is not uncommon for us to move through a wide range of emotions in a short span of time, bouncing from up to down and everything in between. Sometimes it is our own emotions we are feeling, and sometimes it is others' emotions we have taken on.

☐ We often struggle with fatigue, especially after a lot of social interaction (whether for work or pleasure), or chronic fatigue if we aren't engaging in enough self-care, alone time, and downtime.

☐ We require regular time alone to decompress and reconnect with our center.

☐ We often require downtime or time alone after being in crowds, with large groups, or at family and social events.

☐ We cry often and feel our own (and others') emotions very powerfully.

☐ We commonly turn to a variety of escape mechanisms (often addictions) to give us a reprieve from the intensity of the world and our own feelings.

☐ We can be perceived as quiet, introverted, brooding, a loner, unstable, fragile, or even antisocial because we are constantly being overwhelmed or overstimulated, or we need to get away to sort out what is ours and what isn't and clear our energy field.

☐ We are often misdiagnosed by Western medicine or Western psychology as depressed, bipolar, agoraphobic, or other inaccurate labels because, other than those paradigms, there is no way to describe the collection of experiences we live through on a daily basis.

3. **We were born with great sensitivity to the energies around us and the ability to perceive or access subtle information stored in the energy fields of all types of life-forms.**

☐ We are drawn to professions that naturally dovetail with our sensitivities, such as being a massage therapist, energy healer, medium, psychic, therapist, shaman, health care worker, member of the clergy, or tarot or other divinatory system reader, because it is so easy and natural for us to tune in to the metaphysical and unseen realms. On the casual side, it may not manifest as a profession, but we are usually the one our friends always come to for advice and insight.

☐ We have a highly developed intuition and powers of perception and often experience psychic or paranormal events, usually starting in early childhood.

☐ We are great listeners because we hear with our whole being, not just our ears. Our ability to relate draws people to us and makes them feel they can trust us.

☐ We often know what's going to happen before it happens.

☐ We often have the experience of complete strangers telling us their life story while standing in line at the grocery store.

☐ Distance doesn't matter; we can feel or sense when something is going on with a person close to us. Sometimes this expresses as premonitions.

☐ We are natural bullshit detectors and can tell when someone is lying or being deceptive or disingenuous almost to the point where we feel a repulsive reaction in our body or nervous system. If we are in denial of our gifts or have stopped listening to our intuition, this aspect may be shut down.

☐ We are usually animal lovers and can just as easily tune in to the needs and feelings of animals as those of people.

☐ We talk to rocks, trees, birds, plants, fairies, bodies of water, angels—anything with a life force, seen or unseen.

☐ We make decisions very instinctively and will often "feel into" the energy of an item we are considering purchasing (like clothing or knickknacks), a location we are considering visiting, a program or group we are contemplating joining, a menu item we are considering ordering, et cetera.

☐ Shamanic journeying, astral traveling, altered states of consciousness, traveling to different dimensions, et cetera, tend to be very easy for us.

4. **We were born placing high value on peace and harmony in relationships, our environment, and our own energy field.**

☐ We seek harmony in relationships and our environment and devote a lot of effort to creating and sustaining this harmony.

☐ We tend to be peacemakers.

☐ We do not like confrontation and can even shut down when conversations get too intense.

☐ We hate arguing or witnessing an argument.

☐ We tend to avoid tense or harsh situations and shrink away from any situation that feels tense or intense.

☐ It takes great effort and motivation for us to rock the boat; we don't like friction or conflict.

☐ Our home space is our womb space, our place of rejuvenation and rest, our sacred battery-charging station. Hence, it is very important that our environment (including office, car, yard, and so on) gives off a peaceful and harmonious vibe and supports a calm nervous system.

☐ We are sensitive and hyperattentive to the energies in our environment. This includes the arrangement of furniture and decorations, music that is playing, temperature, light (sunlight or artificial light), smells, texture, colors, et cetera. We will often tweak our environment to ensure that it remains congruent with our energetic requirements, which can lead to a regular and frequent need to reorganize, redecorate, paint, get rid of things, and do energetic clearings.

☐ Beauty is a form of harmony for us, and we love creating space. Decorating, designing altars, putting outfits together, and arranging our environment are all acts of creating beauty (and thus harmony) in our lives.

☐ We are often drawn to creative expressions—art, music, dance, crafts, et cetera—through either personal expression or appreciation (going to art exhibits, theater, concerts).

☐ We highly value and thrive in cooperative environments. Competition can feel awkward or exhausting to us.

5. We were born with a big, open heart and a desire to serve others.

☐ We often put everyone else's needs before our own.

☐ We care for ourselves last, being woefully negligent of our own wants and needs or devaluing them.

☐ We are often found working as volunteers with people, animals, or the environment.

☐ We deeply feel the plight of the less fortunate and those who are struggling and often care for them or support causes to our own detriment (going into debt, not taking care of our basic needs, ignoring other relationships, and so on).

☐ We are often found in an advocacy role; oddly, we find it easier to defend others because of our deep compassion and because it is much easier to stand up for the needs of others than for our own.

☐ We are often trusting and have an innocent nature, which can lead to being gullible or easily taken advantage of.

☐ We tend toward service-oriented professions such as nursing, massage therapy, counseling, administrative support, health care, etc.

☐ We say yes too often and struggle to balance our obligations and responsibilities with enough downtime.

☐ We keep the focus on others and suppress or deny our own needs, rationalizing them away or feeling like we don't deserve to be satisfied. Sacrifice, self-denial, and martyrdom can show up as major life patterns if we're not careful.

☐ We can feel uncomfortable and awkward when we are in the spotlight, receiving a compliment, being acknowledged in some way, or having "too much" attention paid to us, especially if we have internalized the message that it is important to put everyone else first and ourselves last.

☐ We get confused when we try to lead with our heart and other people don't operate the same way. This can cause us to shut down or become jaded.

☐ We often find people "dumping" their emotional baggage on us or coming to us for advice all the time, or we attract energy "vampires" because people intuitively recognize our big heart, compassion, and desire to help.

Clearly, there are many dozens of ways these five key traits can manifest themselves in the life of an empath. This list of behaviors and experiences is always a massive eye-opener for my clients and students. For many, these experiences have never been packaged together in one place, and they haven't encountered a comprehensive list that so accurately captured their life experiences. There are many echoes of "I am not alone!" "This describes me perfectly!" "Wow, there really isn't anything wrong with me!" And the always popular, "I'm not crazy!"

As I shared in chapter 1, without healthy guidance or awareness of these traits, it is natural for us to be predisposed to certain coping mechanisms, challenges, and unhealthy expressions as a result of our empathic bestowments. When we are unconscious of something, we have no ability to walk in awareness with it. It doesn't happen this way because we are "bad" or did something horribly wrong to deserve it. If we don't understand our underlying motivations, they will be acted out through the shadow until we become conscious of them.

Consequently, what usually happens is that we end up living from the unhealthy aspects of those five qualities, which can manifest as experiences of codependence, losing ourselves in relationships, feeling responsible for other people, putting everyone else first, struggling with boundaries, suppressing our authentic self, denying our own needs, and feeling regularly depleted. Most empaths do not have parents, models, or teachers to show them how to live with their sensitivities or give them a context for what being an empath is, let alone how to embrace it, develop it, and relate to it as an asset. Only after we recognize and accept our empathic nature can we make new, healthy choices and begin to relate to these aspects of ourselves as positive.

So Are You an Empath or Not?

After all of this exposition, what I'm about to say next may surprise you or sound contradictory.

Being an empath is not a specific diagnosis with a specific set of criteria that will determine whether you are unequivocally an empath or not. The presence or absence of any of these five qualities does not decisively include or exclude you. Each of them lies on a continuum, and not every empath will exhibit exactly the same qualities in exactly the same proportions. Some people will resonate with and experience one particular characteristic strongly, while not identifying nearly as much with another. For other people, the entire set of qualities are dormant or deeply buried through conscious or unconscious life choices. There are a lot of closet empaths out there starting to wake up. Someone might look at this list today and proclaim, "Nonsense!" Six months from now he or she might realize, "Oh God, that's been me all along."

I understand our human desire to label and categorize. We love our *Cosmopolitan* surveys and bite-size questionnaires whose results proclaim to definitively describe us. I'm not putting these down—it's human nature to desire belonging, and these types of systems help us understand ourselves and identify with a group. However, using the checklist I just presented as an ultimate measure, while seductive, is an oversimplified way to decide, "Yes, I'm an empath" or "No, I'm not." Yet I feel it is highly valuable to include because it serves a purpose in helping to establish the energetic field of this phenomenon—a particular frequency or totality—so that people can locate themselves inside of it and understand more about who they are and what their motivations, soul purpose, and woundings may be. You won't see me offering a rating system of "if you answered yes to so many questions, then you are a such-and-such level of empath."

Being an empath is a resonant field. You might still be considering and feeling into its relevance and resonance, but for most people it registers as an immediate intuitive hit—*yes, yes, I know this to be true.* My charge is to try to explain a difficult and esoteric concept in a way that is accessible to as many people as possible so they can then insert themselves inside the idea and decide if it resonates with them. From that point they can make choices about how this material can serve them. I honor each person's individual choice and path. Take what works for you and leave the rest.

What I also know is that on a grander scale, as we evolve, our collective sensitivities will increase. The heart is still a new filter through which to run all of our life decisions, values, and experiences, and we need new tools and mind-sets—a total paradigm shift, really—to help us make the transition. And, while we are evolving into greater consciousness and awareness, these sensitivities are not new in the history of human development. In one aspect, we are returning to ancient ways and ancient wisdom. For many past cultures (and some present ones), communicating with the unseen realms and using their bodies as finely tuned instruments to transmit and receive energy was routine and practiced. A skill that was valued and honed. These societies knew how to live in balance and harmony with the natural world and sought to be in sacred relationship with, rather than in domination of, the world around them. Our evolution includes reclaiming some of these lost ways.

Regardless of the degree to which you identify as an empath, the life tools I explain in subsequent chapters are sorely lacking in the world and desperately needed if humankind is to evolve and practice heart-centered living. This book is not just about understanding your empathic nature. It is about recognizing where you fit in the grand scheme of humanity's evolution and owning your choice to incarnate *now*. And with that comes the understanding that you are an emerging leader of the New Earth. Labels aside, you are here to experience your God-self in human form and to contribute to the evolution of this planet and all her inhabitants.

THE EMPATH AS A LIFE PATH

There remains one final critical piece to weave into this comprehensive exercise of defining the term *empath*. This last component is what I consider the key ingredient and is something I haven't found in other materials that talk about being an empath. I am creating the distinction that being an empath is a *life path,* a choice that was made in spirit form when we were deciding what characteristics and experiences we wanted for ourselves in this incarnation.

So the questions then that beg to be answered are: Why in the world would we choose to lose ourselves in relationship? Put ourselves last? Struggle with figuring out where we end and the next person begins? Fail miserably at maintaining boundaries? Dwell in codependence? Live in an almost constant state of overwhelm?

Walking the path of an evolutionary empath is a choice to deeply engage this full spectrum of characteristics—everything it means to be an empath—to gain further insights into the nature of life in human form for our soul's highest growth and expression. It is the choice to experience in a human body all the unique challenges and gifts associated with having an open energy field, a highly sensitive nervous system, the ability to perceive and access subtle energies, an openhearted desire to serve others, and a profound need for peace and harmony.

In addition to our own experience of incarnating as an empath, our soul contracts include anchoring this vibrational field on planet Earth and being in service to humanity's ascension as a whole. We, along with legions of other empaths, sensitives, conscious elders, and next-generation youth, are here to establish the energetic frequency we are evolving toward as a species. Somebody had to be first. We may have been incarnating in increasing numbers over the past several decades, but on a geological scale, all of us make up the genesis of the empathic big bang.

As we empaths progress through our life's experiences, we are discovering, developing, and refining our *medicine*. In shamanic terms, our greatest wounding—our greatest tribulation or challenge—has the potential to become our greatest medicine later in life. Meaning, our greatest challenge becomes a gift we have to offer the world, born of our unique path and the wisdom we have gained from the highs and lows on our journey with that challenge. What is your distinctive medicine? Have you ever considered that through your empathic experiences you have been cultivating and refining your medicine gift to the world?

Once we start to walk in consciousness with this quality of being an empath, we can begin to see it as a gift. We will see what we have learned from the experiences it provided. We will walk in harmony with it. We will come to value it. We will carry its medicine. This book is designed to help empaths move out of living from the unhealthy aspects of being an empath to thriving in the world and embracing this part of themselves as the gift that it is. Moreover, it is about owning the awareness that we came here as wayshowers and anchor points for the return of the divine feminine (more on that in chapter 10) and the ascension into heart-centered consciousness and for holding the frequency of the new human blueprint on planet Earth.

To be thoroughly clear, it is important for me to state that I believe that every human is born with the ability to perceive subtle energies, communicate with the unseen realm, feel all emotions, and sense the world around them. Every human being has empathic abilities. But not every human has incarnated as an *empath*. And not everyone makes the choice at a human level to express their empathic nature. They may have signed up at a soul level, then incarnated, looked at the state of things, and punched out. They might have deemed it too risky or treacherous to expose that aspect of themselves in this lifetime, so they repressed it and took a different life path. Remember, we have free will.

I also want to acknowledge that not everyone struggles with their empathic abilities. There are some cultures (and households) that actually cultivate these qualities from early childhood, and the entire tribe or community operates in this way. For them it is normal to be an empath, and it is supported, encouraged, and mentored. They are acknowledged and respected for their sensitivities and taught how to develop, manage, and apply them. And because they have experienced nothing but support, being an empath is not a struggle or a point of conflict or shame and, consequently, probably not a major vehicle for deep soul growth. However, while they may not have chosen a life where they experience the struggles of an empath for soul growth, they are most certainly still here to help anchor these frequencies in the energetic grid of our planet and hold the space of fourth chakra consciousness.

Most empaths perceive at least the early period of their life's journey as a hardship. The vast majority of us did not have parents or mentors who recognized our abilities or knew how to guide us. Our life can feel solitary, and we are often ostracized, made fun of, or treated like an outsider. We have to hide much of who we are, and we are forced to develop extensive coping mechanisms and wear masks to appear "normal." We pretend we are fine when we're not. We shove our feelings and reactions deep below the surface. In some cases we bury our empath so deep inside that what we present on the outside is quite the opposite: stoic, emotionless, mechanical, detached, or hypersocial.

At a more profound level, empaths choose to engage this very challenging mantle to hold the higher vibrations of love, heart-centeredness, and expanded consciousness on the planet. So, while there is a long list of qualities, characteristics, and behaviors that, taken collectively, do a good job of defining empaths, we do ourselves an injustice and miss a critical component in understanding ourselves if we don't acknowledge that we chose to be an empath at a soul level. And hence, we chose all that came with living the life of an evolutionary empath.

WHAT AN EMPATH IS—
THE FORMAL DEFINITION

Being an empath is a state of being, 24/7. It is part of our personality, part of our psychological makeup, and part of our energetic physiology. It is a choice we made at the highest soul level.

Here is the formal definition I have crafted from all the aspects I have presented in this chapter:

An empath is a person who chose, at a soul level, to incarnate with a specific set of qualities expressing in varying degrees: an open energy field, a highly sensitive nervous system, the ability to perceive subtle energies, a strong need to create peace and harmony, and a deep desire to be of service. Empaths easily perceive nonverbal communications and subtle energies from life-forms—physical or nonphysical—either through feeling, knowing, physical sensations, or a combination thereof. Empaths are often born to families and communities that do not recognize their abilities or know how to mentor them. The unique challenges that these qualities present were accepted by the soul to serve their highest growth and to serve the planet by anchoring the new human blueprint and fourth-chakra (heart) consciousness on Earth during this early period of ascension.

Unpacking the
Five Qualities of an Empath

In this chapter we'll unpack each of the five qualities of an empath and consider examples of what they look like in real life.

OUR ABILITY TO MERGE WITH AND ABSORB THE ENERGY OF OTHER BEINGS

As empaths we have the uncanny ability to tune in to and feel other people's emotions, feelings, and states of being. We not only feel what they are feeling, we can also take on what they are feeling like it is our own, actually experiencing those emotions in our bodies and then expressing them. We can also insert ourselves inside other people's circumstances, seeing everything from their point of view. When we don't know we're doing it, we think what we're feeling and expressing are our own emotions and viewpoints.

Empaths also have very open energy fields, often with no boundaries or sense of limitations. Our psyche remembers what it is like to be in spirit form, where there is little need to protect ourselves and no concept of struggle, conflict, or competition. We are vast and expansive when we exist in pure consciousness. When we incarnate in human form, this memory of how we are one with everyone and everything is preserved, though usually at a subconscious level. This memory creates an idealistic, loving, open, expansive, trusting state of being that translates into the energy we carry and thus into our energy field.

This open energy field, coupled with our predisposition for heightened sensitivities, makes it so easy and natural for us to merge with others and absorb their energy patterns that we often don't realize we're doing it. And, to our detriment, when we are unconscious of it, we think that everything we are feeling is our own. It doesn't even cross our mind that we are feeling—and expressing—someone else's emotions or pain.

When we don't know any other way than to become the other, the idea that we are separate and distinct can be a confounding notion. To then begin practicing boundaries and engaging in activities to determine who we really are and to center ourselves in our own core can feel as foreign and unfamiliar as walking on our hands. I'll cover this in greater detail in chapters 8 and 9, where I talk about the importance of boundaries.

Additionally, when we are reprimanded for or met with strict denial of what we feel, notice, or intuit in another or a situation, it creates immense confusion and usually behavior modification. As children, we are still developing (cognitively, physically, emotionally, etc.), trying to figure out how the world works and learning to correlate what we're thinking, feeling, or intuiting with reality. For us, what we see, feel, hear, or sense is real and clear as day, and as children, we don't stop to think that other people can't see, feel, hear, or sense the same things. We rely on our parents to help us sort this out, but when they don't have a context for or understanding of our sensitivities, they usually chalk up our strange experiences to imaginary friends, daydreaming, making something up, trying to get attention, eavesdropping, lying, or any other "rational" explanation. It is incredibly invalidating, and as a result, we begin to kill off the parts of ourselves that are not met with approval and acceptance. However, these parts don't go away. They just go into the shadow. Codependence, addiction, and other unhealthy behaviors become our coping mechanisms when we can't reconcile our experiences.

Wendy's Story

As a child, Wendy remembers feeling a chronic sense of shame and being wrong no matter what she said. "As I got a little older I always seemed to be speaking things no one else expected or wanted to acknowledge." She had the experience of her mother being angry, asking why she was angry, and her mother denying it. Many times people told her, "That's not a true experience," but then later they came back and realized it was true. For her this created a tendency to walk on eggshells and a fear of speaking things that seemed crystal clear to her. She learned to close off her consciousness and was accused of daydreaming from as early as she can remember. She said, "It was an escape mechanism to keep me from saying something that would somehow get me in trouble. It's much easier to have someone yell at me because I'm not listening than to tell me I'm wrong."

Leah's Story

Leah described how she was tuned in to her mother as a child and teenager. Her mother was a narcissist, addict, and rageaholic, so she was never sure what to expect at any given moment. As a child living in a large house, it didn't matter where her mother was in the house, Leah could feel her location and what mood she was in and then decide if she needed to stay away or do something to soothe and manage her mother.

This sensitivity and ability to connect to another's energetic state continued on in her romantic relationships. Leah was so connected to one partner's energy in particular—a man with whom she broke up and got back together several times—that even during periods of breakup, when he would travel for his job she could feel precisely when he boarded the plane and left the city as well as when he returned to the city.

Rebecca's Story

Rebecca shared a specific example from about twenty-five years earlier when she first noticed that she took on other people's physical symptoms. She would ride the bus back and forth to work and revealed, "One day there was a person behind me who was coughing and sneezing and by the time I got to work I had a sore throat. I called myself a hypochondriac. I knew this wasn't possible [to catch their affliction so quickly]. The next morning the sore throat was gone. I came to understand that I was taking on other people's physical experiences. This was my first experience of it and I was very critical of myself for it."

My Story

When I was in the Air Force I was stationed in Saudi Arabia for three months. I was twenty-five—way before I knew I was an empath. While in that country, I absorbed all the heightened tensions from all the countries and branches of service that were present. I absorbed all my coworkers' fears as well as their homesickness and how much they missed their families. I felt the discomfort and sometimes downright hostility projected on me—and the other women I worked with—just for being a woman. My nervous system registered every danger and potential threat while trying to manage my own emotional overwhelm. I had several unusual reactions to the stress, including bleeding gums. While I loved the job I performed, I was so distraught and cried so hard that my throat swelled up and I could hardly breathe. I had no idea how to process my own emotions and certainly had no clue that I was absorbing the stress and tension from everyone around me.

Dorian's Story

During a college English class, the discussion turned to the female body and sexuality, as both were prominent parts of the story line of a movie the class was assigned to watch. One female student who had dwarfism had a very strong emotional reaction to the conversation as it was clear that her body didn't allow her the "normal" sexual experiences of a young woman. She was confined to a wheelchair and quickly wheeled herself out of the room. Dorian's entire body was taken over by what the student was experiencing. He got flashes of her life experience, felt what she was feeling, and was overcome with sadness and isolation. When the class was over he had to go home and cry. These kinds of experiences create symptoms of nausea, body tremors, sweating, and general overwhelm for him. When he takes on another person's state, he can't handle anything else that goes on around him. He has to isolate as quickly as possible in order to shut out the outside world and nurse himself back to balance.

Amy's Story

Amy recalls a period in her early twenties when she had something scheduled every single night for three weeks. She didn't yet recognize that she could say no and hadn't gotten to know herself well enough to discern what she liked and didn't like doing. She also felt a sense of obligation to those who asked her to participate in the various events. That period was a turning point, as it pushed her to the limit and left her completely exhausted, and she realized, "This will kill me if I keep it up." When she was in this pattern she would crash hard and often get a migraine. She didn't yet have a concept of or know how to be more mindful of managing her energy field or establish boundaries, so this three-week period helped create a critical awareness.

Willow's Story

Willow is always aware of where her children are emotionally, even if they aren't overtly expressing themselves. When she was a young mother, she struggled with discipline because she could feel their emotions so strongly. In one particularly difficult example, her son was at the dinner table but wouldn't eat his food. She and her husband gave him a timer and told him he had to eat before the timer went off. Willow could feel him getting more and more anxious and her anxiety increased as her son's did. Even though she and her husband were calmly talking to him and explaining the consequences of his behavior, he wouldn't eat until the last minute. At that moment he wolfed down as much food as he could but then vomited because he tried to shove everything in before the timer went off. Willow had to leave the table because she was so overcome with his emotions. She went to another room and sobbed, taking some time to regain her composure to be able to come back into the "parent" role.

In addition to feeling other people's feelings or tuning in to their emotional or energetic state (and not enforcing clear boundaries), we can absorb other people's personality traits, preferences, and values. Said another way, we can lose our identity in relationships, and not just romantic relationships. Our natural inclination is to connect to other people on a deep level. This type of connection brings us great fulfillment and reminds us of the oneness we experience in spirit form. However, when we are unaware that we are empaths and unconscious of our ability to merge with another life force, we have not yet developed our homing beacon or internal compass to keep us centered in our own selves, so we run the risk of absorbing and taking on the qualities of others, such as our parents, lovers, bosses, in-laws, and sometimes even acquaintances or strangers.

This can show up in myriad ways as unwitting adjustments to your sleep habits, hobbies, spending habits, involvement with pets or children, social activities, what and when you eat, or points of view concerning politics, the environment, or parenting. These modifications can be so subtle that you may not even realize they have happened, or it may not register that these habits or qualities really aren't your own. When you are so used to soaking up the energy patterns of everyone you closely interact with, you may have no other experience to compare it to, so carrying around other people's emotions and habits feels "normal" to you.

Lydia's Story

Lydia has taken on her partner's personality traits, beliefs, or habits in multiple relationships. For one ex-husband in particular, whom she described as a straightlaced judgmental individual, she found herself excluding important people in her life because he didn't approve of them. According to Lydia, he was not domineering and never asked her outright to stop seeing certain friends or relatives. She just so completely absorbed his views and opinions of others that she began to relate to them as he related to them. This culminated in Lydia almost excluding her own sister from her wedding because he had strong judgments about her.

Lydia's first marriage was to a drug addict, and she immersed herself in his addictive behaviors and habits and began doing drugs as well. She did not do drugs before they met and was not coerced by him to participate. In her desire to merge, she took on his habits as a way of trying to deeply relate to him and create greater intimacy. Instead, she created her own addiction. As Lydia described it, these relationships were examples of "me twisting myself outside of my comfort zone to make sure the person I paired myself with was as comfortable as they could be."

Even now, when Lydia goes to a restaurant where the server has an accent, her children have made a game of counting how many seconds it takes before she starts talking in the same accent. For years she was completely unaware that she did this. It used to cause problems because people in her party thought she was making fun of or insulting the server. She had no idea that she could identify with and take on the qualities of another person so easily and almost instantly.

Raquel's Story

Raquel had a friend who learned to play the Native American flute. Whenever he played the flute in her presence, she was enthralled and *picked up strongly on his joy and enthusiasm. This influenced her so much that she decided to purchase a flute for herself and learn to play. As the weeks went by she recognized that it didn't speak to her, and she wasn't nearly as excited as she thought she would be. She certainly didn't feel as enchanted and joyful as when she heard her friend play. She had completely absorbed his interest and zeal, which became obvious to her through her lack of excitement and passion when she played the flute herself.*

Mary's Story

One of Mary's coworkers made the comment, "Mary acts like the person she's with." Mary thought about this and realized that she patterned herself, her demeanor, and her communication style after those of the person she was talking to. If someone was funny and joked a lot, she made sure she said funny things, too. She also observed that she would think of someone she knew whom the other person liked and would take on their qualities to gain favor and be liked herself.

Wendy's Story

Wendy speaks of her marriage as being short-lived, unhealthy, and unhappy. Yet it was eye-opening for her when she recognized how much of herself she denied and how many of her husband's preferences she took on. She said, "I really got to see in action how immensely codependent my whole life was and how I chameleoned myself so forcefully that I not only became unrecognizable to myself, but my friends thought they had lost me, too. I would speak in terms of 'we' (as opposed to I), and I talked like he did and used his turns of phrase. (He had a very unique way of explaining life and I became very attached to using those turns of phrase so we could be recognized as a couple.) My entire diet changed from vegetarian to carnivore. He ate huge portions of food but was very active. He always encouraged me to have seconds, so I did. He wanted to be a member of the Society for

Creative Anachronism and do medieval gaming. I couldn't stand it and didn't want to but would go camping with the kids and cook. I became very active in alternative communities. He was very interested, I was not. He wanted the relationship to become polyamorous. I tried to twist myself into a pretzel for a year to become that and accommodate it. I pretended to practice it with him for a year to save my marriage. I actively tried to keep his family away at his behest because he didn't like his family and didn't want to be around them. I helped him make excuses and told lies for him to avoid seeing them. Conversely, I also lost my own spine and ability to hang out with my own friends because he felt they didn't like him."

Jocelyn's Story

Jocelyn was married three times, each time thinking, "What am I doing?" She knew it wasn't going to be a forever decision. She said, "I would immerse myself with that person for three to seven months. I would stop whatever I used to like to do, such as journaling or dancing, and would stop doing joyful things. I was so needy of wanting to feel deeper. I was seeking intimacy with myself and deeper connection with myself but mistook losing myself in them for this experience I was longing for."

Being able to merge so completely with others almost always creates the unfortunate by-product of not knowing who you are, how you feel, or what you want. Said another way, we suffer from an identity crisis, often for decades. As unconscious empaths, it is incredibly difficult for us to figure out where we end and the next person begins. When we live this way and don't even know it, we lose track of our own wants, desires, feelings, and values because they become consumed and overridden by the swirling tempest of everyone else's wants, desires, feelings, and values that we have locked into. In chapter 14 we will explore ways to define yourself separately from others and to create a solid self-image so you can always return to your center.

It is also important to understand that, while most of these examples show human-to-human interactions, as empaths we don't just absorb energies and emotions from other humans. Empaths can often take in energies from animals, plants, rocks, bodies of water, and more. When asking yourself, "Is this mine?" don't forget to consider that you might be picking up on nonhuman sources.

OUR HIGHLY SENSITIVE NERVOUS SYSTEMS

There is practically no end to the ways in which our sensitivity can present. Most commonly it shows up as getting easily overstimulated or overwhelmed. The source can be anything: too much noise, harsh or artificial lighting, large crowds, violent programming, too many projects or tasks, being subjected to constant arguments or loud talkers, sensitivity to electronics or power lines, the weather, chemicals, and strong or artificial scents, to name a few. This attribute is practically universal among empaths, no matter what form it takes.

Natasha's Story

Natasha has such a sensitive nervous system and is so empathic that she struggles greatly in large groups of people. On multiple occasions, she has had to leave gatherings, workshops, or social events, panicked and practically in tears because being with so many people created a massive anxiety attack. Her nervous system gets completely overstimulated, and she feels everyone else's energy so intensely that she immediately becomes overwhelmed and loses her ability to make good self-care decisions. All she can think about is getting out, to the point that she doesn't look people in the eye, she doesn't tell them what she's feeling, and she doesn't even tell them where she's going. She just makes a beeline for the door. Until she and I worked together, she did not understand the cause and effect of this behavior or that her energy container was full of holes and she was taking on everyone else's energies.

Leah's Story

Leah is highly sensitive to the change of seasons as well as the presence or absence of the Sun. During each quarter, her digestive system shuts down and goes "wonky," and she feels like she can't digest anything for a couple of weeks. It has to go through a period of adjustment as one season gives way to the next. She is also highly sensitive to the winter season and has to engage in multiple tactics to keep from spiraling into depression during the colder and shorter days. She uses therapy lighting, plays uplifting music, chants and sings, and puts a lot of effort into keeping her mood high, especially on cloudy days. When the Sun is out, her system responds strongly and positively.

Bridgette's Story

Bridgette was prone to intense migraines and had to have it cold, dark, and quiet to sleep. When her children were young, she had blackout blinds in the bedroom and a window-unit air conditioner. Her children could not make a peep until she got out of bed, especially on the weekend. Even then, it took her a long time to wake up and be ready for noise and energetic activities. If she didn't get enough sleep, her eyes would hurt terribly, and she would wear sunglasses even at work. Bridgette was a product of the Valium generation, and her doctor prescribed Valium for decades to help manage her sensitivities.

Raquel's Story

Raquel cannot watch violent movies or television shows. She went to see Kingsman with her husband and, she shared, "I was so altered that my husband and I had a fight. I was so unsettled that I couldn't speak. I *bit his head off. It was like disassociation. I left my energy and my body so much. I had to find a way to get back to myself."*

Rebecca's Story

Rebecca shared that she doesn't do well in closed spaces with a lot of people and conversations. She tends to disassociate in those circumstances. She says, "I go elsewhere mentally. This is not a conscious process; it just happens. I have a lot of difficulty with all the sounds going on at once. I'm good at shutting external stimuli out, but it's hard when a lot of voices are talking at once, and I can't make heads or tails. I'm gone before I know I'm gone."

Dorian's Story

Dorian said, "I need to have a certain level of management over my environment. The amount of stimuli in my environment will make me explode. The way my brain works, I bring in an insane amount of data. For example, at a restaurant every sound would be pervading my consciousness (clinking of plates, music, plastic wrap crinkling, assessing each person and their energy, noticing the spiritual essence of a place, picking up on entities, and possibly even getting flashes of the present or future of the place)."

In addition, Dorian's wife and children know that after a certain hour in the evening, the sound level needs to be nil because it takes him a couple of hours to settle in and fall asleep. "My ears are always absorbing information."

Lexi's Story

Lexi is highly sensitive to smells, especially if they are artificial or chemical based, which can trigger an immediate migraine. If a scent is natural, like pure essential oils, she is okay. She long ago removed from her home any artificially scented candles, air fresheners, perfumes, colognes, and anything else that triggered her. In public, she has to

visualize thick shielding and calls upon her many angelic guides to help
keep her safe and functional.

Managing our sensitivities is key to staying functional, and it is done through multiple methods including tending to our energy field (see chapter 7) and engaging in radical self-care (see chapter 12). It's vital to recognize that we aren't wired like other humans and no amount of denial or aversion training is going to make us "toughen up." That is a form of committing violence upon ourselves. Our sensitivities are a gift, but we must learn how to adjust our environments (and probably a relationship or two) to maximize peace and harmony and minimize overwhelm.

OUR SENSITIVITY TO SUBTLE ENERGIES AND INFORMATION

As empaths we are highly sensitive to subtle energies, which means we can perceive and/or access information from the subtle realms.

A radio is an electronic device that receives radio waves and converts the information carried by them into a usable form. All radios use some type of an antenna, which is the mechanism that collects the radio waves. As empaths, we have a massive antenna, and we are constantly processing thousands of pieces of data that our sensitive receivers are collecting. And we have the ability to receive transmissions from "stations" that other humans may not be tuned in to.

Our particular brand of sensitivities combined with our open energy fields make us empaths prone to paranormal, psychic, or otherworldly experiences as well as chillingly accurate intuition. We are highly predisposed toward seeing apparitions, communicating with angels or the dead, seeing or feeling other people's energy patterns or auras, tuning in to and "reading" the future or the past, communicating with animals or anything with a life force, working with and understanding energy fields and energy therapies, achieving naturally induced altered states of con-sciousness, receiving premonitions, and astral traveling, to name a few!

Lydia's Story

Lydia was one of those children who used to freak her family out by what she "just knew" without anyone telling her. She recalls several specific examples of knowing things without having any way to know them. In one instance, before the age of five, a mentally disabled aunt was attacked at her mental health institution, and she became pregnant. The family, being Catholic, made the aunt carry the baby to term. The family didn't talk about it in front of Lydia, but she knew that there was something going on that involved her aunt and a baby. One day she asked her grandmother why Aunt Barbara's baby couldn't come and live with them. Her astonished grandmother demanded that she tell her who told her this information.

In another instance, as a four-year-old, Lydia knew that her uncle was having an affair. One day her aunt (the cheating uncle's wife) was distraught, sitting at her grandmother's kitchen table, ruminating as she smoked and drank coffee. Lydia came right up to her and said, "Aunt Margaret, don't be sad. He doesn't love her like he loves you." Flabbergasted, the aunt just pushed her away, asking whom she had been talking to. Lydia said that because she had so many of these types of encounters, her family told her she had an overactive imagination, was a liar, or was just plain weird.

In an example from second or third grade, Lydia remembers playing the game Heads Up, Seven Up. In this game, a few children are asked to come forward and stand at the front of the room. The other children close their eyes and put their heads down but leave a fist on the desk with a thumb sticking up. The children at the front of the room then quietly go around the room, tucking everyone's thumbs back into their fists. When they are done, the children sitting at their desks open their eyes and try to figure out who specifically tucked in their thumb. Lydia was accused of cheating numerous times because she always, without fail, knew who did it. The teacher didn't believe her when she said she could just tell who was touching her. So the teacher tested her several times, to the point of covering up Lydia's eyes with her own hands. After that incident, the class never played Heads Up, Seven Up again.

Willow's Story

Willow can feel the consciousness of inanimate objects. Her children often tease her, for example, when she tells them to be gentle with putting their plate in the sink. When she's dusting or cleaning, she talks to things. She thanks the pictures for being beautiful, the fireplace for providing warmth. She has a relationships with the things in her environment, and they communicate with her.

Hazel's Story

Hazel is a sixteen-year-old who has been able to see the dead for a couple of years. She didn't really talk about it with anyone except her parents until her beloved grandmother died and began visiting her a few weeks later. On that day, Hazel came home from school. Her parents were not home, but she heard footsteps upstairs. She went tentatively to her bedroom and found her grandmother sitting in a chair as plain as day. She could clearly see every detail, such as her clothing, face, hair, and glasses. She remembers being so thrilled to see her. They began talking and went downstairs so Hazel could make herself a snack. However, when they heard the garage door opening (her dad coming home from work), her grandmother said she had to go. That evening her dad took her to Burger King, and she ordered exactly what her grandmother would have ordered. She even cut her burger in half, just like her grandmother did, and saved the other half for later. They took the half burger home and put it in the refrigerator. The next day the box was still there, but the burger was gone.

In another vivid example, Hazel shared that on multiple occasions she saw a woman in her house looking desperately for a gold dove necklace. The woman would actually go into her parents' room and rummage through her mother's jewelry. Hazel remembers very precise details: the woman was tall, had her brunette hair secured in a low ponytail with bangs swept to the side, and wore glasses, a green V-neck sweater, and long khaki pants. When she was a child, Hazel had bought the necklace for her mother at a garage sale. Hazel didn't know what to do, so she did a bit of research and read that if a dead person comes around looking for an item, you should put it outside the house, but nearby, so they can find it. She and her mother sat on the deck one evening talking about the incident and decided to leave the necklace on a table on the deck. The next day the necklace was gone, and they never saw the woman again.

Amy's Story

Amy is particularly sensitive to disasters and tragedies that happen on a global scale. She has learned that if she becomes irritable and agitated (not her normal state), she treats it as a red flag and assesses if what she's feeling is hers or not. She will check the news to find out what's happening in the world, and usually some form of natural disaster, bombing, terrorist event, or something that involves many souls crossing over at once has occurred.

Amy is also able to detect the presence of her pets that have passed. On regular occasions she has heard the thump of a dog lying down (where there wasn't one) or a dog sighing or felt a cat jump up on the bed. This phenomenon has been confirmed by an animal communicator who has shared that her past pets often visit her.

I know numerous healers, massage therapists, energy workers, and intuitives who are able to read or "just know" what is going on in their client's body, mind, or energy. I have heard countless reports of clients saying, "How did you know to put your hand there?" "How did you know that was going on with me?" "How did you know I was having an issue with my [body part, relationship, pet]?" This has happened to me numerous times in my client practice as well as with coworkers or friends. As empaths, we are able to tune in to more than just the realm of our five senses.

My Story

When I worked at the medical examiner's office, one of my coworkers was stressed, and I offered to do a little energy work and clearing on her. One of her friends was sitting there with us. As I worked on her, I perceived some unsettling emotional and energetic patterns and asked if I could ask her some questions and share what I was picking up in her energy field. I don't remember precisely what I said, but I told her what I was picking up about her relationship with her boyfriend and the unhealthy dynamics between them (she was okay with her friend being present). She was incredulous and a bit speechless. Her friend told me later that what I shared freaked her out because it was so accurate.

Wendy's Story

Wendy became a massage therapist before training became formalized. She learned by being an apprentice to another woman therapist who did not teach her about boundaries or energy transference. Wendy had been working on people for almost ten years when she started seeing a counselor because she was having dreams and memories of events that had never happened to her. She would have vivid dreams of child abuse, but there was none in her family. She dreamed that she was a man experiencing family tension with people who were not in her family. She had dreams of spouses fighting or fights between parents and children. Fortunately, her therapist helped her identify that she was taking on other people's experiences and taught her energy and grounding practices. Now, with her energetic practices in place, the gift

shows up as impressions of people and not specific details. She said,
"Mostly I would just find myself saying something that felt completely
random to me, and the client on the table would come unglued in a
positive way, 'How did you know?'"

The natural world (humans included) is always communicating, but so many of us don't pay attention. Empaths pick up signals and signs that others don't, though they could. And for many empaths, part of our disillusionment during childhood was having parents who didn't understand or believe what we were so naturally able to see and sense. Depending on what coping strategy you deployed, you might have trouble "turning off" your abilities or, on the other end of the spectrum, might have buried them so deeply that you need to coax them out of hiding. There's no obligation for you to do anything with these gifts, but remember that anything that remains in the shadow (unacknowledged, unloved, disowned) will continue to seek expression and strive to be reunited with the whole.

THE PREMIUM WE PLACE ON PEACE AND HARMONY

As empaths, our heart-centeredness has a constant traveling companion: the desire for peace, cooperation, harmony, mutual support, genuine caring, and teamwork. This premium we place on peace and harmony shows up in two areas: our relationships and our environment. Let's look at the first aspect in more detail.

In terms of relationships, this characteristic affects how we interact in our relationships, workplaces, families, and social groups. It usually translates into devoting a great deal of time tending to our relationships to keep peace, calm, and harmony and to promote cooperation. We thrive on meaningful relationships and crave intimate connection, so this investment of our time and energy is a priority we don't begrudge.

We are fed by connecting deeply with another's true essence and by that person reciprocating in kind.

When we are conscious of this quality, it makes us exceptional mediators, facilitators, coaches, negotiators, partners, and team leaders. We are excellent at reading a group, understanding everyone's point of view, and being sensitive to people's triggers. With practice and conscious engagement, we can monitor and manage any tendency to fall into codependent behavior and maintain our boundaries so we don't lose ourselves to the group. In one-on-one settings, we can create a sense of safety and connection that allows the other to share deeply and feel valued and heard. We value cooperation and equality over force and competition.

When we are unaware of this aspect of ourselves, however, we usually deny our needs in favor of keeping everything together for the family, workplace, friend, or social group. Maintaining the illusion of peace and harmony requires that we do not acknowledge our own intuition, disappointment, unmet needs, lack of fulfillment, disagreement, or overwhelm, or it would obliterate our precarious house of cards. This behavior is almost always accompanied by lots of pretending, followed by resentment and projection. Until the value we place on speaking our piece overcomes our fear of disturbing the peace, we will stay in a pattern of complicity.

Aaliyah's Story

Aaliyah was living in New York City, living her dream as a professional dancer. She roomed with a fellow dancer whom she had known for ten years. However, Aaliyah was working for a big, reputable ballet company, and her roommate was with a smaller company. This made her roommate jealous and created tension between them. In preparation for an upcoming weekend of multiple performances, Aaliyah cleaned the apartment for her roommate in a way that would please her and went to the grocery store to get items her roommate would like. All of this was to potentially stave off any jealous outbursts or lessen the intensity of whatever resentment her roommate might throw her way because of her big upcoming weekend. In the process, Aaliyah compromised her own mental and physical preparation because she was focused on keeping the peace with her roommate instead. Aaliyah said, "My performances in general that weekend were disappointing to me. In one particular performance, I wasn't present. My body did what it was asked to do by the choreography, but I didn't get to enjoy it and I didn't get to let the audience see me. I was a body doing shapes on the stage instead of being a vessel for spirit."

Aaliyah shares another example of how she has modified her behavior during long holidays such as Thanksgiving and Christmas when she visits her family. She says she used to binge drink to put herself in a good mood so that when she got triggered by her family or had to deal with their judgments of her, she could let it roll off her back and not affect her. In her family, great value is placed on respecting your elders, which, in her words, means you are to defer to your elders at all times. Standing up for yourself or your beliefs is considered disrespectful. So she would compromise herself and her health by suppressing her own truth to keep the peace. After each of these incidents, she was exhausted, hung over, and depleted. It would take her an entire week to get back to normal, which would affect her work and her relationships.

Raquel's Story

When she was still a young child, Raquel took on the role of peacemaker in her family. She said she was always trying to calm everyone and make peace. She accomplished this mostly by trying to anticipate everyone else's needs, but it became overwhelming because she felt responsible for everything. When she was in the first grade and her brother in the third grade, she tried to intervene during a playground bullying incident. Her brother was being bullied, and even though she was two years younger, she came over to break up the tension and prevent a fight.

As an adult, the overwhelming feeling of responsibility still crept in for Raquel. Whenever she would leave town for a few days for work, she would do as much as she could to try and make it as easy as possible for her husband and daughter while she was gone. This involved making everyone's lunches, sending emails, coordinating activities, and handling whatever other business she could. Because she was so tuned in to her husband's energy, if he was upset, she would feel his pain in addition to her own. She didn't want to hear about how hard it was for him while she was away on business, so she would try to set up her whole world to avoid those explosive feelings.

My Story

A couple of years into my first marriage, I remember my ex-husband remarking, "Where did the Stephanie go who used to be so cocky, outrageous, and unafraid to say what she thought?" I replied something to the effect of "Well, there's more at stake now." I didn't know I was an empath and didn't understand my deeper motivations.

For almost fourteen years I suppressed aspects of my personality in favor of maintaining coveted harmony. I was massively codependent and had no confidence recognizing or asking for what I needed, even when the request was completely reasonable and fully justified. It wasn't worth the potential risk (real or imagined) of upsetting my husband.

When our marriage started coming apart, my ex was at a difficult point, as life—his job, finances, status—didn't look the way he had hoped, and with my career transition and not being able to sell our home, there was much boiling beneath the surface. I was highly sensitive to his moods and whenever I needed to speak to my needs, bring something up we needed to decide as a couple, or discuss something potentially prickly, I always milk-toasted it down. I walked on eggshells, trying to pick the right time to bring it up. I sanded off the edges so that it would land more gently and not provoke a blowup. Oftentimes, if it was about my own needs or wants, I wouldn't bring it up at all.

I called all of this behavior "compassion." My husband was disappointed, struggling, and frustrated. I was his loving wife trying to be sensitive to his circumstances. It all sounded good in my head.

Our need for peace and harmony as empaths translates directly to our home and office environments, not just our relationships with other people. It shows up in the way we arrange our physical environment and tend to our physical and energetic needs. Our sensitive nervous systems can pick up very subtle levels of discord and dissonance in the energy field of other people as well as the energy of every item in our home, workplace, or wherever we spend time.

The color of our walls, our decor, the arrangement of furniture, the sounds inside the home, music we play, lighting, and more all either positively calm or negatively stimulate our nervous system. As empaths, it is not uncommon for us to constantly be tweaking things and clearing energies in our surroundings to create the most harmonious environment for our sensitive nervous systems.

Amy's Story

Amy is clairaudient and very sensitive to sound. When she is home alone she rarely has the TV on and enjoys the peace and quiet. She is very discerning as to when she can handle the TV being on, and even when she's engaged in a show or her husband is watching something, she will sometimes need to leave the room or ask that the volume be turned down. Crowds are difficult for her to manage because of the overwhelming noise and the energy of so many people. She loves live music but can't go to concerts because of the way the sound (and crowd) affects her.

In terms of her home space, Amy has a nightly routine where she carefully clears her own energetic field and sets a field of protection around her home and property. If she doesn't do this, she experiences a subtle but clear feeling the next day that something in the house "isn't right" and registers a sense of discomfort. As soon as she tends to her practice, everything goes back to "normal." One of her biggest triggers inside the home is clutter, and if clutter begins to build up she stacks it, labels it, and puts it out of her visual range to deal with later. When her home is in disorder she physically experiences minor anxiety, and her entire body tightens up until she can manage the clutter.

Lexi's Story

Lexi is highly sensitive to the energies of people, alive or dead, as well as to dark forces. For many years as an unconscious empath she was regularly overwhelmed, taking on others' emotions (especially sadness, fear, anger, and hopelessness) and experiencing multiple physical symptoms, such as migraines and feeling nauseous and light-headed, when she did. When she became aware of her sensitivities, she started making changes and created a thorough energy self-care and protection routine. She tends to the energy of her home, land, and car on a daily basis, and the protective shield she visualizes goes thousands of feet above and below her home and property.

Whenever she has gatherings or even family at her home, she always does a thorough cleansing of the home and property afterward to return the vibratory field to a state that is harmonious for her; otherwise the discord will create physical symptoms of distress.

Lexi also directed the refurbishment of an old building into a public venue with therapy offices, a café, and larger spaces to rent for events. Before the space was opened for business, she spent many hours clearing out old energies related to the building, land, and neighborhood and even helped many souls cross over from the funeral home that used to be across the street. In the beginning she said the dense, chaotic energies there used to kick her butt, so she created a crystal grid on the roof and on each floor and now employs comprehensive cleansing and shielding processes similar to those she does with her own home.

Willow's Story

Willow does dream interpretation in her work, so she often relates to her waking life as she does her dreaming life. She said, "I am constantly interacting with everything around me to get my point of reference. I believe the house (with regard to psychology) represents the psyche and different parts of the house correspond to different parts of a person's makeup. When things are not in their proper place, I don't feel like I have a reference point to keep me on track. When this happens I feel scattered and less efficient. I have a sense of feeling lost until everything is put back in its proper position." She is also affected by color and feels most calm and at peace with very muted colors in her home as well as for her clothing.

This sensitivity to the resonance or dissonance of the energies in her home shows up in other ways, too. In particular, Willow shared, "If I am going through any kind of huge transition (healing, death of family, children going from elementary to middle school, any kind of transition), I need to move furniture around to help me process. I am always trying to release things and behaviors that don't serve me. I use transitions as an opportunity to reflect inwardly and then it is reflected externally. I need to move things around to help shift processes and energy."

My Story

Over the past decade, I have observed a particular phenomenon in my relationship to my energetic and physical environment when I go through any kind of accelerated spiritual program. Upon returning home from a deeply transformative workshop, my vibration shifts so much that I often walk into my home and proclaim, "Oh, this just won't do." I have painted rooms, rearranged furniture, swapped entire rooms, and completely reorganized my mesa (Peruvian altar), all in an effort to realign my physical and external world to be in harmony and synchronicity with my new frequency and internal landscape.

I am very sensitive to disturbances in the energy field of my home, so I also tweak furniture and knickknacks on a regular basis. Like adjusting the dial of a radio, these alterations ensure that my inner and outer worlds are harmonious and in complete resonance.

OUR BIG, OPEN HEARTS AND A DESIRE TO SERVE OTHERS

Empaths are very "other" oriented and come into the world with a natural attunement toward service. Because we are so empathic, it is easy for us to put ourselves in another person's shoes. We can understand what another is going through and therefore, of course, want to help them. We have big hearts, which means we tend to be very caring, compassionate, giving, generous, understanding, and thoughtful.

These qualities incline us toward careers in service, or some outlet through which we can care for, attend to, support, and serve others. We are quite frequently found working in health care, in support functions, or as therapists, counselors, clergy, teachers, or artists. We are often the person whom everyone comes to with their problems. Strangers tell us their life story in the grocery store. Our home can have a revolving door—for people, animals, or both.

Unfortunately, our big heart and desire to serve also predispose us to overgiving and putting ourselves last on the list. In our desire to make sure everyone else's needs are taken care of, we neglect our own needs. We become accustomed to running on an empty tank or being in constant deficit. Because we have no boundaries, we take on everyone else's feelings and problems as our own to solve, which often leaves us feeling drained and exhausted.

Raquel's Story

Raquel admits that she has had great difficulty taking time for herself. Just recently she has begun scheduling time on her calendar to do things for herself. She shared how hard it is for her to stay committed *even when she schedules the time: "I paid $500 for an online course for myself. I did the first class and then got behind. I didn't catch up because I chose to do work instead and didn't hold that time sacred." Raquel also acknowledges that she's not a big exerciser. She loves to walk, but she has to put it on the schedule. She has learned that it helps if other people are involved. Because her daughter doesn't drive yet, Raquel is responsible for taking her to the gym. This gives Raquel the opportunity to work out, which she normally wouldn't take, and thrills her because "I can put my daughter first and that benefits me."*

Star's Story

Star said, "I used to put everybody else's needs in front of mine, especially when the kids were younger. My husband's needs came first. My sons' needs came first. I wasn't aware that I even had needs. I rolled along with life the way it was not knowing I had a say in the matter."

Dorian's Story

Dorian grew up with a very devout Christian mother (and grandmother) whose whole life was about service to Christ. Although conservative and fundamental, he was always inspired by that devotion and modified it to his own truth—service to "The Christ," which he described as "this energy that lives within all of us that is about serving all of humanity." He started out his work career as a nurse's aide and was always fascinated by (but not afraid of) death. He said, "As a child I always had dreams of me and God or The Christ battling demons or protecting people. As a kid I grew up a with a superhero mythology. I was always attracted to it as a superhero paradigm (knowing it is not about being a perfect human). With great power comes great responsibility." Dorian serves his community now as a shamanic healer and teacher.

Wendy's Story

Making sure her mother was always emotionally safe and balanced (a highly codependent behavior) led Wendy to follow that pattern as a teenager and adult. From the eighth grade on, her way of navigating was to put people first: "If someone had a headache, pain, PMS, I was always the person to help them, give them a massage, tend to them. If I am giving to people and they feel better, they will not yell at me and will also want me around." She later became a massage therapist and energy healer, but it took her a long time before she felt comfortable putting her hands on her family members in a healing way.

Natasha's Story

Natasha and her husband chose to help out their friends (who were both addicts) by agreeing to take care of their two young sons full-time for over two years. Natasha admits that she has a difficult time buying things for herself and can always think of someone who needs something more than she does. She had gotten to the point where her underwear and bras were ripped, ragged, or full of holes, so her husband gave her money to buy new ones. She couldn't do it. She spent the money instead on the two boys.

Taking care of these two boys created great difficulty in their lives, which was hard for them to admit. Every time they made progress with the boys, seeing their dysfunctional parents would throw the children back into old habits and cause them to regress in their behaviors. Natasha and her husband had to admit that they were overwhelmed and over their heads. They originally agreed to take the boys because they felt they could provide a better and more stable home. Yet they were deeply embedded in codependent and enabling behaviors themselves. This was a huge lesson for both Natasha and her husband, who ended up working with the state to take custody of the boys until they could find the children's grandmother. Yet even after this, they continued to give money and support to the parents and children. Eventually they stopped their support, when they realized they were being taken advantage of.

SUMMARY

Taken in totality, as empaths we all exhibit some degree of the five qualities I have presented. As with any set of characteristics that describe a group, not everyone exhibits every characteristic in the same measure. There are bound to be a few of these qualities that stand out above the others for you personally. As I mentioned earlier, you can think of these five as a continuum—you might register high on some and low on others. And, depending on how conscious you are of your empathic nature, you may have already begun to counter some of the unhealthy tendencies (like losing yourself in relationship or your inability to say no) and develop tools for survival.

As I stated before, some people have shoved their empathic qualities so far down that it is difficult for them to consciously connect with or even recognize them. If that is you, then allow this information to percolate for a while. You might assign yourself the casual task of noticing how any of these qualities show up in the coming weeks or months. Just reading this material is like shining a light on a dark corner. Consciously or subconsciously, contact has been made with your inner empath by engaging with this book.

If you want to take a deeper dive, I recommend exploring how these five qualities have shown up over the course of your life and what you learned from them by journaling about it over the next several weeks. Task your subconscious mind with recalling examples from your life and offering them for you to consider and integrate.

No More Denial: We Are the New Human Blueprint

If you've made it this far in the arc of your life, I know that you recognize, on some level, that denial isn't going to work for you anymore. Denial of your nature, denial of your gifts, denial of your power, denial of your purpose . . . these are all roads you have already traveled. You know them well. Remember the definition of insanity? Doing the same thing over and over and expecting different results. In your heart, you know that doing what you have already done is not going to get you where you desire to go. Your soul has been calling you forward into the next highest expression of your Self . . . into greater authenticity and consciousness. Whether crisis or curiosity brought you to this point, you're ready for a change.

GROWING CORN AND POTATOES

One of the pillars of my work is to make whatever I am offering practical. I might start out with the esoteric, spiritual, or conceptual, but at the end of the day what I do needs to grow corn and potatoes. This phrase comes from the Peruvian shamanic lineage I practice. Growing corn and potatoes is a concept in this culture that refers to anchoring or planting your spiritual wisdom in the earth—in this dimension—so that it creates nourishment for your community. Corn and potatoes are staples in the diet of the Peruvian culture, so this metaphor is about creating everyday sustenance—something people can sink their teeth into, something practical and useful, something in physical form they can see, touch, and smell, something that benefits and grows roots in the physical realm. It's about embodying the wisdom and sharing it with others in a way that is meaningful to their existence.

While this book is focused on empaths, on a deeper level it is focused on life skills for an evolving species. Whether you currently identify as an empath or not, the need for a new human life skills toolbox is undeniable. The hard truth is that, on the whole, humans suck at trusting our intuition, acknowledging our feelings, drawing clear boundaries, asking for what we need, saying no, caring for ourselves, cooperating, sharing, and honoring the dignity and sovereignty of every life-form. As we move into heart-centered consciousness, the well-worn tools of the patriarchy will need to be relinquished. All of the old fail-safes will fail. Value systems will shatter. Duality will—eventually—give way to unity consciousness. The old navigation tools are about to run our collective ship aground. True north is being redefined, and we are in desperate need of a new compass and map.

WHAT IT'S GOING TO TAKE—A PACHAKUTI

Moving forward as a conscious, evolutionary empath is going to take a paradigm shift, individually and collectively. As one of my coaches taught me, paradigms don't stretch, they break. We can't just take the current model of human interaction and values and tweak it a bit here and there. It needs to be thrown out and an entirely new one created in its place.

Oscar Miro-Quesada, who created the Peruvian shamanic tradition I practice, named it the Pachakuti Mesa Tradition. *Pachakuti* is a

Quechua term that means "world reversal." According to Oscar, it is an "Incan notion of a shift in spiritual, magnetic and energetic currents of the Earth brought about by a critical mass or matrix of high-vibration transformed and transformational consciousness (usually human), causing massive upheavals and cosmic changes in both the activities and consciousness-reality paradigm of humanity and leading to a distinct, more 'whole' or all-encompassing world and world-view."[1]

We need a Pachakuti.

On a collective level, the "world reversal" is coming (really, it's already here) as a natural by-product of the period of ascension that we are in. As ignorance gives way to expanding consciousness, the old systems will crumble and new ones will take their place. Remember the example of winter giving way to spring? Each day isn't necessarily warmer (better) than yesterday, but the trend is inevitably moving us toward expansion. So what does that mean for you?

On a personal level, this Pachakuti, or paradigm shift, will involve changes in your daily habits—how you talk to yourself, care for yourself, and view yourself. It will take installing a new operating system, compelling you to look at outmoded belief systems and to release relationships that no longer serve you. It will take surrendering to and embracing your nature. It will take an entirely new relationship with boundaries and an awareness of subtle energies. It will require a fresh relationship with the masculine and feminine. It will ask you to look at relationships and community in an entirely new way. And it will take expanding your perspective to recognize the cosmic influences at work. It will take much practice and diligence. And it will most certainly take courage. It will take planting new seeds that will grow the corn and potatoes in your life necessary to fulfill on your soul contract. Through all of it, we will need each other's support more than ever.

Sitting back and meditating won't do it. Daily affirmations are not enough. Sequestering yourself from others won't produce the growth you desire. Burying your head in the sand will not eliminate unsupportive forces from your life. Staying in "victim mind" will not develop your personal power. All of your old go-to moves of spiritual bypass—being disembodied, blaming, ignoring, pretending, forcing yourself to fit in, keeping yourself small, and hiding out—will no longer be effective or useful. Unless you want to stay in denial.

This book is not a spiritual "fad diet"—the next short-term fix with short-term results. This book is about acknowledging and claiming your nature, embracing your place in the bigger picture, instituting a systemic lifestyle change, and re-creating how you live your life from the ground up. Installing this new paradigm will involve critical mind-set shifts and fresh practices to help you build a solid, conscious, and loving foundation for yourself and your fellow humans, so we can all thrive together in the new world heart consciousness.

As with any type of transformation, becoming conscious to the old habit, pattern, or belief is the first step in making a change. In twelve-step programs, or any program designed to help one change behaviors, the first instruction is always to admit the problem: "I am an alcoholic." "I am addicted to painkillers." "I am codependent." There is great power in stating what is so because it eliminates all the energy and effort spent denying, defending, justifying, rational-izing, hiding, and pretending. When you say, "I am an alcoholic," all the games you play to keep from admitting the truth to yourself get a massive spotlight shone on them, and they shrivel and die like the Wicked Witch of the West doused with water. It is very freeing and clarifying to state what is so. And yes, it is terrifying, too.

Yet a thing is not nearly so frightening when you can call it by name. It is the crucial first step because you will not be able to shift your patterns or have a new relationship with yourself without first clearly owning your truth and acknowledging what is. Otherwise, you will continue to operate as a victim and perceive the events in your life as "being done unto you" or "not having a choice." The sooner you can move out of victim energy, the sooner you will become empowered.

Some people resist stating what is so because it doesn't sound very "spiritual." They think it is equivalent to setting an intention or making a declaration, which is naturally intended to then manifest. This is inaccurate. Not stating what is so is like trying to map out a trip to Colorado Springs without knowing where you are starting from. Saying, "I am in Kansas City and I will travel to Colorado Springs" does not affirm that you will stay stuck in Kansas City. It simply gives you a reference point from which to begin your journey. The Universe knows that your intention is to get to Colorado Springs.

Your own personal world reversal is upon you. I encourage you to start by admitting where you are in space-time. "Hi, I'm Stephanie and I'm tired of hiding my true nature. I am an empath. I want to live in a world where we honor and value all life. Everything in my life is falling apart. I don't know where to begin. I want to embrace my soul's calling to help human consciousness ascend." Whatever your truth is, own it. Tell yourself the truth about what you want and what isn't working for you. Remember, it's not a proclamation of how it will continue to be. It is simply an acknowledgment of where you are starting from. If you've been walking the path of the empath consciously for many years, your truth might be different. But there's still another octave. What is the next step for you? Wherever you fall on the consciousness or adeptness scale, there is always another level on this spiral path.

As you contemplate what it means to be an empath, what it means to be anchoring the new human blueprint onto the Earth grid and to be individually and collectively participating in humanity's evolution, the implications can seem weighty and almost impossible to grasp. Taken in totality, the sheer size and gravity of it can easily shoot you right out of your body. It does for me sometimes. The enormity of it is hard to take in all at one time. Yet at a soul level, you knew you would be incarnating at a very precarious, highly charged time in human history. I know you are up to the challenge.

Having all the answers is not a prerequisite for change. It requires trust . . . trust in yourself. All you need to know is that you are ready and willing. Are you ready? Are you willing? Then simply put one foot in front of the other. Think of it like driving at night. You can't see the entire road, yet you trust that your headlights will illuminate the road far enough in front of you that you can comfortably continue moving forward. That is trust. Take step one—even if you don't know what step two is—and trust that the next step will be revealed to you. Your soul knows where it is going. And the tools in this book will help you bring substance and flesh to the bones of our new consciousness.

WHERE WE BEGIN—THE SPIRAL PATH

I would love to tell you that this transformation will be a linear path: simply do A, then B, then C, and you will achieve D. But I think you already know that that is not how transformation works.

One of my shamanic teachers, Linda Star Wolf, has taught on the subject of the spiral path of transformation for many years and says,

> The simple truth is that our culture doesn't offer a healthy model for change. Change is not a linear process; it does not follow a straight line, nor does it happen in a circular fashion. . . . The spiral path is really an alchemical transformation map of shamanic consciousness. The spiral movement takes us through sequential experiences of symbolic death and rebirth on the pathway of changing something in our lives. Change travels in a circular motion on the spiral path, but it is more like orbits than circles, and each orbit moves us beyond the present situation to a more expanded level of awareness or consciousness.
>
> The spiral path may not travel in a straight line, or what is often referred to as a masculine or yang-like manner, but neither does it move in a circular, feminine, or yin manner.[2]

Star Wolf also says,

The spiral path is the sacred marriage of the masculine (yang), linear path to the feminine (yin), nonlinear path. When the circular
feminine and straight-line masculine energies merge, the result is the
spiral path.[3]

When massive change occurs in our life, we often experience multiple aspects changing all at the same time. It's certainly not linear! When
my spiritual awakening began, I was dealing with change in practically
every area of my life, examining and redefining everything from my relationship with God to what it meant to be a woman to what my life's
ambitions were. My career, marriage, finances, and self-concept were all
in flux simultaneously. Unfortunately, I didn't have much guidance to
help me through it and spent quite a lot of time angry, in despair, confused, lost, bumping into walls, and cussing at God. That's why I do the
work I do in the world now—to help other people through those agonizing world reversals so it is not as painful and confusing as it was for me.

Where I suggest you begin is in first accepting that this transition
will be messy, and it will take time. You're going to get your hands
dirty. Embarking on this level of a shift—with repercussions in personal
as well as planetary consciousness—is no small feat. Yes, at one level you
are embracing your empathic nature and installing tools and systems
to help you thrive in the world. But on another level, you are embodying an anchor point for the new frequencies of consciousness that the
human race is evolving toward. This work—and its repercussions—will
be felt on many levels in many dimensions.

I can also tell you that it doesn't matter where you start. If you look at
the rest of the chapter titles in this book, you'll see where we are headed.
I had to choose some order in which to present the information because
I couldn't state it all at the same time. But make no mistake, all of these
elements will work you simultaneously as you begin to engage, change,

and embrace your nature. Whether you start with understanding your relationship with the divine feminine, learning to clear your energy field, or figuring out how to say no doesn't really matter—they are all helpful and they are all necessary. And there is no right order in which to pursue them. You will eventually get around to all of them, and they are all interconnected in one way or another. You will probably find, too, that as you focus on and make progress in one area, it will translate into progress in other areas. Just pick an area in your life and begin.

RESISTANCE IS FUTILE— YOU CAN'T ESCAPE YOUR OWN DEATH

This isn't meant to be as foreboding as it sounds. I am referring to metaphorical death and rebirth. Many times throughout our lives we die to our old selves. When a piece of us no longer serves our growth—whether it's a belief system, a set of values, a habit, or how we view ourselves—we let it go. This also includes things outside of us: relationships, careers, homes, friends, possessions.

When something no longer serves us, we muster the courage to release it. And thus we go through a type of death process. We release the old, mourn it, and express gratitude for how it served us, and we make room for the new. Everything in life has a natural life cycle. We see this in the micro as well as the macro. On a simple level, each cycle of breath is a form of death and rebirth. Think of the words we use to describe the out-breath: exhalation, expiration. And the words to describe the in-breath: inhalation, inspiration. Our breath dies and is reborn in every moment. Nature is constantly showing us cycles of death and rebirth—in the seasons, the transition from day to night and back to day, and the interconnectedness of ecosystems. And she moves through these cycles with much more grace and trust than we do.

Too often we get in the habit of artificially animating or repeatedly attempting to infuse life into something that is already dead, has already served, and has completed its life cycle. We do this because we either don't want it to be over or we don't know how to get out of it. This is called resistance.

Much on the subject of resistance has been taught and spoken about, and in many cases it is misconstrued as a negative force. I like to think of it less as negative and more as instructive. If you are experiencing resistance and willing to examine what it's about, there is always something important to uncover.

In this instance, I am clarifying resistance to mean rigidity, closed-mindedness, and a refusal to accept what is. When we resist the cycles of nature, the natural ebb and flow of life, the natural sequence of death and birth, we create suffering. And I promise you, suffering only prolongs the inevitable. Death will come no matter how much you ignore, resist, or fight it.

So how do we move past this resistance and suffering? First, we investigate the resistance. We ask ourselves the hard questions: "What am I afraid of?" "What is underneath my resistance?" "Am I really resisting the thing or am I resisting something I've made it mean?"

Second, we embrace its opposite: allowing. Allowing—along with accepting, being open, receiving, and trusting—is the currency of graceful change. And of graceful death.

There's another concept that is sometimes used interchangeably with allowing: surrendering. However, this word tends to elicit more defiance (more resistance!) from people than the concept of allowing because we don't understand what it truly means to surrender. We think surrendering means to give up. Admit defeat. Be conquered. Forever forfeit or relinquish our dreams and desires.

This is a highly masculine way of interpreting surrender. If we take a more feminine approach, surrendering and allowing are about releasing attachment and creating space for the new that is seeking expression. When we surrender, we are simply getting out of our own way and making room. It doesn't mean giving up, nor does it mean settling. One of the tapes I constantly have to monitor in my own head is the one that tells me that allowing or surrendering means I don't have a say in the matter. But this is not true. Manifesting is a co-creative process, and we create as partners with Spirit. My heart knows this, but sometimes my old beliefs creep in, so I know firsthand how challenging it is to practice surrendering.

Part of walking intentionally into your own personal world reversal will be to consciously die to your old self, and even to initiate it. To surrender to what wants to be birthed through you takes faith. Spoiler alert: you won't die just once. This type of death process is a natural part of human existence, and you will experience it many times over your lifetime. With time speeding up, we are experiencing way more "life" in the course of a lifetime than our ancestors did even a hundred years ago. It takes immense courage and vulnerability to recognize when a thing has run its course and to consciously release it. We are used to walking away from something only after we have been bloodied and beaten by it. If someone cheated, lied, left you, fired you, betrayed you, or abused you, it is much easier to say, "I'm done! This is over!" But can you release something or someone simply because you know its time has come and nobody did anything wrong?

Navigating conscious death is a critical—and much overlooked—skill. And as with any skill, it takes time to develop it. As you tune in to what your soul is calling you to do, can you die to the old forms and structures to make room for the new? You can keep fighting it, or you can learn to accept it and release yourself into your death with your eyes wide open. Either way, your life will give you many opportunities to practice. Stepping into the role of conscious evolutionary empath is one of them.

WE ARE THE NEW HUMAN BLUEPRINT

We are the new human design. We are what humans are evolving toward. All of our energy bodies are being refined, and dormant aspects of human potential are being activated. As we reembrace the feminine and purge the heavy-handed, unhealthy masculine expression from our collective system, our empathic qualities will blossom and flourish and become mainstream. As we accept and embrace our intuition, sensitivity, and open hearts and place value on harmony, open communication, and true equality, the very nature of the way we "do life" will be forever transformed. The decisions we make as a global community will follow suit. From the movies we produce to the way we hire employees, the news headlines, our industrial processes, what we choose to eat, and our values will change.

The divine feminine is seeking to return to this planet, and we are major anchor points for this energy. Now I don't mean to imply that as empaths we have an exclusive contract. There are millions of us from all walks of life serving to anchor the divine feminine, living as edge-walkers and wayshowers, and embodying the new evolutionary human design. As empaths, we are one set among many who are pioneering the way into heart-centered consciousness. But it is important to recognize that you chose—at a soul level—your particular body, your specific sensitivities, and your individual set of life circumstances because they *uniquely qualify you to appreciate and carry this higher frequency!*

What's ironic is that in the future, where the human race is headed, we are *normal!* But right now we are the pioneers. We're the ones cutting the path. We are outnumbered, and by most of society's standards, we are currently judged as abnormal. But we are here to stay. And what it will take for us to thrive is the application of a few, but potent, game-changing tools, which are the focus of part 2 of this book.

NUTS AND BOLTS—WHERE TO BEGIN

While transformation and change occur in a nonlinear, spiral path, we have to start somewhere. So, if I had to choose which tools to focus on developing first in your Evolutionary Empath Tool Kit, they would be tending to your energy field and establishing boundaries. Both are equally vital. These are the two most important practices that empaths must engage in to stay sane and healthy. And they are massively important in establishing a strong foundation for our human evolution into higher consciousness and greater awareness. In the next two chapters I will explain both of these tools in great detail, along with providing exercises and daily practices you can begin to engage in immediately. These two skill sets are what I would focus on developing first.

Along with tending to your energy field and establishing boundaries, evolving into a healthy empath is going to require a combination of the following concepts, mind-sets, and practices that complete the complement of your new Evolutionary Empath Tool Kit:

- Recognizing, understanding, and accepting that this is your nature and that you chose this path. You came here to hold this new frequency and pave the way for others. You are embodying the new human blueprint. You are an evolutionary empath, and that comes with unique gifts and challenges. (See this chapter and chapter 5.)
- Understanding and managing your energy field. This involves being conscious of what you are letting in and out, tending to energy leaks, building your container, establishing protection, and clearing your field regularly. (See chapter 7.)
- Drawing healthy boundaries. This has many aspects to it, including creating safety, saying no, asking for what you need, engaging the divine masculine principle, deploying and maintaining your energetic boundaries, and recognizing the consequences of squishy boundaries. (See chapters 8 and 9.)
- Walking in conscious equal partnership with the masculine and feminine within you. This involves doing the work of releasing the patriarchy, understanding the masculine and feminine principles

and embracing them as equals, and reconciling/cultivating your inner marriage. We are experiencing the return of the divine feminine, and you are an anchor point for this frequency. (See chapter 10.)

- Practicing radical self-care, which involves listening to your body, developing trust, making adjustments to your physical environment and to your relationships, giving yourself plenty of downtime, honoring natural rhythms and cycles, drawing boundaries, and caring for your nervous system. (See chapters 11 and 12.)

- Becoming more fully embodied. This means doing your inner work to heal unresolved issues and emotional wounds, practicing being present with your body and emotions, recognizing and avoiding spiritual bypass, accepting that you are a full-spectrum human being, and fully inhabiting yourself with your life force energy. (See chapter 13.)

- Creating a solid self-image. This includes activities that begin to define who you are separate from others, finding and maintaining your center, releasing codependence, and embracing your empathic nature as a gift and not a liability. (See chapter 14.)

As a groundbreaker, you're not just here to break ground by *being* a new kind of human; you're here to *act* from that new human blueprint. And in so doing, you set an example for others, offer inspiration, and show humanity a new way of living. In part 2 of this book, I will shift the focus to the development of your Evolutionary Empath Tool Kit, breaking down each of these concepts and giving you exercises, examples, and mind-set shifts to help you begin your transition. These tools are designed to help you evolve your beingness (feminine) as well as your doingness (masculine).

Let me also reiterate that while this book is directed toward empaths, these awarenesses and tools are designed for every human being who desires to embrace heart-centered living and develop the necessary mind-sets and skills for engaging in conscious relationship with humankind. Can you imagine what the world would be like if we were all clear in the communication of our needs, limits, and expectations, were responsible for our own energy fields, trusted each other to ask for what we need, valued intuition and feelings as part of decision making, embraced the masculine and feminine qualities (and therefore genders) as equal partners, and honored the sanctity of all living things? I want to live in that world!

In the upcoming chapters, I will take a more tactical approach, focusing on the practical application and giving you tools and mind-sets that you can put to use right away. I will intersperse topic explanations with exercises that you can engage in to explore the concepts I am presenting. While this book includes a plethora of exercises, meditations, and journaling questions, additional supplemental materials are available to download for free on my website. I have also created eight guided meditations to provide you with a more experiential engagement with the material. These eight tracks are available on the Inner Traditions • Bear & Company website. Please refer to "How to Use the *Evolutionary Empath* Audio Tracks" at the end of this book for instructions on how to access and use these tracks. If you're looking for a more comprehensive engagement experience, I do work with a limited number of private clients as well as offer virtual and in-person workshops.

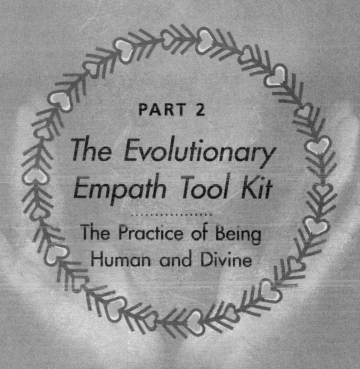

PART 2

The Evolutionary Empath Tool Kit

·················

The Practice of Being
Human and Divine

Change takes enormous energy. A rocket burns roughly 80 percent of its fuel during takeoff. This fuel is spent overcoming the force of gravity and creating enough momentum to maintain an orbit around the Earth. Sustaining momentum takes significantly less effort than liftoff. In choosing to embrace your soul path and be a leader of the New Earth, you will expend most of your effort overcoming the inertia of your current life patterns, but the fuel will not be spent in vain. Each step toward greater consciousness, healing, and wholeness will help you gain—and sustain—momentum.

The new human consciousness is a practice of unifying "opposites": humanity and divinity. We are both human and divine, and we as a society can no longer afford to fight about which aspect is better and waste precious energy pitting one against the other. They are both necessary and crucial. In the Iron Age, man forgot that he was a spiritual being and thought of himself primarily as a material being. During the Bronze Age, however, as Walter Cruttenden says, the focus on materialism began to fade, and man discovered that he was more than just flesh and blood; he was also an energy form. Man began to understand that all matter was an expression of energy, vibration, and electrical qualities.[1] Stepping into higher awareness demands that you learn to reconcile the limitations of being in human form with your limitless spiritual nature. It means surrendering to the cosmic influences guiding us toward expanded consciousness and an ascending cycle of humanity.

The second half of this book provides you with the mind-sets, perspectives, tools, and practices to help you embrace "both/and"—both human and divine. It focuses on practical, rubber-meets-the-road life skills that we must all become adept at to walk the human aspect of our life path. In Native American parlance, these are skills to cultivate when walking the "red road." In many Native American cultures, the red road is a metaphor for living a conscious and spiritual life as an incarnated human. Oglala Sioux medicine man and holy man Black Elk spoke of all the people on the red road as being one interconnected circle of people who made a sacred hoop. However, while many are on the road, only *you* can walk *your* journey. This part of the book is intended to help you walk your red road with more grace, consciousness, humility, clarity of purpose, and peace.

The Earth experience is most definitely a human mystery school. My favorite definition of a mystery is "the infinitely knowable." This is what you will find as you explore and work with these practices in your own life. You are a mystery, and you are your own mystery school!

7

Your Energy Container: "Shields Up, Mr. Sulu"

As with the content of most of the following chapters, the subject of the human energy field is complex and voluminous enough to warrant a book of its own. It is not my intention to educate you on the different philosophies or systems of energy (such as the chakra system) or to teach you specific energy healing modalities. This chapter will focus on introducing you to the *concept* of your energy container and give you visualizations, exercises, and mind-sets that you can use to develop your awareness as well as maintain your energy field on a daily basis.

UNDERSTANDING YOUR ENERGY CONTAINER

Quite simply, you are more than just your physical being. You have a field of energy that surrounds you—your personal energy field. It is unique to you, just like a fingerprint or a snowflake pattern. Basic physiology teaches us that each cell in our body has a charge. The very fact that you are alive—from electrical impulses traveling throughout your body to your cells converting food to energy—creates an energy field.

Yet your energy field is comprised of more than just the by-products of human biological functioning. Thoughts and actions also have a frequency. Everything you are, think, and do contributes to the distinct frequency or vibration that is you. The law of conservation of energy applies in the context of this discussion. In essence, the law states that matter is neither created nor destroyed; it just changes form. The most significant implication of this is that your thoughts, feelings, and words structure your reality, converting, over time, into your physical reality in a process we commonly refer to as "manifestation." As humans, we are manifesting machines. It's what we came here to do—to experiment with and experience our creative self.

Your energy field is made up of everything you can possibly imagine that makes you, you—your beliefs, desires, experiences, unresolved issues, passions, dreams, creative expressions, disappointments, physical ailments, shadow aspects, and more. All of these things have a vibration to them—a life force of their own—and they combine to create your individual, unique energetic signature.

The size of your energy field is ever changing and not at all static. Humans are dynamic beings who are acted upon by multiple internal and external forces thousands of times a day. Our energy fields are constantly responding to our thoughts, reactions, emotions, circumstances, environment, and the degree of wellness or illness we are experiencing, as well as other people, marketing messages, the weather, and much more. And the effects on our energy field are not restricted to events or people in our immediate vicinity. Factors that affect our energetic state are not limited by space and time. Think of talking to someone on the phone halfway around the world. From ten thousand miles away your energy fields are still interacting with and affecting each other. Recall someone from your past whom you loved or even someone who has died. Just connecting with their memory and the effect they had on you affects your energy field right now. In this way, space and time are an illusion.

To drop into the even more esoteric, energy patterns from your past lives are accessible to you and influence you now in the present moment. Though you are inhabiting a "new" body in this incarnation, the common denominator between your lifetime now and any past or future lifetimes is your soul, which stores the records of each and every incarnation. You are more than just the body you inhabit. Your human consciousness is seeded with the consciousness of your soul, as well as the consciousness of the Creator and the cosmos. Within you lies access to all of these dimensions, and all of this contributes to the unique energetic signature that is your energy field.

How far does our energy field extend? The answer to this question has several components. In one aspect, our energy field is vast and limitless. We can communicate (and thus interact on an energetic level) with people on the other side of the planet, traveling in outer space, and in other dimensions (such as those who have died). We can send our consciousness—and hence our energy—anywhere in space-time.

And yet it is also crucial as human beings to understand and apply the concept of boundaries, making conscious choices about what or who we let into our field and what or who we don't. So while our energy field is boundless, part of partaking in this Earth school is exploring and understanding both our *boundless* nature and the appropriate *boundaries* we need apply for our health and safety.

You have probably already surmised that as empaths we require much more effort and focus to establish and maintain boundaries than we do to be boundless. You would be correct. Without mentors or an understanding of the fluid nature of our energy field, we are prone to arbitrarily allowing any energy into our field and leaking vital life-force energy into the ether.

Please listen to track 1 of the audio tracks, "Where Are My Edges," for a simple but effective visualization meditation that I use in all of my empath workshops to introduce people to the concept of their edges and to play with expanding and contracting their energy container.

For simplicity's sake, I'd like you to think of the shape of your energy container as being a bubble, cylinder, cocoon, or any other shape that's roughly oblong or spherical. I have a client who likes to imagine it as a hamster ball that rolls around as she moves. However you visualize it, your energy field consists of everything inside that container, including the space "inside" your body. This internal space is sometimes referred to as your etheric double. It is an exact "copy" of your physical body except that it exists in nonphysical reality and overlies your physical body precisely.

Every day, with every interaction we have, our energy field comes in contact with hundreds and even thousands of other energies. Think of it like this: Pretend that we are all a different color of paint, and with every interaction we have—in person, over the phone, through social media, or by any other method of interacting—we get a little bit of our color on whomever we interact with. So, if I'm red and you're blue, and we have a conversation in the grocery store, you walk away with a smudge of red in your blue, and I walk away with a smudge of blue in my red.

Can you imagine how many different smudges of paint color we would have all over us at the end of each day?! It would be difficult to figure out what color we started out as if we didn't already know. And, to be clear, we aren't judging any paint color as good or bad here. Whether we like the person or not, agree with them or not, touch them physically in some way or not, have a happy interaction with them or not, we still exchange paint colors.

Being an empath, we naturally have very open energy fields, which, when we're unaware of it, usually translates to loose, sloppy, or non-existent boundaries, meaning that the edges of our container are not well defined, if they are defined at all. When we don't recognize we're an empath and aren't conscious of our energy field, we tend to let everybody into our energetic (and even physical) space, indiscriminately. There are many reasons for this. On the healthy end of the spectrum, it is because we are naturally kind, helpful, compassionate, and thoughtful. On the unhealthy end of the spectrum, it can be because we are codependent, define ourselves by how others view us, or have no idea how to say no. Either way, it is not uncommon for unconscious empaths to walk around carrying everyone they know in their energy field.

I often send private clients right back out of my office as soon as they arrive and instruct them to leave outside the threshold everyone they walked into my office with. Sometimes I give them a handful of crystals to create physical representations of the people they are leaving outside the door. This creates some breathing room and gives them greater access to their own voice and their own truth as we engage in our private counseling or healing session.

Now, to the *who* in your energy field you need to also add the *what*. In addition to all the people you cart around, you also carry problems, health issues, pets, decisions you're trying to make, obligations, old belief systems, unforgiveness, and so much more. No wonder we all feel cluttered and claustrophobic! Fair warning: once you become aware of these energies, it will be almost impossible to go back to being ignorant of them.

☼ Who Is in Your Energy Field?

This is a great exercise that illustrates very clearly just how much you are carrying around with you at any given time. It is easy to become numb to all of the baggage and energetic clutter we accumulate over time. We acclimate to it and don't recognize how bogged down, confused, and exhausted we have become in the process.

For this exercise you'll need to create a circle around you that is approximately four feet in diameter. You can use rope, a Hula-Hoop, scarves strung together, or whatever you can come up with. The idea is to create a visual boundary or container. You will also need a pad of Post-it Notes or paper you can cut into small pieces, and a pen.

Write down whatever comes to you for each of the categories

listed below, one item per note/slip of paper. Then place each one inside your circle.

- ♥ Everyone who is currently affecting your life or whom you carry in your consciousness: family, friends, coworkers, et cetera
- ♥ Animals/pets
- ♥ Decisions/issues/problems you are sitting with
- ♥ Health concerns
- ♥ Major stressors, whether ongoing (paying down debt) or one time (a death)
- ♥ Things you feel responsible for
- ♥ Unforgiveness
- ♥ "Shoulds"
- ♥ Wants/desires
- ♥ Regrets
- ♥ Obligations
- ♥ Anything else that's affecting you at this time

Now look at the totality of all your notes, all the names and categories, and take a moment to let the impact sink in. What initial reaction are you noticing in your body?

You will discover that some of these people or things in your energy field are legitimate, right, and necessary, and some are invasive, draining, and nonessential. These are energies that you've let into your space whether you're conscious of it or not. Some of these people or situations give energy back to you, meaning there's a partnership or equal investment in each other, but many of your notes will represent people or situations that are not supporting you. Either they are taking or expecting something from you or telling you what to do, or you're overgiving or in some form of codependence or taking responsibility for them when the responsibility isn't yours.

Journal now about all the things you've written on your notes, asking yourself the following questions:

- ♥ What needs to change?
- ♥ What actions do I need to take related to all of the people and situations drawing upon my energy?
- ♥ What boundaries do I need to draw?
- ♥ What decisions do I need to make?
- ♥ Where do I need to ask for support?
- ♥ What kind of self-care do I need to engage in?

ENERGY LEAKS

To understand the concept of energy leaks at a visceral level, close your eyes and call up the sensations that arise in your body when you are feeling powerful, solid, grounded, confident, energetic, and excited about your life. Take a moment now to fill yourself with those energies and feelings. Look around inside yourself and at your energetic container. Take note of whatever there is to notice. How do you feel? What is the consistency, structure, or content of your container? What does it look like? How big is it?

When you are in a positive and powerful state, fully embodied, alert, and present, your energy container is solid and defined, with no holes or leaks. You are able to discern the edges. Your container is able to fully contain you, and you have clear boundaries. Your container is in integrity.

Imagine now what it feels like in your body when you feel weak, disempowered, or codependent or when you're suppressing your truth, doubting yourself, and feeling afraid. Again, take note of whatever there is to notice. How do you feel? What is the consistency, structure, or content of your container? What does it look like? How big is it?

Now take a deep breath to clear that visualization out of your energy field, shake out your hands, and return to a neutral state.

When you are in a disempowered or fearful state, it usually means that you are partially disembodied, not fully present, acting on autopilot, and often regressed. In this condition, the integrity of your energy container is obliterated. It looks like Swiss cheese, leaking energy like a sieve. Boundaries are nonexistent, and you probably feel exposed, weak, and vulnerable.

When your container has leaks, it means that you are either venting vital energies out into the ether or allowing compromising energies from others or the environment into your space. Or both. Leaks show up as all kinds of unhealthy behaviors, including squishy boundaries, disempowering money habits, codependent relationships, taking on problems that aren't yours, not speaking your truth, suppressing your authentic self, feeling responsible for other people's emotions, and letting people take advantage of you, to name a few. And you will often find that if you have a leak in one area of your life, there's probably a leak in other areas of your life as well.

As I mentioned earlier, our energy field is always in a state of flux as we process and respond to all the stimuli we encounter on a daily basis. I'm sure you can recall a time when you were feeling amazing, happy, and solid only to receive a piece of news that completely deflated you seconds later. Our state of being (and thus our energy field) can turn on a dime. Part of the spiritual and emotional maturation process is learning to tune in to, manage, and care for your energy field and employ practices to keep it as stabilized as possible.

With attention and practice, you can sustain a more consistently intact container and develop the skills to restore balance (plug up leaks), clear your field of unwanted or unfavorable influences, and stabilize your field more quickly after a destabilizing blow. I will cover energy leaks more in chapter 8, which discusses boundaries in greater detail.

DAILY PRACTICES FOR MANAGING YOUR ENERGY FIELD

There are simple daily practices that can make a world of difference in becoming attuned to and managing your energy container. These include checking in and clearing your energy field. Checking in is really about cultivating consciousness. Consciousness is always the first and most important step in making any significant change because you can't change what you aren't aware of. Clearing your energy field is part of daily maintenance. Think of it as a priority, just like eating, drinking, and sleeping. If you find that you have difficulty remembering to do this, set a reminder on your phone or watch.

It's essential to our well-being that we give ourselves the opportunity—daily—to purge our nervous system of the chaos we've been exposed to throughout the day. The rings and beeps of electronic equipment, the noise of traffic, engines, or machinery, the din of constant background conversations, the vibrational assault of unhealthy electromagnetic frequencies, challenging arguments—whatever the source, if we cannot release this energy, then we become stressed. More importantly, these loads can build up in our energy body and, over time, can become locked in our physical body. A deep or extended purge is highly recommended at regular intervals to release the stubborn stress and to help restore your natural biorhythms.

Checking In

The most important habit to develop is what I call checking in with yourself. This only takes a couple of minutes, and I encourage you to do it several times a day and especially before bed. Checking in means taking a moment to assess your physical, mental, emotional, and energetic state and then to make whatever adjustments are necessary.

In assessing your physical state, you want to notice how your body feels. Are your shoulders tense or hunched? Is your breathing shallow? Is there a knot in your gut? Is there an ache or pain somewhere? Are you slouching? Are you present in your body? All of these can be clues that help you understand what you're feeling, thinking, or processing at any given moment. Our bodies physically manifest our fears and patterns of belief. If we will just listen, they will give us all the evidence we need to recognize when we have something to address or work through. Taking one or two deep slow breaths can then act as a reset button.

In next assessing your mental and emotional state, you want to notice what you are thinking and feeling. If you've already checked in with your body, chances are that you have a hint of your emotional/mental state because your body will reflect it. Are you feeling empowered or disempowered? Clear or confused? Overwhelmed or eager? Is your inner dialogue giving you encouraging messages or ripping you a new one? Are you running old arguments over and over in your mind? Are you in the future, planning your day or making your grocery list? Did you let someone tear you down? Did you say or do something you regret? Is something trying to get your attention that you are ignoring?

Assessing your energetic container involves looking at what and who is in your field that doesn't need to be there. After you've investigated your mental and emotional state, you'll probably know if you let something or someone unhealthy creep back into your field because your emotions and inner dialogue most likely referenced it. The next step is to clear your energy field of what isn't serving you. See "Clearing Your Energy Field" below for a selection of clearing techniques.

The point of checking in is to give you the opportunity to notice your patterns and make any necessary adjustments. My check-ins always include deep breathing. I use my breath often as a tool for moving energy—in fact, it is my most powerful tool for moving energy. It happens so automatically now that often I will be going about my day, and my body will just pause and take a giant, deep, clearing breath all on its own.

Daily check-ins are also important for noticing your habits and patterns, which will give you clues as to where you might need to do some deeper inner work. It is vital that we as *humans,* not just empaths, pay regular attention to our physical, emotional, mental, and energetic state. In doing so, unresolved issues, wounds, traumas, and daily accumulations don't fester and compound into disease, pathologies, resentment, bitterness, intractable attitudes, rage, and victimhood.

Clearing Your Energy Field

Think of clearing your energy field as like brushing your teeth: you can skip brushing your teeth, and you won't die, but it leaves a really bad film and taste in your mouth if you do, and prolonged periods of dental neglect can lead to gum disease and many other issues. It is the same with your energy field. As I said earlier, dis-ease begins in the energetic body and, if not addressed, will lower in vibration and manifest physically.

Once you become attuned to your energetic state, you will immediately notice when you need to do some clearing. There are dozens of methods for clearing and tending to energies, so this list is not exhaustive. However, it does offer a wide variety depending on your personal preferences, the availability of supplies, and the environments you spend your time in.

Method I—Deep Breaths

"Have breath, will travel" is a motto I like to say. Our breath is one of the most powerful tools we have for moving energy, and it doesn't cost a dime. We already possess this tool; it's just a matter of applying it consciously.

Multiple times throughout the day, and especially before and after working with a client, I will take a series of deep breaths to clear and center myself. I imagine the exhale combing down my energy field like the rake that runs through an automatic self-cleaning cat litter box, picking up any "waste" and releasing it into the earth.

When you take deep, conscious breaths, breathe in slowly and deliberately, pause for a few seconds, and then exhale slowly and deliberately, directing the flow very specifically instead of haphazardly. When I move energy using my breath, I can hear the air moving, and it's not uncommon for me to have shivers, tingling, or other bodily reactions as my energy field clears itself.

There are all manner of visualizations you can use to accompany your deep breathing, too, from inhaling through your crown and exhaling through your feet to inhaling a color and sending it to the tight or heavy parts of your field and then exhaling the waste as gray or black. You might also bring your in-breath to each of the seven chakras to clear them one at a time. Experiment and choose what works best for you.

Method 2—Smudging

Smudging means lighting a natural material that smokes, like sage, sweet grass, palo santo, or something similar. I use all three frequently, using a smudge fan (usually made with feathers) to waft the smoke through my entire energy field. I also use the smudge fan as a tool to brush away clogged spots on my physical body. Smudging is a great technique for clearing a room, sacred object, your office, or entire home. Almost every workshop or program I offer includes smudging participants before we begin. I am partial to ceremony and resonate with the ceremonial aspect of burning sage to consecrate the space, clear the area, and call in the supporting energies. You don't have to go to this level of detail, but I offer it as an extra practice.

Method 3—Dry Brushing

This is a handy method when you're in public or not near your cleansing tools. You can simply run your hands over your body, breathing intentionally, and then flick or shake your hands to release what you have cleared off. You can also use your hand to scoop out your heart (or any other place where dense energies have collected) or to pull energy off you, much like pulling burs off a dog's coat. Some people like to imagine the ends of their fingers as paintbrushes and run their hands around the edge of their auric field (like a bubble), brushing, cleansing, clearing, and tending to the edges.

Method 4—Affirmations and Intention Setting

Affirmations are a way to consciously release any unwanted energies from your field and call in a higher, more supportive frequency through a repeated phrase. When I use affirmations, my breath always accompanies them, much like an automatic response. An affirmation I say regularly after I get in bed is "I release everything that is not mine," and I repeat it three times, while breathing deeply. Then I imagine my guides surrounding me on all sides brushing my aura with wings to clear anything I've picked up.

Similar to affirmations, intentions set a conscious field, a reminder of what you aspire to. While this may seem obvious, it's easy to hit the ground running as soon as you get up in the morning and forget to take a moment to pause, pray, offer gratitude, or set intentions. When I'm working to adopt a new habit, behavior, or mind-set, I will often write my intentions down and read them every morning so they stay present in my consciousness.

Set your intention every day to not take on other people's energies, emotions, or problems, but be sure to phrase it in the positive. For example, "My energy container is solid and has structural integrity" or "I choose whom I let into my energy field" or "I am my own sovereign being." You can use them like you do affirmations, creating an intention that you repeat throughout the day. If you write it down, put it where you will see it. One of my favorite places is to stick it on my bathroom mirror.

Method 5—Epsom Salt Baths

Epsom salts are known for absorbing or drawing out toxins from the body as well as sedating the nervous system, reducing swelling, and relaxing muscles. Bump up the clearing and soothing factor by adding your choice of essential oils, tea leaves, or dried flowers to your bath. If you're not much of a bath person, you can put Epsom salts in the tub when you shower and plug up the drain so the tub fills with water. Though the salts are only making contact with your feet and lower legs, you can consciously intend for your system to release through your feet into the salty water.

Water itself is incredibly healing, so just getting in a bathtub (or river, lake, ocean, or pool) and engaging with water consciously can do wonders, Epsom salts or not.

Method 6—Crystals and Stones

While this is a more passive method, I love the support that the mineral kingdom provides. You can carry crystals in your pocket, wear them as jewelry, or place them in your home, office, car, desk, et cetera. I have stones all over my home and office, as well as lots of jewelry. The important thing is to remember that these stones are acting in your service, so be sure to clear them regularly. You can clear crystals and stones in a variety of ways, such as placing them in the sun or full moon, burying them in the ground, placing them in salt, smudging them, or running water over them (be sure to check that the composition of the stone remains stable in water). If you want to work with a specific energy or stone but don't know which one to choose, there are tons of references out there that will provide you with the properties and benefits of a variety of crystals.

Method 7—Essential Oils

The plant kingdom, just like the mineral kingdom, loves to be of service. You can put oils derived from plants directly on your body, in a diffuser, or in your bathwater, or you can ingest them (depending on the type and purity), cook with them, and more. Just like crystals and stones, they raise the vibration of your environment, addressing specific maladies and helping you clear your energy field.

Method 8—Prayer and Incantations

Some people use daily invocations that include anything from prayer to spoken mantras to intentions. All of these are similar tools, with the most important commonality being that they are used with consciousness. Incantations, mantras, or repeated phrases—often uttered in foreign languages (Sanskrit or Quechua, for example)—can be powerful tools for clearing your energy field, setting up a protective boundary, asking for guidance during boundary-challenging circumstances, and anything else that supports you in keeping yourself clear and separate from others. My prayers often include calling in my spiritual team, animal-helper spirits, or higher self to assist me.

BUILDING YOUR ENERGY CONTAINER

Building your energy container means developing the ability to hold space for yourself—all of you. To understand what it means to hold space for yourself, let me start by illustrating the opposite. In this case it will help to imagine your container as something solid, like a jar. If you put something such as sand or water in a jar that has holes in it, can the jar contain its contents? No. The contents leak or spill out. No matter how much you keep adding to the jar, you cannot fill it up.

The idea of our container—specifically what we can hold—is much like this. If you think about your own capacity to hold the bigness of your dreams, to receive, or to sustain joy, how do you do it? Do you get excited about big ideas and then become deflated and dejected within a matter of days? When someone offers you assistance, love, or support, do you allow yourself to deeply receive it or do you brush it off or reject it? How long can you maintain positive feelings?

The answer to all of these questions points to the integrity of your container as a major contributor. If your dream container has holes, then it is difficult to sustain a dream into manifestation. If you have leaks, then joyful, happy experiences become fleeting because your ability to hold space for your own happiness is diminished. If you have difficulty receiving, then you don't fully allow yourself to experience the gift of a compliment, a surprise present, or emotional support. These are all leaks in your container (and point to some inner work that needs to be addressed).

Building our container is most definitely like building a muscle—it takes regular practice and exercise. Many of us are used to playing small. We have worn masks and pretended that we were someone we are not in order to fit in, be accepted, and gain love. Most of us don't have a lot of experience holding a big container for ourselves, but we have lots of experience holding a small, erratic, or compromised container.

Women, in particular, have a tough time holding a sizable container for themselves because of the suppression of women that has occurred for millennia. We have been programmed to fit in, stay small, submit our will to others, and keep quiet, and we have been told that we are less intelligent, capable, qualified, or hardy than men. If you regularly self-sabotage to keep yourself small, you might look further than just the messages of your upbringing. Almost every woman holds influences from the collective in her consciousness that silently tell her she can't do it, whatever "it" is.

Exercises for Building Your Container

Working to build your container is more of an advanced activity that I recommend you add after you have practiced checking in and managing and clearing your energy field regularly. I include it because you can begin building your container now, even if you are just getting acquainted with your energy field. It is also a natural by-product of working with your own energy field and developing the awarenesses offered in this book.

☼ Pay Regular Attention to Your Container

This exercise can be combined with your daily check-in process. You can do it by asking your psyche to create a visualization, or, if you are not a visual person, asking your psyche to give you impressions or feelings. Using whichever method works best for you, you want to evaluate multiple aspects of your container. Is it solid, meaning no leaks? Does it feel/look strong or weak? Does it feel buoyant or deflated? Are there holes? Are you aware of anything you've been trying to hold that has already begun to slip away and lose momentum or potency (such as a good feeling or creative idea)? How long are you able to hold on to positive or life-affirming feelings or ideas?

Notice any patterns, such as feeling strong and solid in the morning but weakening as the day goes on. Or feeling strong and solid in general, but like Swiss cheese when you are in certain situations or around certain people. You can even journal, asking yourself the following questions: "What knocks me off my center?" "When do I feel strong and when do I feel weak? "What energies can I hold for a long time, and what energies dissipate as soon as they arise?" Journaling will help you raise your awareness of the types of circumstances that cause you the greatest difficultly in maintaining the integrity of your energy container.

☼ Allow Yourself to Hold Positive Feelings for Longer Periods of Time

Set your intention to practice holding on to joy, pleasure, abundance, or any form of positivity or expansive energy for longer periods of time. Don't try to do too many at once. Pick one to start, so you can clearly distinguish when you are holding the integrity of your container and when you are not.

For example, let's choose joy. Expanding your container means allowing yourself to feel joy fully. Whenever something happens that brings you joy, feel it in every cell and with every sense. Be completely present with it. Tell yourself, "I deserve this. I love this. This makes me happy. Thank you." Let it fill you up.

As your day goes on, notice what types of external or internal events deflate your joy. For me, my Inner Critic is one of my worst perpetrators. When you notice that your joy has been deflated, be gentle with yourself and don't beat yourself up. Be compassionate with yourself as you ask, "What just deflated my joy? Why did I allow this to affect me? What am I telling myself about this?" Then, connect back in to a recent event that brought you joy, or find something in the moment that can fill you up, even if it's just stepping outside to feel the sunlight on your face or look at the beauty of a flower.

As you become more adept, you can work on building additional aspects of your container. As with strength training, it is something you have to attend to regularly if you want results. This is not a "one and done" kind of endeavor. Tending to your energy container will be a lifelong practice. It is important to remember this adage from Vince Lombardi: "It's not whether you get knocked down; it's whether you get back up." You will get "knocked down" (deflated) many times when tending to your container. Just keep getting back up. This is how you build your strength.

☼ Expand Your Capacity of Appreciation

Appreciation is an expansive energy, and the effectiveness of gratitude exercises is well documented. One of the simplest is a gratitude journal. Keep a notebook by your bedside or at your desk—someplace you will be every day at the same time (the actual time of day doesn't matter)—and make it a habit to write down five or ten things you are grateful for.

If you are a person who prays on a daily basis, a variation on the gratitude journal is to speak your gratitudes during your prayer time. Again, give yourself a number to shoot for, such as five or ten.

☼ Loving Yourself in the Mirror

For some people, looking at themselves in the mirror is one of the most daunting things they've ever done. And not just looking at yourself like you do when you're getting ready in the morning or checking to make sure your outfit looks good. I mean deeply looking into your eyes, taking yourself in, and speaking to yourself out loud.

There are three levels of mirror work. Try these out:

Mirror exercise 1: Stand in front of a full-length mirror and take in every aspect of yourself that you see. Do your best to look at the back of you as well. For each body part, tell yourself,

"I love my (body part)" or "Thank you, (body part), for
_____." Touch each part as you speak about it.

Mirror exercise 2: Do exercise 1 naked.

Mirror exercise 3: Stand in front of a mirror and stare deeply into
your eyes. Get to know the person staring back at you. Allow
yourself to be vulnerable and to be seen. Take this person in
like you've never seen them before. Then say out loud, "I love
you" ten times. For the advanced version, do this every day
for a week.

PROTECTING YOURSELF

This can be a tricky subject, as there are many different points of view
on how to protect yourself and why you need to protect yourself, and
even more methods of deploying protection. Some people feel that they
are personally prone to psychic attacks or attract dark energies. Some
believe that your intention is the most critical factor. Some conduct
their lives as if there is always something out to get them. There is an
entire spectrum of beliefs and subsequent practices regarding the need
for protection, what we're protecting ourselves from, and the best way
to do it.

I must be clear that I have no one special technique to offer you
that works in every situation. I am not a "there is only one way" kind
of person. It depends. You have probably gathered that my style is to
offer you a variety of tools and then have you trust the wisdom inside
you to decide which is the most useful or valuable tool to employ in any
given situation. And my philosophy always includes an assessment of
your belief system and the lens you see the world through.

So while I won't go into great detail, it is important to address this
topic because the subject of protection is just another forum to help us
recognize that we are responsible for our own energy. While we cannot
control what's going on outside of us, we can control how we respond to

it, which includes both offensive (preparatory) and defensive (employed in the moment) measures. How we react to the concept of protection is fed by several factors, including our beliefs, the type of person/people we are interacting with, the energies present in our environment, and the tools we have at our disposal to manage our own energy field.

Belief Systems

It may not be obvious at first how our belief system is related to protecting our energy field, but to me, one clearly feeds the other. Our perceptions color our reality, and we cannot ignore the influence of our beliefs when we consider how we view the world and, subsequently, how dangerous we believe that world to be.

One of the most important aspects to consider is what was instilled in you from childhood. Here's an example: Some people were raised in an environment of chaos, unpredictability, and boundary violations. This could be a product of alcoholism, sexual or physical abuse, or parents who just had no concept of privacy, respect, or personal space. This would then become the template for the child's life, and as an adult, these people would continue to attract chaos, drama, disrespect, and people who violate their boundaries. It is the lens they see the world through and the types of experiences they continue to attract. Though unhealthy, it is familiar and known. And it certainly breeds a belief system that is preoccupied with the need for protection. This is how we tend to construct our world before we "awaken." We repeat old patterns and habits, not realizing that they aren't giving us the intended results. We can feel as if the events of the world are "being done unto us," and it throws us into a victim space.

If you are programmed to believe that everyone is out to get you, then there's a good chance you will look at everything in your life with suspicion and distrust, wondering exactly how and when you are going to get screwed. It's the cause-and-effect wiring that gets laid down in our brains as we develop. We see the world through the lens we were handed until we recognize that the lens might be defective, and we begin to do the work of creating a new lens. This is part of the awakening process.

Yet shifting beliefs is not simply a matter of rattling off a set of affirmations every morning or just changing a few habits. Belief systems are insidious and multilayered and take work to transform. Nonetheless, embracing a new belief can be one of the most powerful choices a person can make. I have seen many people who, through doing their inner work, no longer relate to their *need for protection* in the same way as before. They begin to show up in their lives less defensively. This type of inner work almost always restores people's personal power, releases the victim mentality, and helps them understand that they have a choice in every moment. All of these shifts create a greater sense of wholeness in people, vastly changing how they relate to the world and transforming how they view and deploy their need for protection.

The Nature of People

People aren't inherently bad or ill-intentioned, meaning they don't come out of the womb that way. But unconscious people are rarely aware of—and therefore don't take responsibility for—the state of their energy field. These people come in all kinds: manipulators, energy vampires, complainers, gloomsdayers (think of the character Sadness from the movie *Inside Out*), loud talkers, gossipers, constant critics, people who "dump" all their emotional baggage on you, and the list goes on. And what bothers you may not bother the person next to you, and what bothers you today may not bother you on other days. The methods you employ to protect your energy field will change from situation to situation.

This is where it is important to recognize that you can't control other people; you can only control yourself. Now, can you control the types of environments and circumstances you expose yourself to? Absolutely. Only you can determine when, where, and in what circumstances you feel safe. Taking responsibility for your own energy field and energetic environment definitely includes making decisions about what and who you expose yourself to. Sometimes protection comes in the form of avoidance—of a person, an environment, or a situation. In all cases, employing a regular and robust energy-clearing and boundary-drawing practice is crucial and should most likely include your office, home, property, and car in addition to yourself.

The Physical Stuff

There are actual physical, measurable influences in the world, such as certain electromagnetic frequencies, chemical off-gassing, noise pollution, solar flares, and more, that assault our energy fields on a daily basis. These are things that physically exist in our environment that we can see, smell, or touch and that we can measure in some way. I often rely on the mineral kingdom for help with things like this. For example, I keep a piece of pyrite near all of my computers, laptops, and TVs to protect against harmful electromagnetic frequencies

The list of common offenders in our environment and potential remedies is long. People are highly affected by smells, plastics, cleaning supplies, power plants, power lines, oil refineries, pesticides, and so on. The best method of protection is avoidance, but this isn't always practical. I refer you to the different ways of clearing yourself that I offer in this chapter, as many of our nature helpers (the mineral kingdom, essential oils, etc.) can work in an offensive or protective capacity in addition to clearing.

Harmful Entities

Though I have minimal direct experience in this area, I do know that dark forces exist. There are practitioners who work in black magic or the dark arts and will happily put a curse on a family member for you. There are disembodied entities who are lost and confused and might find a human to plead with or torment. There's an entire world of paranormal and unexplained activities. People who work with the "light" and who open themselves regularly as a channel or portal to higher frequencies can be offering an unintentional invitation for energies of "less than pristine intent" to come through.

There are specific techniques I have learned as a shamanic practitioner to clear people and work with attachments. The techniques are too complicated to go into here and would require an apprenticeship in the shamanic arts for you to employ. However, this doesn't mean that you are out of luck. Sometimes "sticky" energies actually point back to an attachment within us—a belief system, an expectation, a resentment, an addiction—and not a dark entity. If you ever find that your own personal energy practice isn't sufficient to resolve the issue you are dealing with, find a practitioner you resonate with who can assist you. It doesn't matter how conscious we are, how long we've been doing this work, or how huge our toolbox is, we all need help, including me. We all need support in our blind spots.

Tools of Protection

The most fundamental tool of protection is consciousness. You must do your daily practice of checking in, maintaining your awareness, clearing your energy field, and setting your boundaries because if you aren't aware that someone or something is affecting you, then it doesn't matter how many tools you have to protect yourself. Developing a practice of awareness is key, as I addressed earlier in this chapter and remind you below. Once you become aware, then you can make a decision about how you want to handle the situation. I divide the options into two categories: offensive and defensive.

An offensive strategy simply means anticipating what you might need and preparing in advance. You can think of it as preplanning. My husband and I joke whenever we get ready to go into certain big-box stores, "Shields up." If I take a moment to prepare myself, clean my field, check the integrity of it, firm up the edges, stay in my center, and go in with a smile (instead of preparing for a fight), it always goes better than if I walk in without taking a moment to pause and prepare my field first.

Preplanning can also involve more long-term protective measures, such as placing crystals around your home or office, setting up an energetic or physical grid, drawing symbols, wearing certain pieces of jewelry, or performing your daily spiritual practice. Offensive protection includes anything you do *ahead of time,* whether it's for a single use or for a long-standing need. And don't underestimate the importance of clearing your field several times a day.

Defensive options include what you do *in the moment* to respond to a "threat." The offending energy could be in the form of a person, loud noise, electromagnetic frequency, large crowd, or any number of external circumstances. Don't forget, too, that things happening inside of us can also affect our container and require us to fortify our field. Events like being triggered (and potentially regressing), a drop in your blood sugar, or being overwhelmed can cause us to call on additional support to stay in our center and maintain our faculties.

In-the-moment responses include things like walking away, clearing your field, taking a deep breath, saying no, eating or drinking something nutritious, taking a few moments by yourself, or going outside to connect with nature.

If there are long-term offenders, such as certain coworkers, unhealthy relationships, or dysfunctional belief systems, then you might consider reaching out to a therapist, shaman, energy healer, or trusted teacher to help you work through a strategy and do the inner work that is related to your trigger.

IT BEGINS—AND ENDS—WITH AWARENESS

Your energy field is a complicated and complex living organism. It is intelligent and communicative. It is constantly in flux, adjusting to your mood, your physical state, the environment, your inner dialogue, and people you interact with. The most important and fundamental tool in working with your energy field is awareness, which comes from simple repetitive practice. Being aware of how you are feeling and how something is affecting you is the first step. Change cannot happen without conscious recognition of what is occurring in the moment. From there, you can make a choice about how to rebalance or clear your field and how to respond to any external factors. It is most certainly a daily—if not hourly—practice. With this practice, you will be able to catch yourself sooner and more frequently when something is affecting your energy field. The power is always in the awareness.

8

Boundaries: You and I Are One, but We Are Not the Same

The subject of boundaries is so extensive and essential that I could fill volumes exploring every aspect of them. For the purpose of this book, I intend to explain why boundaries are so important and how they are related to your energy field and give you tools for enforcing and strengthening your own.

Boundaries help you create safety, say no, and ask for what you need. They help you get clear about what is yours and what is not yours and assist you in staying grounded in your center. Boundaries help you stay out of codependence, overwhelm, and confusion and stay "clean" in your interactions with others. Boundaries keep you comfortably contained inside yourself, creating a base—a place you can always come home to—and give you the opportunity to spend time in your authentic self. Becoming proficient at drawing and maintaining boundaries is vital to your energetic, emotional, spiritual, and physical health.

As the title of this chapter implies, from a cosmic, summit-level perspective, we are all one. We all come from the same source, and we are all individuations of the Creator. Our physical bodies are made of the same stuff, and we have a shared consciousness—what happens to one affects us all.

Yet at a human, rubber-meets-the-road level, we are not the same. We have individual energy fields, sensitivities, preferences, values, skills, beliefs, physical appearances, tolerances, strengths, and flaws. We have a personal frequency that is the amalgamation of all of our individual parts combined into a unique energetic signature. When we interact with other distinct frequencies, some are in resonance with us and some are not. At an individual level, we don't desire to let everyone into our space, be friends with everyone, or even talk to everyone. And that's perfectly okay.

Tending to our needs as humans, and especially as empaths, involves drawing boundaries that make it clear where we end and the next person begins. Boundaries require us to know ourselves, to know what we want, need, think, and feel and then to act on that knowledge. For people who are naturally designed to merge with others, figuring out boundaries can be as foreign as eating with your toes!

Boundaries can be an especially confounding concept when there's a part of us that remembers what it is like in spirit form, where this distinction doesn't exist. As I mentioned in chapter 1, the human constructs of division, separateness, and the need for protection don't exist in spirit. We are grounded in the knowledge that we come from the same source and therefore don't perceive another soul's energy as a threat. Nor do we need to worry about keeping our energy field clear, being overwhelmed, or merging unhealthily with others. These are trappings of the human experience.

Holding the truth that we are both spirit and matter can be baffling, disorienting, and just plain hard. For many, it can be easier to identify with one or the other ("I am spirit" or "I am human") because we live in a planet of polarities. Most things in our environment tell us that we have to choose. That one is good and the other bad, or one is more advanced or better, or whatever description we use that creates a split between the two opposites. It is still an emerging concept that we can be "both/and." Even when we recognize and embrace that we have a physical, human existence and a multidimensional (spirit, energy, consciousness) existence, walking in both worlds simultaneously takes skill and practice.

Our boundaries can be squishy or nonexistent for a number of reasons. Some of us have gone through life believing subconsciously that we are victims, or we didn't have any modeling of how to draw healthy boundaries, or we just never gave any conscious thought to it. If we didn't have anyone in our life to show us boundaries, how would we know what they are or that they even exist? Many of us hoped that others would rescue us or stand up for us. Or we tried to run away from uncomfortable situations and bury our head. Or we stubbornly hung in there while our own energy field was getting decimated in the process. No matter the cause, we now realize that none of these options are healthy or empowering.

Drawing boundaries takes practice. It's not something you're just going to be immediately adept at, especially if you have spent most of your life with squishy boundaries or no boundaries at all. In the earlier, unconscious stage of our lives, being an empath and having good boundaries are mutually exclusive. It takes conscious effort and time to learn how to powerfully own your empathic abilities and maintain good boundaries (the "both/and"). It is important to give yourself permission for this venture to look messy, for you to make mistakes, and especially to let go of expectations.

Think of a child learning to walk. Do you scold them every time they fall down? No. Do you expect them to walk perfectly the first (or even fortieth) time? No. They'll get up and try again and will naturally get stronger and more adept as they continue to practice. They just need you to encourage them, give them space to try, and keep them safe. This is the role you need to play for yourself as you learn to step powerfully into drawing and maintaining clear boundaries in your life.

ENERGY LEAKS—BLOWOUTS AND CAVE-INS

As we discuss the concept of boundaries, it will be useful to recall your understanding and practice of managing your energy field and identifying the edges of your container. Boundaries are closely associated with the management of your energy field, and I will use many references from chapter 7 in this discussion.

Think of your energy field as a semipermeable membrane. There are two directions that energy can flow: toward you and away from you, into your container and out of your container. For easy reference, I call these *cave-ins* and *blowouts,* respectively. Your energy field is intelligent and communicates with you every second of the day. Sometimes you are aware of what you take in or send out, and sometimes you are not. The more adept you become at consciously managing your energy field and registering its communication, the more adept you will become at understanding and applying good boundaries. They go hand in hand.

When you fall into unconscious patterns with your energy, they will show up in the form of leaks. A leak is an unconscious, unhealthy stream of energy (usually a pattern and not a random occurrence) and can occur in both directions. Energy leaks are unproductive, unhealthy, and often detrimental.

So what does an outward energy leak, or blowout, look like in daily life? Here are some examples that aren't appropriate or healthy:

- Interrupting other people when they're talking, talking over other people, or needing to always have the last word
- Thinking about what you want to say in response instead of listening and being present with the other person
- Having to comment on everything everyone says, including laughing, making faces, or making other noises
- Being pushy, getting in other people's faces, standing too close
- Touching people or energetically invading people without their permission or without waiting for their answer
- Saying whatever comes to your mind without filters, censoring, or consideration of the other person

- Sharing every experience, conversation, or crisis you have with everyone you know (your hairdresser, your massage therapist, your neighbors, your manicurist . . . usually everyone except the person you need to address the situation with)
- Being overly protective of someone (think of energetic claws gripping at them)
- Having temper tantrums or violent outbursts or being demanding
- Being smothering or clingy (hovering; constantly giving advice or direction when it isn't needed or asked for; not leaving someone alone)
- Being obsessed—with a person, thing, activity, or belief system
- Not allowing others their own process and their own space (i.e., not containing your need to soothe them, give them a tissue, give them advice, say something encouraging, touch them, hug them, or otherwise get in their space and interfere with their process; this behavior is about your *own* insecurity)
- Leaking sexual energy through inappropriate flirting, manipulation, or seduction (overtly leaking sexual energy shows up as one-night stands, seeking sex as an escape, and harassment)
- Doing anything that might cause the other person to have to set a boundary with you

In these examples, think of your energy like water leaking out of holes in an aboveground pool. What's happening in these situations is that you are not containing your energy. You are not being conscious or deliberate in what you are saying, how you are behaving, or even what you are thinking. You are letting your energy (in the form of your words, behaviors, actions, etc.) leak out all over everyone else, and you are not being responsible for its effects or consequences.

Here are some examples of inward energy leaks, or *cave-ins,* that are not healthy or appropriate.

- Tolerating gossip or disparaging comments about other people
- Letting other people manipulate you into doing something that you don't want to do through guilt, blackmail, coercion, bullying, or intimidation
- Allowing people and situations in your life that drag you down, sap your energy, and only take but don't give (think of any friends, relatives, coworkers, or others in your life who drag you down)
- Letting people take advantage of you
- Not standing up for yourself or not stating your point of view or opinion (essentially deferring to the other person's decision, feelings, or opinions by not stating your own truth)
- Not asking for what you need, want, or desire
- Drawing a boundary and then caving in, wavering, or changing your mind about it
- Allowing other people to define who you are
- Tolerating abuse of yourself by other people
- Being generally passive
- Secretly "vampiring" energy off other people (i.e., hanging around certain people or groups because they make you feel good or because you cannot hold your own worth or value, so you "suck" their energy in; this one is tricky and could go in both categories of energy leaking out and in)

In these cave-in examples, think of your container as a boat, with the leak being water flowing through holes into your boat. Other people's needs, demands, expectations, or unconscious thoughts and actions are flowing into your container and overwhelming and collapsing (essentially sinking or caving in) your own sovereign energy field.

We can leak in both directions, and each dysfunction has its own consequences and points to a different remedy. Generally, however, leaking outward is akin to an *explosion* and points to the need for proper *containment*. Leaking inward is akin to *implosion* and points to the need for *fortification*.

Containment for Blowout Leakers

If you recognize that the majority of your leaks are blowouts, then your practice needs to focus on creating containment for yourself. Containment is about applying a measure of conscious restraint. It isn't a negative concept, such as when your parents might have said, "Stephanie, contain yourself!" It doesn't mean you are bad or wrong and need to go into lockdown. Containment is not about shutting down your life-force energy, squelching yourself, or hiding your feelings. It's about keeping your energy inside you, where it belongs, instead of in everyone else's face. Containing yourself means questioning why you feel the compulsion to interrupt, invade people's space, take over the conversation (or the room), smother, overnurture, flirt, or always be doing something.

As one of my colleagues and dear friends Rima Bonario says in her classes, "Listen from here, not from over there." Meaning, stay inside yourself. There's no need to leave your body and go occupy the other person's space. Whatever you desire to say, convey, or accomplish, you can do so staying safely tucked inside your own energy field. As empaths, we often have no idea that our essence is floating around, unchecked, overrunning other people's energy fields. We have no sense of what it is to be with ourselves or to even know ourselves in the absence of another. Our (dysfunctional) comfort zone has been in blending and merging with others.

Sometimes people who leak energy outwardly are using these (and other) behaviors as a way to bleed off energy because they haven't learned to hold space for themselves or develop the strength of their energetic container. Learning to hold our own container is like building a muscle. Our life-force energy has a charge, like electricity. Energy can build up, like pressure in a lidded pot. It is literally a force. If we're not used to that pressure (and in this instance, pressure is not bad), then we'll do whatever we can to get rid of the discomfort. For a variety of reasons, as we developed, we never learned how to hold our own energy, how to contain or direct our own life force, or even how to recognize ourselves as distinct from another. So when we feel our energy building, our life force increasing, it can feel intense and overwhelming, causing us to discharge it as soon as possible. This can be in the form of discharging sexual energy, joy, anger, long-term dreams, or grief.

Common traveling companions of this outward-leaking energetic pattern include the inability to manifest and difficulty with seeing things through to completion, focusing, being with other people's—or our own—discomfort, and speaking about our feelings in a measured way instead of blowing up. Does this make logical sense? If you are unable to contain, manage, or direct your own life-force energy, then it makes sense that it would be difficult to hold your containment long enough to direct your life-force energy toward a specific end. These types can be well defined by a term my pilot friends used to say when I was in the Air Force: "All thrust and no vector."

The easiest method to employ in learning to build containment is pausing. Pause, pause, pause before you say or do anything. Ask yourself, "Why am I doing this?" Journal about it, engage in self-reflection, and get professional support if you need it. The unconscious outward-leaking behaviors will almost certainly point to unconscious wounds and the lack of development of certain filters, awarenesses, or skills. You can also refer to the practice in chapter 7 titled "Allow Yourself to Hold Positive Feelings for Longer Periods of Time."

Additionally, outward-leaking types need to practice patience and pacing. They are the sprinters. They call upon their life-force energy in bursts. Pacing requires that they take that life-force energy and apply it in small doses over time to sustain a feeling, cause, or dream.

Fortification for Cave-In Leakers

People who leak energy inward (cave-ins) will benefit from practices that fortify their energy field, but in a different way. Fortifying your energy field in this case is about reinforcing it, like adding stabilizing braces to a building that is collapsing. Fortifying your energy field helps strengthen it so that the pressure of the energies, expectations, and opinions coming toward you doesn't crumple your field. People who leak energy inward tend to implode on themselves. The influence they feel from those outside of them is translated into weight, and that weight overpowers their fragile container, which causes it to collapse.

People who implode also need to question their behaviors and reactions, just like those who explode. Fortifying your container will result from introspection and understanding your motivations. This means questioning why you allow others to take advantage of you, why you tolerate abuse, inequality, or unfairness, and why it is so difficult for you to ask for what you need or stand up for yourself.

Like blowout leakers, they too can benefit from learning to hold their own life force, but with a different focus. People who leak energy outward, overexpress, or bleed energy off need to contain their energy and become comfortable with feeling—and holding the space for—their life-force energy. People who leak energy inward or underexpress can hardly generate enough life-force energy to keep air in their balloon. They need to strengthen their field so they can begin to build up their life force, like air pressure in a tire, to prevent outside forces from decimating it.

Here's another way to think of the difference between these two types of leaks: People who leak energy outward need to concentrate on the *inside* wall of their container. They need to focus on controlling what goes *out* by establishing filters, applying conscious restraint, and pacing themselves. People who leak energy inward need to concentrate on the *outside* wall of their container. They need to focus on strengthening their container to allow their life-force energy to build up enough charge and substance so that they can speak their truth, hold their center, and advocate for themselves.

Common traveling companions of this inward-leaking energetic pattern include many of the same aspects as the blowout leakers: the inability to manifest and difficulty with seeing things through to completion, focusing, being with other people's—or their own—discomfort, and speaking about their feelings. But these occur for *different reasons* and, thus, require different remedies. Other traveling companions include avoidance behaviors: where outward types tend to confront, inward types abdicate. No one is sitting on the throne ruling their sovereign state. Therefore, anyone else who happens by can pretty much take over the kingdom.

For inward-leaking types, exercises to stay grounded, present, and in body are crucial (refer to chapter 13 on embodiment). These people tend to leave their bodies when confronted with difficulty or challenge.

Sessions with a professional therapist of choice conducted in a safe setting can help these types work through woundings and practice standing up for themselves. This is necessary and important work if they are to reclaim their inner throne and fortify the "outside" of their container to prevent future leaks.

Though I have distinguished two clearly different types of leaks, most people aren't strictly blowout leakers or cave-in leakers. What's more accurate is that people will have a primary pattern but experience leaks in both directions over the course of their lives.

LEAKY ENERGY BREEDS DISTRUST IN OURSELVES

How many leaks in the above two lists could you identify with? Almost certainly there were a few. This doesn't make you a bad human; it just makes you human. As you grow in consciousness and awareness, your energy leaks will diminish. But first, you need to understand a fundamental consequence of years of unconscious energy leaks.

Regardless of whether our leaks are blowouts or cave-ins, we are unconsciously participating in a behavior that is detrimental to our well-being and the health of our relationships. We unknowingly become our own perpetrator, allowing certain energetic patterns of thought and behavior to perpetuate. Energy leaks can produce all kinds of unwanted results, such as loss of friendships, destruction of relationships, misunderstandings, resentment, poor job performance, people not liking or trusting us, holding ourselves back from our goals and dreams, and much more. But all of these can be boiled down to one common core: loss of trust in ourselves.

For example, when we don't stand up for ourselves, when we invade another person's space or interrupt them because we couldn't wait to speak, when we let other people's expectations cloud our truth, or any number of other leaky patterns, then we lose trust in ourselves. On some level, usually an unconscious one, we recognize that our behavior is not in alignment with our true, authentic self. This misalignment creates an internal rift in the form of loss of trust. This trust in ourselves degrades over time as we continue the leaky behaviors.

If you're not clear on the relationship between energy leaks and self-trust, let me illustrate it this way: Take the behavior(s) in question (choose one you resonated with from the list above) and pretend it is being acted out by another person. This method is called externalizing. You take internal qualities and pretend someone else is doing or saying those things. In this way, it is much easier to get a clear read on your reaction to how those actions or words affect you. Pretend that someone else is not standing up for you. Pretend that someone else is invading your personal space or interrupting you. Pretend that you are observing another person shutting down his or her authentic response because of others' expectations or intimidation. It makes you not want to trust that person, doesn't it?

We have grown accustomed to our own internal dialogue and ensuing reactions, so when this interaction occurs inside of us, we can't clearly register the cause and effect. We can't recognize that our own behaviors are having a destructive effect on us; we don't see or feel the impact. It just feels like status quo. However, when we pretend that someone else is treating us or another person in the way we treat ourselves, it is much easier to register a reaction and thus make the connection of how our inauthenticity breeds distrust in ourselves.

Almost certainly there is some amount of damage to the relationship you have with yourself (you wouldn't be human if there wasn't). But there's good news. Rebuilding your self-trust does not happen on a 1:1 ratio, which means that you don't have to perform an act of restoring trust for every act you performed that destroyed that trust. Just a handful a trust-building actions can begin to massively restore your self-trust and, consequently, your self-confidence, which helps you build the strength of your energetic container, which then helps you more consistently draw and maintain boundaries.

These trust-building actions include saying no, asking for what you need, speaking your truth, and creating safety. For instance, when you say no to your neighborhood association's request for you to be their treasurer (where you might have previously said yes, even though you didn't want to), it builds trust in yourself. When you ask your partner to split household chores more evenly because night school is taking all your time, it builds trust in yourself because you asked for what you needed. When you tell your adult son that he can come back and live at home for a while but that he needs to pay rent, it builds trust in yourself because you aren't letting him take advantage of you, where you might have otherwise.

Another way of restoring trust is listening to the needs of your inner child. So often our destructive and unproductive behaviors are a result of our wounded inner child. If as a child you learned that children are meant to be seen and not heard, then one of your inner child's wounds is most likely about not being heard, which can lead to believing that what you think, desire, or believe is not valid or valued, that people don't listen to you, or that what everyone else says is more important. However we internalize messages from childhood, until they become conscious (meaning that we identify them and work to understand and heal them), they will continue to drive our behaviors. It is often from this unconscious, wounded place that we make the decisions that contribute to the creation of our primary leaks.

An often unexpected but corollary benefit of these trust-building actions is the corresponding reduction in resentment. When you don't ask for what you need, draw boundaries, or say no, resentment builds up inside. This resentment often escalates into anger, irritability, passive-aggressiveness, and a whole host of other unpleasant behaviors that confound your friends and loved ones and push them away. But when you begin to rebuild trust in yourself, you will notice over time that the anger, resentment, irritability, and other behaviors dissipate. Building trust in yourself is a major component of drawing and enforcing boundaries.

Projections as a Tool

The uncomfortable but revealing practice of owning your projections can really show you where you need to stand up for yourself or speak your truth. Noticing your projections can actually help restore your self-trust. If you find yourself saying, for example, "Why won't anybody give me a break? They keep asking more and more of me, and I can't do it all," then it's time to look at where *you* are not giving yourself a break and why *you* can't say no. If you have been saying, "Nobody listens to me. I ask for support, and I say no when I need to, but people just blow me off," then it's time to look at where you blow yourself off. Maybe you do decide what you need and want, but if you don't believe that you deserve it, then you'll back down and there will be no substance to your requests. People are perfect mirrors for us. If they aren't listening to you, then you want to look at where *you* aren't listening to you.

People are constantly reflecting our state of being back to us. And all of this happens at a mostly unconscious level. People don't think, "Hey, I don't really believe her when she says she's tired of doing all the cooking, so I'm just going to ignore her request for my help." But energetically, their system is parsing and decoding the energetic emissions that you are unconsciously sending out. Likewise, you are not consciously thinking, "Hey, I am tired of doing all the cooking, so I'm going to ask for help. Except I really don't feel like I deserve help. Plus, I'm a control freak, and I'd really prefer to do it myself. It helps me feel like I'm earning my keep." These are the messages encoded in our energy field, and our systems are highly tuned receivers. This goes for all humans, not just empaths. This is why doing your inner healing work is so critical.

The Effects of Drawing Boundaries

As you begin to practice all the ways in which boundaries can be drawn, you will notice a decline in your resentment of others, an increase in self-trust, and a corresponding fortification of your energy container. Do remember that this will be a lifelong practice and that your energy field is dynamic and ever changing, which means that your relationship with setting boundaries will be a journey, not a destination.

Further, remember that the key to any behavior change is the pivotal moment when you become aware that you are in the pattern, and you can then make a new choice. The power is always in the choice. Once you become aware that you're in the old pattern, you can stop and make a new choice. Do I choose to continue this pattern, or do I choose to draw a new boundary? You can task your subconscious mind with the job of flagging you when you are engaging in leaky behaviors or squishy boundary patterns. As with any behavioral change, the more you practice, the sooner and more frequently you'll be able to identify when you're in the pattern.

THE ROLE OF THE MASCULINE
IN CREATING SAFETY

One of the most important results of drawing good healthy boundaries is creating safety. In terms of the masculine and feminine archetypes, the masculine is the one who is responsible for creating safety. To understand how to create safety through establishing boundaries, we need to explore the role of the masculine as well as its many forms. Chapter 10 covers the masculine (and feminine) in great detail. After you read it, you might choose to come back and reread this section.

Personal Masculine, Archetypal Masculine, Divine Masculine, and the Influence of Culture

The masculine takes on many forms, and I want to distinguish some terms so as not to create confusion. We will delve, briefly, into the *personal masculine*, the *archetypal masculine*, and finally the *divine masculine*. It is important to understand how these three interrelate so you can be clear on which aspects you are working with at any given time and how they influence your life. Further, it is crucial to understand the corruption and distortion of the masculine principle that has occurred through millennia of patriarchal influence.

The Personal Masculine

Our personal inner masculine is formed through our interpretation of all of the modeling we observed as a child; hence the reason it is called *personal.* It is important to recognize that your inner masculine is an amalgamation of the male *and* female influences in your life. It might seem like our masculine would be patterned after our father and other male forces, but consider that the influences of your mother and other female figures also contributed significantly to the development of your inner masculine. You absorbed all of your female role models' *reactions* to masculine energy, which again contributed to the totality of the expression of your inner masculine.

Your personal inner masculine is the expression of the masculine that is unique to you. Your inner masculine is a "human" characterization. It has a specific personality, just like a person. You have a relationship with your personal inner masculine (whether you are aware of it or not), and your inner masculine impacts your decisions, behaviors, thought processes, and actions. In this way, it operates in the physical realm of the manifested world because the influence of your personal inner masculine shows up in how you live your life.

The Archetypal Masculine

The archetypal, or transpersonal, masculine is a collection of qualities that we generally agree defines the masculine model or standard. It doesn't define what a *man* should be; it defines the masculine *principle*. It is not unique to an individual person but rather an idea in the collective human consciousness.

I cover these traits in more detail in chapter 10, but they are listed below in a condensed version. The masculine principle is generally associated with the following:

- Directness
- Logic
- Taking action
- Defining boundaries
- Being assertive
- Tending to details; planning
- Thinking in a linear or sequential fashion
- Being results-oriented
- Being competitive
- Dealing with the concrete or tangible
- Creating structure, safety, and security

The masculine principle is also associated with the left brain (and, correspondingly, the feminine is associated with the right brain). According to neuroanatomist Dr. Jill Bolte Taylor in her book *My Stroke of Insight,* the left brain:

- Perceives things as being solid
- Helps us identify personal physical boundaries
- Is concrete enough to stay a path
- Defines boundaries
- Is responsible for taking all the energy, information about the present moment, and magnificent possibilities perceived by the right brain and shaping them into something manageable
- Is the tool used to communicate with the external world
- Believes everything has a place, and everything belongs in its place
- Focuses on differences and distinguishing characteristics
- Perceives shorter wavelengths of light, increasing its ability to clearly delineate sharp boundaries (as a result, our left brain is biologically adept at identifying separation lines between adjacent entities)[1]

You can see from these two lists that the qualities needed to identify and hold good boundaries are clearly found in the left brain and, hence, the masculine as well.

The archetypal masculine is not good or bad; it is simply a set of qualities that can be considered neutral. If these qualities are overexpressed or underexpressed, then they can certainly become harmful and throw an individual, or an entire society, out of balance. But in their "pure" neutral form, the masculine and left-brain attributes serve important and necessary functions.

The Divine Masculine

Finally, there is the divine masculine. The divine masculine is the blueprint or ideal version of masculine energies. It resides in the archetypal realm as well, but it is different in that it is not a "human" created stereotype. It is not influenced by culture, though to be thorough, it is influenced by consciousness and humanity's understanding of highly conceptual ideas based on where we are in the cycle of ascension or descension. The divine masculine is an emerging concept; it is what we are evolving toward. It holds a collection of high-frequency patterns that include creating safety, holding space, and witnessing without judgment.

This doesn't mean that the other qualities of the masculine principle that I listed previously are now discarded or obsolete. They are still present, but they are in the process of reorganizing themselves into a different focus and expression. As the concepts of the sacred marriage and conscious equal partnership begin to shift the collective energies, the masculine will *show up* in a different way. If he no longer needs to rescue the feminine or play the role of "completing" her, if he is no longer concerned with domination or defending, he is then freed to show up in his full sovereignty, partnering with the feminine in her full sovereignty. The qualities of the left brain/masculine will still serve a purpose (just as the right brain/feminine will), but they will no longer be trapped in the current stereotypes, which are based in a lack of inherent wholeness.

The Influence of Culture on the Masculine Principle

The myths of Western culture have distorted the archetypal masculine, turning up the volume so that the once neutral attributes are now blasting us with excess. And in looking at the influence of culture on the masculine principle, we must also bring the feminine principle into the discussion because these two are inseparable poles. What happens to one affects the other.

The factors that have influenced the distortion of the masculine (and feminine) are too numerous to go into here, but it is clear that, instead of conscious equal partnership between the masculine and feminine principles, there is a vast imbalance in the way in which the two archetypes are portrayed in our collective consciousness. With the influence of the patriarchy in Western society, the archetypal male qualities have been perverted and inflated and then projected onto the men in our culture. We expect our men to be rescuers, knights in shining armor, breadwinners, and heroes. To be superhuman and made of muscle. To show no weakness and to conquer all. Along with these unrealistic expectations, we have perpetuated values that reflect the same disparity: men are smarter than women, men work and women raise the children, men assume leadership roles, women are too emotional and can't handle stressful situations, only men can be in the military, women are sexual objects. These are all examples of the myths our culture continues to maintain.

In short, this gross imbalance in the masculine and feminine principles at the archetypal level has infiltrated their expression at the human level. Anything that is related to the masculine principle is highly valued; anything related to the feminine principle is devalued. Masculine qualities are upheld and praised. Feminine qualities are denigrated and dismissed.

This distortion of the masculine principle and its corresponding relationship to the feminine principle feeds into and helps create the personal expression of your own personal inner masculine. Your inner masculine was created from a combination of influences that included your parents, religion, school, social structures, the media, and the greater society. Each of these influences enforces and reinforces the same expectations, stereotypes, and messages, almost in lockstep. These messages are pervasive, sometimes overt, and sometimes deceptively subtle. We aren't always aware of what these messages are, but aware or not, we are most definitely influenced by them.

Calling upon the Divine Masculine

At some point, doing your inner work is going to lead you to an examination of the masculine and feminine archetypes and how they have manifested in you personally. If you want to understand boundaries and learn to establish and maintain them, it is necessary to recognize the influence of the masculine (and feminine) at all levels. I have focused on the masculine because, as I have established, it is the masculine principle that is associated with boundary drawing. Whether you are familiar with the varying aspects of the masculine or are reading about them for the first time, there are tools you can use right away to support you in establishing boundaries.

One of the ways in which we can interact with the concept of the divine masculine is to imagine it being the blueprint we download into our circuitry to act as the new template for our personal inner masculine. This doesn't mean our inner masculine is bad or wrong or needs to be killed off. I'm making an assumption here, but I'm presuming that when you begin to investigate your inner masculine, there will be qualities in your relationship with him that are not serving you. As a place to start, it's important to know what you *don't* want. Yet sometimes it is more difficult to know what you *do* want. Allow the divine masculine blueprint to act as the "do want." When your human inner masculine gets stuck in an old pattern, you can gently remind him of the role you would like him to play for you instead of the role he has been playing. The masculine is an action principle. He likes to have a job.

When it comes time to draw a boundary, such as saying no, asking for what you need, or creating agreements, call upon the divine masculine to assist you. This might be a novel concept at first, and maybe even a bit awkward. If most of the perpetrators or abusers or abandoners in your life were men, it might be a long stretch to call upon anything resembling a man to create security for you. But remember, you're not calling upon a *man,* you're calling upon the divine masculine principle, the archetypal *ideal.* If there are any masculine deities, angels, or guides you work with, ask them to assist you. In petitioning the divine masculine, you are calling forth an energetic field. This field contains the pattern of creating safety. Open yourself to this support.

I encourage you, especially if this is a new concept, to find some kind of sacred object to hold the divine masculine archetypal energies for you. Working with physical objects that represent intangible concepts or energies is very helpful to me. I have a sizable altar and make use of many medicine pieces. There is a large Shiva lingam stone that holds the energy of the divine masculine for me. I have a collection of smaller items grouped together that hold different aspects of the masculine principle. Carry your object with you if you can. Put it someplace where you will see it and interact with it daily. Touching it can help you remember that the power to stand firm in your own sovereign space is accessible to you at any time.

Another way to work with the masculine energy is to examine your personal relationship to your inner masculine. Take the time to contemplate this relationship and the influences that shaped him, as it can reveal volumes about your beliefs, decisions, and actions in the world. Maybe you don't trust him. Maybe you feel he abandoned you. Maybe you never acknowledged him or developed a relationship with him. How much was he influenced by the collective consciousness? How many of his beliefs do you agree with or disagree with? Wherever you are in your relationship with your inner masculine is fine. Just begin the dialogue.

Additionally, as a next step, or in combination with the above inquiry, you can examine the balance of the masculine and feminine principles within you. Be forewarned; this whole process of investigation can be a harrowing, teeth-gnashing journey, and one you might choose to work on with a coach or teacher. As you begin to look inward, the pieces can become shifty and confusing. Living in a patriarchal society for as long as we have has created a tangled web that most of us stay caught up in for our entire lives. Understanding your relationship to your personal inner masculine is a difficult enough task. Looking at the expression of the masculine and feminine within you requires looking at the familial as well as societal influences, which means deconstructing the patriarchy within. This is no small feat, but it's one worth accomplishing. And one certainly worth mentioning as we learn to reclaim our own authority and ability to create our own safety and draw clear boundaries.

Boundaries:
The 3-D Application

One of the greatest gifts that evolutionary empaths give to the world is an open, loving heart. We are deeply committed to holding the vibration of love and heart-centeredness on this planet, often to our frequent detriment when we walk the path unconsciously. The goal is not to close down the heart, but to develop trust in ourselves to apply the necessary tools to create safety and boundaries. This way, when we begin to feel vulnerable or get knocked off our center, we can right the ship but keep our heart open.

What often happens in the earlier, unconscious years is that we project our need for safety and protection onto others. And to be fair, it is right and normal to expect our parents to protect us! But through their humanness and their own wounds, unmet needs, and unresolved issues, they invariably made some missteps that had significant consequences for us. None of us make it to adulthood unscathed. Our wounds then feed into the different coping mechanisms and strategies that we employ, which in turn feed into the construct of our energetic container and, subsequently, our ability to create safety, ask for what we need, speak our truth, and draw boundaries.

We can overcome the influences of our childhood! In fact, empath or not, that's part of our spiritual maturation process as adults. Drawing boundaries is a skill, and anyone can learn how. But know that it will take time. You will be honing these skills for the rest of your life. But make no mistake, your mastery in this area is crucial for your own well-being and for showing the way for generations coming up behind you. At the soul level, you came here to be a leader in your own life, which also means you are leading by example with your family, friends, work group, and community.

Learning to live in the 3-D is one of the hardest challenges for any soul. We are limitless beings! We are timeless, dimensionless, and formless. *Thunk!* And now we are crammed into a physical body with limitations, linear time, and physical stuff to maneuver around. It is clunky and confusing down here on Earth. Yet this is what we came here for: to experience life in human form and to contribute to the evolution of humanity in the cosmos.

THE ENERGETIC IMPACT OF SETTING BOUNDARIES

So what happens at an energetic level when you draw boundaries? You are essentially changing some aspect of your relationship with a person. You are showing up differently, and this will most definitely show up in your energy field, which will subsequently register in that person's energy field. The change could be as simple as saying to your partner, "I'm not folding your clothes and putting them away anymore and here's why" to "If you don't get sober I'm leaving this relationship" to "I will no longer allow you to speak to me this way (giving examples), and if you do I will hang up the phone or walk away, and if you continue, I will no longer maintain a relationship with you."

When you change your behavior, shift a belief, make a new decision, or resolve yourself to a particular action, your energetic signature changes. Your personal vibration shifts to a measurable degree.

Measurable by whom? By the people you interact with and especially the person or people the changes are directed at.

On multiple occasions I have had clients report similar results back to me when they draw a clear boundary and enforce it. Experiences of cord cutting with an ex often resulted in unexpected contact from that person, usually in the form of a random-seeming "Hey, you were on my mind." Sometimes cord cutting resulted in an amplification of the other person's manipulative or codependent behavior. For example, a client's cord cutting with her mother (who was very manipulative) created a strong reaction in her mother because, on an unconscious level, her mother perceived that she no longer had her talons in her daughter and felt she was losing control.

In another case, one client chose to stop enabling her husband. I warned her to expect that he might regress into childlike behavior, throwing everything at her that he could to manipulate and suck her back into her old behaviors. This is exactly what happened, but because she was prepared for it, she had measures to lovingly deal with it while her husband made adjustments to this new dynamic in their relationship.

When we draw boundaries, we are using words, taking actions, or employing visualizations. Though this work occurs in the subtle realm of the nonphysical and intangible, there are clearly tangible and physical results. It is imperative to understand that as you begin to draw boundaries, it will affect the people around you, and you won't always be able to predict their reactions. Remember that what you're doing will register at the level of other people's energy fields, but it will less frequently register at a conscious level in their mind. Which means that when they react to your new boundary, they will be doing exactly that—*reacting*. It takes highly conscious and practiced people to recognize when they are being triggered and then speak to it rationally. Most times, what you encounter when you draw a boundary is the unconscious, triggered reaction of the other person.

These reactions often include resistance in some form (often anger), which will then immediately lead to some kind of manipulative strategy to get you to renege: accusations, projections, tantrums, guilt, withdrawal, and more. Think of disciplining or enforcing boundaries with a child. He wants to stay up and watch thirty more minutes of TV, and you say no, it's time for bed. That is a clear boundary. The child doesn't like the boundary and will give you resistance. This could be in the form of whining, pleading, screaming, crying, or stomping his feet up the stairs. But when you are prepared for his reaction, you don't get sucked in to countering with your own reaction. You don't get angry, and you don't plead and beg. You simply stay neutral, hold your ground, and weather the short-lived tantrum. You know he'll get over it.

It doesn't always play out this simply and predictably when you set every boundary, but it illustrates the point of resistance and the importance of *you being prepared for the other person's reaction.* This preparation is an absolutely crucial practice when you draw boundaries, especially significant ones. You must understand that people have grown accustomed to you being a certain way. There's a reliable predictability to our actions, and that gives comfort to those with whom we interact regularly. *When I say this, he'll say that. When I do this, she'll do it too. He always says yes to the neighbor's request to borrow something. She always does the grocery shopping. He doesn't get angry very easily. She'll let me do anything I want.* Expectations begin to form. Patterns get ingrained.

It is human nature to put each other in boxes, because it is instinctive to try and quantify our surroundings. This is part of our psyche's mechanism of creating safety. Consistency, reliability, dependability, regularity, predictability—these are all things that help us feel safe. At a transcendental level we might say that these are things that give us the *illusion* of feeling safe, but at a reptilian brain level, it is how we are wired, and we experience it as very real.

So when you draw boundaries, do not forget to prepare yourself for the potential reactions. This way you are not caught off guard. Especially if you are highly sensitive, someone else's onslaught, which is designed to get you to go back to the old way, might do exactly that if you aren't prepared to hold your ground. Again, going back to the illustration of children, it is important to have consequences for disobedience or lack of respect for boundaries. Not punishment, but consequences.

Consequences are matter-of-fact eventualities and can be spoken along with the boundary. For example, "I have allowed you and your two children to live here without paying rent for over six months. When you came, you said it would be for just a couple of months while you got back on your feet. You have not contributed to the rent, groceries, or utilities and continue to expect me to support you. I love you, but I will no longer allow you to take advantage of me. You have thirty days to move out. If you do not, I will change the locks, put all of your belongings in the yard, and call the police if necessary."

In preparing yourself for others' reactions, it is also beneficial to expect that they will need time to process your statement and make a decision about how they will respond, depending on the circumstances. If you're telling a twelve-year-old boy that it's time for him to start cleaning up his own room, then there's not a negotiation happening and he doesn't get to decide if he wants to comply. He can rebel, but you will already have your consequences ready to apply. But in most instances where you are setting boundaries with other adults, they will need time to absorb and adjust.

When you do your visualizing or mental preparation work for setting a boundary, your job doesn't just include figuring out what the boundary is. It includes deciding on the consequences if the other person does not choose to enter into the new parameters of the relationship with you. Taken to its most painful potential outcome, this could include ultimately leaving the relationship, whether it is with your spouse, employer, parent, or friend. As Iyanla Vanzant said on an episode of her television show *Iyanla: Fix My Life,* "You've got to be willing to lose everything to gain yourself."

I realize that this is a bit bleak, but depending on your life circumstances, it could be a very real possibility. When we have spent the bulk of our lives being doormats, taking care of everyone else's needs, avoiding rocking the boat, stuffing our own wants and needs deep inside, and codependently taking on everyone else's emotions and problems, even setting a small boundary can feel like an impossibility. We don't intend to get ourselves mired in these types of relationships and dynamics, but sometimes the answer is as extreme as *get out and get out now.*

It Is Nobody's Responsibility to Comply

Here's another very important fact to remember and probably the hardest to accept: just because you set a boundary doesn't mean the other person has to agree. This is part of exercising free will as humans. And it is an eventuality you should also prepare yourself for. *It is your responsibility to ask for what you need, but it is nobody's responsibility to comply with your needs.* It is a hard truth and one that would behoove you to accept as soon as possible. In the subsequent sections of this chapter I give you tools and practices for this type of preparation.

SAYING NO

If you are a lifelong people pleaser, saying no is one of the scariest statements you can make. If you have spent your existence merging with others, putting everyone else first, or avoiding rocking the boat, then the idea of saying no can feel like standing naked in front of a firing squad. "No!" is a powerful proclamation, and it will get you noticed. William Ury, author of *The Power of a Positive No,* says, "No is the tension between exercising your power and tending to your relationship."[1]

Consideration of other people is necessary when contemplating your response to their request. There are consequences when you say both yes and no. But for empaths it is especially challenging because we tend to—unconsciously—overlegitimize other people's point of view. We feel what they want from us, and it can be exceedingly difficult to extract their influence from our energy field so we can gauge our own response and not feel pressured by their desire for us to say yes. The most powerful tool I have found for creating that critical moment of separation is the pause.

The Power of the Pause

As a recovering people pleaser, I used to feel the pressure of another person's appeal so acutely that I felt compelled to answer right in that moment. It never occurred to me that I had the right to say, "Let me think about this" or "Let me get back to you." This was especially true when it was a relationship I valued greatly, like a boss or lover. And to be fair to myself, in those relationships my pattern was to lose myself and give my authority over to that person. Pleasing that person was especially important so I could maintain love, acceptance, and security.

When I discovered the power of the pause, it changed everything in my ability to regain my center and answer from my authentic truth.

The pause is simply that moment between someone requesting you to do something and your answer. For me, the pause is always accompanied by a deep breath. In this crucial moment, my observer awareness can then come in and remind me, "Hey, you don't have to give this person a final answer right now." It gives me those precious few seconds where I can call back any codependent energies that went shooting out to make the other person feel better and stay in a neutral place centered inside myself.

Pausing—even just a few seconds—gives you time to collect yourself and choose a response instead of reacting unconsciously. Reactions often come from a place of fear. Responses come from a place of careful consideration.

As you are contemplating how to answer the person in the moment, it is important to recognize that no doesn't always mean "no, never." No can also mean the following:

- Not now.
- This doesn't feel right to me now, but I'm open to it in the future.
- I would love to support you in what you are asking of me, but I cannot do it in the way you are asking. Would you allow me to support you in this other way?
- I have other priorities I am tending to; would it be acceptable for me to do this in a week instead of by tomorrow?
- I need some time to think about this.
- I don't have the time to support your cause, but would you allow me to donate money instead of time?

If these types of responses are difficult for you to access inside yourself, you might craft one or two standard lines and keep them in your mental back pocket for just such an occasion. This will serve you well when you're caught off guard, when the other person is in a hurry or state of chaos, or when your energy is low or you feel frazzled. As empaths, we are always walking on the edge of overwhelm, so no is a vital tool for managing our energetic field.

If saying no feels like an almost impossible challenge, I encourage you to begin practicing with easy things—that is, things that don't have much consequence if you don't agree. For example, do you want another helping? "No, thank you. I'm full." Do you want to watch XYZ show on TV? "No, but I don't mind if you do. I'll read my book." Or "No, can we record it and watch ABC show instead?" Instead of saying "I don't care" when your spouse asks where you want to eat, listen for what is true for you and try to feel what your answer is. Maybe you really want Mexican food, but you don't want to risk upsetting the rest of the family. Take a small risk and say, "I'd love to eat Mexican tonight."

These may seem like silly examples, but there are truly some people who are just waiting for the trapdoor to open up and swallow them if they say no in any way, shape, or form. Walk on your growing edge with this one, but take it in baby steps. Your courage and confidence will expand.

At a more advanced level, saying no is a way of creating clarity and focus. When you are trying to make decisions, grow your business, figure out the next step in your life, or undertake any sort of endeavor that requires you to come to a conclusion you can act on, you need your no. No creates space. It eliminates nonresonant possibilities and gives you room to see the resonant options more clearly because your field of vision isn't crammed with every alternative under the sun because you're afraid to commit.

One of my coaches taught me something very important about no that I've used many times: *Sometimes you have to say no to something you like in order to say yes to something you love.* It is much easier to say no to something you don't like at all, can't stand, or don't resonate with in any way. It is hard and even painful to say no to something you like, but it can be the precise surgical tool required to move you closer to bliss.

Saying No after You've Said Yes

Saying no after you say yes is an option! Sometimes we think we've backed ourselves into a corner and don't realize that we have the option to change our mind. It is acceptable to say no after you say yes. The other person will live. And I promise, it will happen at some point.

Saying no takes practice. Here are some examples of what that might sound like, as well as counterproposals you can include if they resonate with you:

- I need to apologize to you; I said yes to your request, but as I thought about it, I realize I can't do a good job (or) I don't have the time (or) I felt how much you wanted me to do this and I didn't want to disappoint you.
- I looked at my calendar and realized I am completely overbooked. Can we reschedule for _____?
- I know this is important to you, but I won't be able to help you

with the whole job. I only have time for _____. Would you be willing to tell me what your priorities are with this? That way I can help you with the most important task.

- Please know that my family loves spending time with your family, but going to large amusement parks is very difficult and exhausting for me. Instead of coming with you, I'd love to plan a day where our families can get together at one of our homes for a cookout.
- I am happy to do this for you, if you can wait three weeks.
- I can give you two hours to _____, but I don't have the time to do all of what you asked.
- I can't take you to the airport, but I know someone else who can.

Saying no after you say yes also means preparing for the other person's reaction. This could be disappointment, anger, frustration, and even projections and blaming. This is where it is important to consider if you are willing and able to offer a counterproposal or alternative plan. If not, then your statement may simply need to be "I said yes, and I really should have said no." And there might be some consequences to that no, which you will have hopefully weighed in your decision process.

The most important thing to take out of this is that you are never stuck. Even if you originally said yes, you still have options. You always have a choice.

ASKING FOR WHAT YOU NEED

Asking for what you need tends to be the next stage of development after getting comfortable with saying no, though they do progress simultaneously to a degree. Asking for what you need, however, requires that you know what it is you need in the first place!

As empaths, many of us have shut down our internal communication grid. As discussed in the first half of this book, there are many reasons why we lost this connection with ourselves. We were given messages when we were young that our sensitivities were not valued and therefore dismissed. We felt shame about our gifts. We experienced a great deal of rejection or ridicule, and it became a coping mechanism to just turn the faucet off. We merged with others so well that we thought other people's needs and wants were actually our own and, therefore, really had no idea what our own wants and needs were. Whatever the reason, the end result is that we have severed the connection between recognizing our needs and our ability to voice them.

Furthermore, we women are typically subject to additional programming that tells us to suppress our needs and put others' needs before ours. We are taught that our needs don't matter or are not as important as those of our husbands, families, churches, communities, et cetera. This influence cannot be overlooked. It is not just empaths who struggle with identifying and voicing their needs.

Early in my spiritual awakening, I did not know how to recognize what I wanted. I didn't even have a model for how to do it. I had a model for suppression, secrecy, and denial from my mother, but certainly not one for standing up for yourself. On the other end of the spectrum, as modeled by my father, standing up for yourself was demonstrated with fist pounding and "by god-ing" at the dinner table and lots of stories of unappreciation from "the Man." Yet Dad tended to be all bluster and bombastic display, and neither parent exhibited much emotional maturity during my childhood. So I had very few healthy skills going into adulthood.

It took mentors and teachers to show me how to ask for what I needed. To give me a context and show me there was a different way, and to help me see how codependent I was and how I had abandoned myself. Before them, I didn't even know that I could say the suggested statements I've been sharing with you! And believe me, the journey to get here was not easy. It was incredibly embarrassing and frustrating being a thirty-something-year-old adult with the emotional skills of a twelve-year-old.

The major task in learning to ask for what you need is getting back in touch with your own needs, preferences, desires, and personality. As you begin to experience yourself more powerfully—through saying no, activating your masculine to create safety, standing up for yourself, and speaking your truth—you will begin to reestablish your internal communication structure. It will become easier for you to recognize when you need or want something. The next step is then having the courage to voice it. Again, this takes time and practice. There's no right place to start. Just begin doing the work.

The Screaming Silence

How we present ourselves when asking for what we need is a skill in itself. It can be very scary to speak your truth and then be quiet. The silence can be excruciating. When we have something to share with someone else, and we're concerned that it might not land well with them or might create a conflict, or when what we have to share is very personal and makes us feel vulnerable, we will try to unconsciously hide the impact.

Here are some ways that we hide the impact and counteract our own power:

- We add in extra filler words, saying things like "kind of," "sort of," "a little bit," "well," or "sometimes."
- We might laugh or giggle at the end of our speaking to try to make our words land more softly and less forcefully. It implies that what we said shouldn't be taken seriously.
- We make noises or even make a face that contradicts what we're conveying with our words.
- After we deliver our message, we don't give the other person a chance to consider it. We quickly say something else at the end of

the sentence, so we don't have to sit in the uncomfortable silence with our words still hanging in the air. What we say often contradicts, softens, or negates the message we just delivered. For example, "I do not like going out to the races with your friends. The noises and smells make me nauseous and give me a horrible headache. I love you, but I won't be going with you anymore . . . *but if you really want me to, I'll still go.*"

- Sometimes we raise our voice at the end (like a question) because we are unsure of ourselves.
- We don't look the person in the eye.
- We speak so quietly that the other person can barely hear us.
- We don't tend to our energy field before we have the conversation, so we are not centered, grounded, and contained.
- We don't speak in our "adult" voice and instead speak in a child-like voice.

We do these things because we are afraid. We're afraid of how our words will land. We're afraid of being rejected, made fun of, ostracized, or abandoned. So we try to lessen the impact for the other person. To some degree, we all exhibit at least one of these evasive measures. It takes a huge amount of awareness and practice to begin eliminating these behaviors from our communication patterns. I encourage you to notice which of these behaviors you engage in and to begin to practice speaking clearly, concisely, and without trying to hide the intensity or significance of your message.

In speaking your truth and asking for what you need, preparation is key. Do your energy practice, clear your field, ground yourself, come to your center, and prepare yourself emotionally and mentally for whatever the reaction might be. Sometimes, in our nervousness and haste to just get it over with, we rush in. In a state of chaos, we fumble around, dilute the message, invalidate ourselves, and end up being completely ineffectual.

If you are exceptionally timid and even blank out when it comes time to say what you need, then write it down. This isn't cheating! This is an exercise in building trust in yourself and moving forward. You can simply tell the person, "When it comes to saying things that are really important to me, I tend to blank out and forget what I want to say. I wrote down what I want to say to you because my relationship with you is important enough to me that I want to make sure you know how I feel." It wouldn't be hard if you didn't care, right? And in case you're tempted, I would advise against just giving the letter to the person. That is an abdication of your power and, in a way, a cop-out. Yes, I know it's hard, but you need to read your own words. It is necessary if you desire to build the skill of asking for what you need.

How to Hear Yourself

Sometimes it helps us figure out what we want if someone else gives us options to react to. It can be overwhelming to choose from an endless selection. This happens to me frequently. I do a much better job of making a decision if I have a small set of options to choose from. If you say the world's my oyster, I get lockjaw.

The simple question of "Where do you want to eat out tonight?" can throw us into anxiety. Many times I've found it hard to decide what I want when my option is "anything." But if someone can give me one option at a time, I can measure my body's response to that single option. "Italian?" Hmm . . . no. "Mexican?" Uhh . . . no. "Indian food?" Mmm . . . no. "Barbecue?" Ahh . . . yes!

Involve your spouse, children, and friends and let them know that you are practicing learning to hear what is true for you and listening to what your body wants. Find easy ways to ask them to help you, like the restaurant list above. Soon, you will be able to give yourself your own list that you can react to, and eventually you will hear your own needs, wants, and desires with clarity. Our wants can speak in small, quiet voices, too. So part of your task of learning to listen to yourself will be to give yourself the space and quiet you need to be able to hear in the first place. Don't be afraid to ask your friends and family for that space and quiet.

LOSING YOURSELF IN RELATIONSHIPS

In a chapter on boundaries I must acknowledge the frequency with which we as empaths lose ourselves in relationships. Oftentimes the first step in establishing a boundary—the precursor, really—is to extract ourselves from the other person's energy field. Because our nature is to merge and absorb, we must develop keen awareness so that, from this point forward, we know exactly where our edges are. This is commonly referred to as knowing where you end and the next person begins. Up to that point, most of us have experienced no such thing. Me and you as distinct? Nope. There's just us. And then, before you know it, you're gone. Any semblance of your individual preferences, personality, and values has been absorbed into the entity called "us."

Maintaining your sovereignty in relationships, especially romantic relationships, is tough. I feel like a broken record, but it is so important to understand that every one of these skills takes practice, and you won't get them overnight. But you will get them! Each one of us is ultimately responsible for our own energy field. The romantic ideas of "you complete me" and being rescued by your one true love are—sorry—false and misleading. They perpetuate the myth that you are not enough, that you are not whole and complete unto yourself, and that you are somehow deficient and need the other to give you something you can't give to yourself.

As I've shared previously, I'm not saying that when we are "evolved" we will no longer want or need to be in a relationship. Not true! However, when we can show up whole and complete unto ourselves, then we can experience love, sex, intimacy, and relationships in an entirely new way. When we are not projecting our unclaimed selves onto our partners, they are free to be who they are instead of feeling the pressure of who we need them to be. We can truly revel in another person's uniqueness and individuality without feeling like we need to change him or her. We're not looking to a partner to heal us, fix us, make up for what our mother or father did or didn't do, or compensate for the errors of our last partner.

All of the practices of saying no, asking for what you need, and speaking your truth will serve you in extracting yourself from the abyss of "other identification." Up to this point you have probably been acting as the absentee ruler of your own domain. When you can reclaim your own center, sit in the seat of your own throne, and manage your kingdom from inside your own energy field, an entirely new experience of relationship will open up to you.

For some, it is easier to do our relationship work when we are single or in between relationships. This can create a sweet space of getting to know yourself—just yourself—without the temptation or distraction of a partner. Others work better in an "on-the-job" setting where they work through their issues while in relationship. Neither way is better and both have their challenges. No matter what your relationship status, being an evolutionary empath is going to cause your soul to "call you on your stuff." It is much easier to be an empath in a vacuum, but that's the same as being a monk in a cave. If you came here to experience a physical existence, you cannot avoid interaction with other humans, and you must do your inner relationship work.

While I have been referring to romantic relationships, we also merge with parents, children, siblings, bosses, clients, and more. Everything I've said above applies. So doing your relationship work doesn't just include your romantic partner, it includes every significant relationship you have. This can be a lot to bite off altogether, so just chew on one piece at a time. Don't choke yourself in overambition. Changes in relationships take time, and the other people need time to adjust, too.

In summary, the skills of saying no, asking for what you need, drawing boundaries, and creating your own safety are key tools in your

Evolutionary Empath Tool Kit. These are competencies you will work on for the rest of your life. Don't get discouraged. As I've stated several times, awareness is always the first step. Once you become aware of your unhealthy patterns, you can begin to transform them. Remember, too, that in this accelerated time, many of us are not doing the work just for ourselves; rather, we are transforming (and transmuting!) patterns for our families, communities, lineage, and planet. *As the one so the many; as the many so the one.* Your empowerment as an evolutionary empath is contributing to more than just your own personal growth.

10

Embracing the Divine Masculine and Feminine as Conscious Equal Partners

The time of the patriarchy is ending. Social systems in which power is held by men and therefore withheld from women have run their course. They are fighting for their last breath. Just like an animal in the wild being killed by its predator, the prey is never so alive as when it is dying. All of its life force is spent trying to stay alive when at some level in its consciousness it knows death is imminent. Don't let the outer appearances of our world fool you. The patriarchy is in its death throes. In order for us to evolve as a species, we need a new model for our communications, relationships, values, and social structures, and the patriarchy won't get us there.

Yet neither will a matriarchy when it is assumed to be the polar opposite of patriarchy. There are those who erroneously believe that the restoration of the divine feminine is about returning to a structure where the pendulum swings mercifully to the other side, with women coming into power and men being vilified as they fall to the margins. On this planet of duality, neither the masculine-dominated nor the feminine-dominated models of community and relationship will evolve us forward. (It's interesting to note that while dictionary definitions of matriarchy indicate that it is a system of government or social organization where a woman is the head and inheritance is traced through the female line, study of matriarchal cultures shows that many of them actually practiced a balance of masculine and feminine energies.)

We are moving into an entirely new dimension that transcends duality and promotes unity. As we make space in our consciousness for "both/and" (both the masculine *and* the feminine, instead of choosing between the two or assigning superiority to one or the other), we begin to resolve the "opposites." Unity consciousness heralds the time of *conscious equal partnership* between the masculine and feminine, recognizing that they can coexist peacefully and are not adversaries. This is the new model, with the masculine and feminine walking hand in hand, co-creating as equals, and honoring and valuing one another's differences.

So how does this relate to being an empath?

To continue this conversation, we must first understand the basics of the masculine and feminine archetypes so we can establish a common foundation. As I mentioned in chapter 8, the terms *left brain* and *right brain* can be applied to this discussion of the masculine and feminine. You might recall from science class that the left brain controls the right side of the body, and the right brain controls the left side of the body. The right side of the body is associated with the masculine and, correspondingly, the left brain and the following traits:

- Directness
- Practicality
- Logic
- Action
- Boundaries
- Consciousness of the mind
- The ego center

- Assertiveness
- Details and planning
- Judgment of good/bad or right/wrong
- Linear or sequential thinking
- Focus on results
- Competitiveness
- The concrete or the tangible
- Structure, safety, and security

Feminine energies are associated with the left side of the body, the right brain, and the following traits:

- Intuition
- Creativity
- Sensitivity
- Flexibility and fluidity
- The body's instinctive consciousness
- Nonjudgment
- Relativity (as opposed to the absolute)
- Abstract or nonlinear thinking
- Nurturing and caregiving
- Present-moment awareness
- Compassion and cooperation
- Receptivity and ability to listen
- Perception of subtle energies and nonverbal communications

If you had to condense these concepts into just two ideas, the masculine energy is related to the *intellect* or *head* and is about *doing,* and the feminine energy is related to the *feelings* and the *heart* and is about *being.*

So you might already be seeing a correlation between our empathic traits and the list of feminine qualities. And because the feminine has been devalued for thousands of years, every quality that defines us as empaths has been devalued right along with it.

Hand in hand with accepting our empathic nature is actually the acceptance and reclamation of the feminine! In choosing to come to this planet, we are embodying and anchoring the new human blueprint on multiple levels. On a grander scale, as empaths we are modeling the best of the feminine: listening, living in harmony with all living things, honoring the natural rhythms and cycles of nature and our own bodies, connecting to and embracing the unseen realms, and understanding subtle energies, along with traits such as compassion, intuition, creativity, peaceful solutions, cooperation, receptivity, nonviolence, and trust.

As I mentioned earlier, humanity is moving into fourth chakra consciousness, which is the place of the heart. The return of the divine feminine and moving into fourth chakra or heart consciousness are different ways of saying the same thing. Though with much resistance, we are making progress away from operating dominantly from the head and toward living from the heart. As the saying goes, "The longest journey you'll ever make is from your head to your heart." This is not to say that we are abandoning the intellect. The left brain and all of its functions are still necessary. We are relearning how to honor and value both equally again. Equality between the masculine and feminine is synonymous with the head and heart living in conscious partnership. The head (intellect) is meant to serve, not lead. We have grown way out of balance in the authority and credence we give to the intellect and masculine/left-brain qualities. Says Robin Sharma, "The mind is a wonderful servant, but a terrible master."[1]

The fourth chakra is also in the center of the traditional chakra system, with three chakras below it and three chakras above it. In this way, the fourth chakra is at home in the ability to hold the space for "opposite energies" or polarities. And more than just holding space, the heart chakra becomes the alchemical furnace in which these opposites are transformed into partners, balancing one another in harmony instead of conflict. From this realigned viewpoint emerges the ability to now recognize the value and significance of these opposites as equal contributors. Transcendence and embodiment, masculine and feminine, shadow and light, and spirit and matter all become necessary and valued partners, equal in their points of view and unique contribution. What was polarized (duality) becomes united (unity) in the space of the heart.

As with any massive paradigm shift, the old establishment is terrified and fighting to the death to keep the status quo in place. It is natural for our egos (which control the tapes of the old patterns and beliefs) to fight hard to stay in place and convince us that change is not only bad, but life threatening. Remember that third chakra consciousness—which we are moving out of—is about ego identity, self-definition, and the exploration and expression of individuality, will, and power. It is important to keep in mind that it doesn't matter how big a country or institution or system is, it is made up of individuals, and the dynamic that is playing out in the mind of each individual person is echoed in the larger system. It is vital to remember that change starts within. So, if the system is going to change, it's going to start with individual people like you and me. As Gandhi said, we must "be the change [we] want to see in the world."

Our first step as empaths will be to love, accept, embrace, and nurture *ourselves,* and these are, not coincidentally, feminine qualities. As the old structures in our minds, thought processes, and belief systems crumble, so too will the greater societal structures of the patriarchy that uphold separateness, inequality, suppression, intolerance, prejudice, rivalry, and domination.

The patriarchy is falling, and we are being asked by our souls to rise in consciousness, reclaim the divine feminine, and live from the heart. This is just the fertile ground needed for the new human empath blueprint to take root and grow.

THE UNHEALTHY MASCULINE OVEREXPRESSES, THE UNHEALTHY FEMININE UNDEREXPRESSES

In taking our understanding of the masculine and feminine one step further, it is important to understand what happens when these qualities are expressed in their unhealthy versions. Being able to recognize the unhealthy (I try to stay away from the word *negative*) expression gives us a clue as to what is motivating us and the opportunity to make a new choice.

Let me digress for just a moment to address "unhealthy" versus "negative." I believe that any quality exists on a continuum. A quality is neither good nor bad; it just is. In this way, hot and cold are just expressions of temperature. Temperature itself is not good or bad; it just is. Hot is not negative, nor is cold. Nor is the middle—warm—always desirable or perfect. How it is viewed depends on the context.

Let's take assertiveness as an example. Pegged to one extreme, assertiveness becomes aggression, hostility, or violence. Pegged to the other end, it becomes passivity, timidity, or hesitance. Assertiveness itself isn't good or bad. Either extreme is almost always unhealthy. In everyday terms we often refer to things as positive or negative, but in my belief system all experiences are occurring for a reason. Who am I to judge the event as positive or negative before I know its purpose? I am the creator of my world—creating consciously or unconsciously—so I cannot deny that what is in my world is there because I called it to me. Every experience serves a greater purpose. So I prefer to use the term *unhealthy* as opposed to *negative*.

Archetypally, the unhealthy masculine overexpresses, and the unhealthy feminine underexpresses. This makes perfect sense if you recall that the masculine principle is about doing, and the feminine principle is about being. Taken to the extreme—like turning up the volume—the unhealthy masculine overdoes it, becoming overbearing, domineering, arrogant, unyielding, forceful, and controlling.

Assertiveness becomes aggression, violence, or attack, and defining healthy boundaries mutates into prejudice, dominance, repression, dictatorship, or separatism. Consciousness of the mind without balance from the feminine cuts off feelings and becomes mechanical, disconnected, and emotionless. In the unhealthy masculine, too much emphasis is placed on functions of the intellect, such as logic, linear thinking, tangible results, concrete concepts, the absolute, and the creation of a simplified world of black and white.

On the other hand, the feminine extreme tends toward under-expression, like turning the volume down. In this way we abdicate our power and become victims—passive, helpless, submissive, and hopeless. Nurturing becomes martyrdom, losing oneself in relationships, codependence, and placing everyone else first. Stifled creativity becomes depression, lethargy, dissociation, and overwhelm. In the unhealthy feminine, without the masculine ability to define edges, our receptivity and sensitivity cause us to become doormats; we lose our center, blend and merge with everything and everyone, and have no ability to take action or to follow through. We become jaded, resentful, and bitter. We lose our connection to our bodies, to the earth, and to our groundedness.

Though I am talking about archetypes and not genders, for the most part women tend to implode, while men tend to explode. Yet the opposite can certainly be true. Women who run a lot of masculine energy might be more prone to exploding, whereas men who run a lot of feminine energy might be more prone to imploding.

☼ Where Do You Over- or Underexpress?

Go back through the last three paragraphs and circle or note which qualities you notice in yourself. Be gentle. This is not about giving yourself another way to feel bad or shame yourself. In striving to become a more conscious human being, we must recognize and acknowledge our patterns. We cannot change what we are not aware of. Remember, too, that we are talking about archetypal energy—patterns. Both men and women have masculine and feminine energies within them, and no matter what body you showed up in, you will most likely identify both unhealthy masculine and feminine expressions in your life.

I want to give a special mention to power and control in this context. Overexpressed masculine energies turn the need for control up to a thousand on the volume dial. The unhealthy masculine is almost always trying to control everything in its sphere of influence: relationships, finances, outcomes, children, business, et cetera. The unhealthy masculine wants to exert power over everything in its world, displaying its authority and asserting its dominance. The underexpressed feminine energies do the opposite; they completely abdicate power and give up the idea that they have any control over their world at all. They suppress their personal power and acquiesce to just about everything and everyone, whether it creates a healthy and happy environment for them or not.

If you expand this on a mass scale, we are bombarded every day with the masculine trying to assert its dominance and control and the feminine constantly being berated, suppressed, and denigrated. And not just by people outside of us. If we look closely at our own programming, it shows up in the voice of our Inner Critic, or ego, our values and beliefs, and our words and actions. We perpetrate the patriarchy on ourselves, often without knowing it. This is one of the reasons that doing our own inner work is so critical. It allows us to begin to create an awareness of what is operating under the surface and why.

Because empaths possess a huge toolbox of feminine qualities, often the rejection and judgment we face aren't just because of our sensitivities or unusual abilities. They arise because our greatest gifts and expressions are so overtly feminine in nature. We face a double whammy of sorts, being ostracized because we are odd *and* because we come bearing the undeniable feminine.

THE DIVINE DISTINCTION

In everyday speech I hear feminine and divine feminine (as well as masculine and divine masculine) used interchangeably all the time. But there is a distinct difference. In talking about the masculine and feminine, we are talking about the human realm. When we speak of masculine or feminine archetypes, we are talking about human qualities. If we were to investigate our own inner masculine and inner feminine, we would find that they are flawed, incomplete, and wounded and express unequally. Our impression—and therefore expression—of each was formed during our childhood, influenced by our parents, teachers, church, extended families, culture, the media, and more. Our masculine and feminine sides have been formed by our human experience. They are what play out in our daily life.

Insert the word *divine,* however, and everything changes. The *divine* feminine (or masculine) is a principle or a blueprint. The divine feminine or divine masculine is an ideal that we strive to embody in human form. It is the most altruistic, virtuous, authentic expression of each. When we have lived from the damaged, deficient aspects of our masculine and feminine for so long, it can be tricky to figure out what to do instead. We can have the desire and willingness to change our beliefs and behaviors, but we need to have a new definition to aspire to. The divine masculine and feminine give us that template to strive for; they are the model.

A HEALTHY INNER MASCULINE GIVES YOU ACCESS TO HEALTHY BOUNDARIES AND RIGHT ACTION

It is important to understand that the masculine aspect of ourselves is what we call upon to draw boundaries. I covered this at length in the previous chapter. This is certainly not the only role that the masculine performs, but as an empath it is critical to develop an understanding of and relationship with your inner masculine because it is the quality of yourself that you will also engage any time you want to say no, deploy your energetic shield, or ask for what you we need.

Please listen to track 2 of the audio tracks, "Meditation to Connect with Your Inner Masculine," so you can begin to develop an understanding of and relationship with your inner masculine.

The individual inner masculine is vastly different from person to person, since we have all been influenced by the unique circumstances of our life. But no matter how you were raised, there are almost certainly aspects of your inner masculine that aren't serving you or are outright holding you back.

Many of us—especially women—have an adversarial relationship with our inner masculine because it was formed under the influence of the patriarchy. Unbeknownst to us, it carries out the patriarchal values and beliefs, often suppressing our true desires, dreams, and authentic expression and influencing us toward "acceptable" roles and aspirations. When I went through the Priestess Process in 2005, I explored my definition of power. What I unearthed deep in my subconscious was that my definition of power was about control, domination, force, suppression, competition, lack, and oppression—someone wins and someone loses. No wonder I was hesitant to step into my power! That was a huge turning point as I then began to develop a conscious relationship with my inner masculine so that I could trust him when I called upon him. From that point I was able to create a new definition of power and recognized that I could be powerful in my gentleness, powerful in my compassion, and powerful in my ability to hold space for another.

As you begin to address and renovate your relationship with your inner masculine, that trust will be a key salve in the healing process, helping to restore your confidence in him and thereby confidence in yourself. Our inner masculine reflects our external experiences of the masculine. For so many of us, our experiences of being abandoned, abused, violated, neglected, disappointed, and suppressed by men as well as by the patriarchy in general (which is conveyed through both women and men) have made us too gun-shy to expect any kind of true support from our inner masculine.

When we reestablish a healthy relationship with our inner masculine, we can then begin to trust him to show up for us when we need him. When we need to say no, he will give us the energy and conviction to do so. When we need to ask for what we need, he will give us the motivation and courage. When we are inspired to follow our dreams, he will act upon the directive of our intention using the principle of right action. We are incomplete without this aspect of ourselves. Our journey toward wholeness must include embracing our inner masculine and restoring our relationship with him to the healthy conscious partnership that was intended by design.

A HEALTHY INNER FEMININE GIVES YOU ACCESS TO SELF-LOVE, SELF-CARE, AND SELF-ACCEPTANCE

Just as it is important to establish a healthy relationship with our inner masculine, it is equally essential to establish a healthy relationship with our inner feminine. When our feminine is embraced and allowed an equal place at the table, it gives us access to immense self-love. This then gives us the ability to accept and care for ourselves with great tenderness and devotion. Instead of putting everyone else's needs ahead of our own, the healthy feminine, supported by the healthy masculine's ability to say no, gives us permission to put ourselves first. In chapters 11 and 12, I go into more detail about self-care and what putting yourself first looks like in real life.

Recalling that the unhealthy feminine underexpresses, our mission in restoring a healthy relationship with our inner feminine is to encourage her full expression. Go back to the list of feminine traits earlier in this chapter if you need a refresher.

Please listen to track 3 of the audio tracks, "Meditation to Connect with Your Inner Feminine," if the inner feminine is a new concept to you or you find it difficult to connect with this facet of yourself.

Many of us are so driven by the values of the patriarchy that it can feel entirely foreign to entertain the idea of listening to our intuition, being gentle, compassionate, and loving with ourselves, slowing down, listening to the subtle communications of the world around us, receiving, making time for creative expression, and just being.

Yet these are the qualities we are sorely lacking, and we desperately need to balance the overbearing masculine traits of do-do-do, achieve, conquer, accumulate, and dominate. Life moves naturally in rhythms and cycles: the days, seasons, tides, and periods of growth and dormancy and activity and rest. The overexpressed masculine thinks he can force everything to happen in *his* time. Believe me, this is how I lived my life for almost two decades. I had no idea how to trust, listen, or wait. I knew how to exert my will and bend things into the shape I wanted them to be (or maintain the self-deception that they were already in the shape I wanted).

When we value the feminine, we make room in our lives to exhale, to pause, and to listen. It means that we recognize our own needs and honor the natural periods of rest that must occur in between every cycle of activity or growth. Integration, reflection, contemplation, relaxation, nurturing . . . how often do you make time in your day for these? Life cannot be all doing and output. But the patriarchy would have us believe that is the way.

Just as we are incomplete without embracing our inner masculine, so too must we restore the feminine within us. Our journey toward wholeness includes coaxing our inner feminine out of oppression—to be held in safety by the masculine—so that she can express herself unashamedly in her beauty, grace, and creativity once more.

RELEASING THE PATRIARCHY

There are many ways to begin to unravel the influence of the patriarchy in your life. What's most important is that you just begin somewhere. Your soul knew that you could handle being here at this point in human history, on the brink of transformation. You are here to herald a new way, a new configuration. At the same time, you are a human, susceptible to the influences of our culture, just like everyone else. It can be confounding to be what I call "the observer and the participant" at the same time. I define this concept as *understanding the bigger picture and the part you play in the whole, while at the same time having to be in a human body, walking through the human experience.* Releasing unhealthy influences, including the patriarchy, is part of this human walk.

How do you begin to release the insidious and far-reaching effects of the patriarchy? By performing inquiry into yourself, working with a coach or healer, reading books, or participating in classes or workshops—any of these will help you begin to identify the masculine/feminine influences, points of view, agendas, and imbalances that exist within your psyche and personality. Examining your own inner masculine and feminine is a potent way to deconstruct the established systems and a great place to begin if you're unsure. Having conversations with different parts of yourself either through voice dialogue, active imagination, or journaling is an excellent way to begin detangling the effects of not just the patriarchy but all the influences that molded you.

There are hundreds of exceptional books that cover everything from the divine feminine to the patriarchy to the arc of religion and its influence on society. All of them would be pertinent to the process of deconstructing the patriarchy within. One book I want to point out that is an excellent resource for women is called *The Shadow King* by Sidra Stone. In this book she discusses the internalized part in our female psyche called the "Inner Patriarch." This is some powerful work, which I have done myself and facilitated for others.

CULTIVATING THE INNER MARRIAGE

The natural follow-on question to the work of releasing patriarchal influence is "What do I replace it with?" I encourage my clients and students to work on bringing their inner masculine and feminine into a conscious relationship with one another, where each honors and values the other. This is called cultivating the inner marriage. To do this, each side must be aware of the other. This means the bigger you is responsible for managing the relationship and relating to each aspect with equal respect and value. Think of it like this: you are the CEO, taking input from everyone at the table (ego, body, feelings, fears, logic, emotion, dreams, past experience, inner voices, aspects of psyche, etc.) and then synthesizing all of the data into a final decision. Every decision you make and action you take derives from a collection of internal contributions, whether you're conscious of who is providing the input or not. Relating to your inner masculine and feminine as equal partners will most likely require some new seats at the table as well as some new awarenesses. They both have valuable contributions to make if you are willing to give them equal consideration.

Cultivating the inner marriage also means recognizing that you can provide for your own needs and that expression of both archetypes is allowed and encouraged. In general, women are encouraged to be feminine, and men are encouraged to be masculine. Expression of the opposite gender is usually determined to be weak or inappropriate, so it is trained out of us. Men aren't supposed to be sensitive, emotional, or nurturing. Women aren't supposed to show anger or be aggressive or ambitious. Recalling the definition of shadow—the unloved, disowned parts of ourselves—our opposite is then relegated to the shadow, ostracized because it was deemed improper. Something that is clearly a part of who we are—our inner beloved—has been killed, extinguished by a society sorely misinformed and misguided in the realm of mature, conscious love.

Once it is banished, we essentially experience the loss of our inner beloved as a death, which contributes significantly to our feelings of incompleteness and longing. This void where our "opposite" should reside causes us to be in constant search of its replacement. The overwhelming pressures of society and our culture tell us that we don't dare go against the norm and restore the lost aspect of ourselves (called soul loss), so we project our needs onto our partner. Since it is not ladylike for women to be strong, independent, ambitious, driven, or highly sexual or to act as the breadwinner or disciplinarian, we abdicate our own power and look for these qualities in our partner. The dreamy notion of "you complete me" is an immature and romanticized representation of love. As long as we continue to look for something outside of ourselves (because we don't believe we are capable of providing it for ourselves), we will continue to enter into relationships from a place of brokenness and incompletion. Because we are compelled to keep searching for that "thing" that will complete us, we won't feel complete even when we have it, because it is still *outside* of us.

This is why so many relationships fail. The partners are each projecting their disowned selves onto the other, desperately hoping the other person will fill the emptiness left from the exile of their inner beloved. That's why it is so critical to do the work of reclaiming your "opposite" gender (reclaiming your inner masculine for women and reclaiming your inner feminine for men), and at the same time healing and redefining your same gender (inner feminine for women and inner masculine for men).

Let me be clear that in all of this I am not implying that restoring your inner marriage means that you will no longer need another person with whom to be in a relationship. This is not the case at all! In *The Shamanic Astrology Handbook,* Cayelin Castell and Daniel Giamario define the sacred marriage as "when a man or woman walks through life with the inner partner on their arm at all times, regardless of whom they are with, or whether they are with anyone at all."[2] Can you imagine the difference between showing up in a relationship already whole and complete unto yourself and showing up needing the other person to fulfill your needs because you are in denial of an entire aspect of yourself?

Tending to your own inner marriage allows you to come into a relationship with an entirely different agenda. You're no longer showing up with unspoken expectations (along with the requisite disappointment that is sure to follow), a slew of projections, desperation, and the talons of codependence ready to grab hold. You can enter into partnership able to fully accept and cherish the other person, allowing them to be who they are, encouraging and supporting their full expression, and having no illusions about their limitations and imperfections. They are no longer a project to fix. They are a unique work of art to love and cherish.

FINDING YOUR INTERNAL MOTIVATION

Make no mistake, walking in conscious equal partnership with the masculine and feminine is a journey, and it will take time to deprogram old beliefs and adopt new values. It is vulnerable work because it is almost always done on a stage where the audience is not rooting for your success or hoping for the same outcome as you. Ensuring that you have a strong support structure is highly recommended. Sadly, the patriarchy is so insidious that even the most loving and supportive people in your life can surprise you with their judgment and lack of understanding, so be deliberate in whom you choose to share your transformation with.

Doing supported processes with a seasoned facilitator is also encouraged so that you don't have to navigate this landscape alone.

Change always begins within. It might be overwhelming and daunting given the current state of affairs in the world, and you might ask, "What's the point of cultivating an inner relationship with my masculine and feminine if the world out there doesn't honor or value this equality?" This is where your personal integrity and value system come in. It has to mean enough to you to make these internal shifts, or else you won't do it. That's the nature of change. If we are not motivated enough, we won't overcome the inertia of what is to make the change.

Motivation that comes from within (doing it for yourself) is always more powerful and enduring than motivation that comes from the outside (doing it for someone else). This is also how we *model change for others*. Part of being a wayshower is trusting our instincts and making the change our soul is calling for us to make, even when the change is unpopular or misunderstood. We are always teaching people how to treat us. You can cause a significant shift in how people treat you just by honoring the sacred marriage within.

Stop Trying to Get Back into the Garden

The straight and narrow path has led us astray. Certainly there are abbreviated times in our life when circumstances ask us to buckle down, make a few sacrifices, put others' needs before our own, and "get it done." But this isn't meant to be a life philosophy! The patriarchal promise of "work hard and get your reward in the end" just doesn't play out with any amount of sustainability. And the old subservient feminine duty isn't so much about service to others as it is about sacrifice of self. There seem to be a multitude of false assumptions circulating in our societal code of conduct as though they were gospel:

- The harder you work (the more hours you put in), the more you are admired and the farther you will get in life and business.
- The more you sacrifice, give of yourself, and put others first, the more it means you care. (Unfortunately, a frequent yet unanticipated corollary that hides in the subconscious is that the more you sacrifice, the more praise, respect, or love you think you deserve in return—that is, I gave everything for you and this is how you repay me?)
- You cannot get ahead or prosper unless you make great sacrifices.

(It's okay to ignore your family, suppress your emotions and pain, and collect a few health problems because, well, it was worth it, right?)

- Life is a trade-off; you can be rich or you can have balance, but not both. (They are mutually exclusive.)
- If you care for yourself, ask for what you need, draw boundaries, or say no, you are selfish and self-centered, and God will certainly be displeased with you. Plus, it means you don't love the other people in your life. (If you loved me or if you cared about your job or if you want to show your appreciation or allegiance, you would do XYZ.)

Are any of these lurking in your belief system, values, or behaviors? You may not realize it, but all of these views set us up for bitterness, disappointment, and resentment. For many it is a mystery as to why they have become so dissatisfied, exhausted, and disenchanted in their life. They feel that they are demonstrating the values they grew up with (hard work, sacrifice, putting others first, or making sure everyone else's needs are tended to), yet deep inside they wonder what they are getting in return and why they are miserable, and they suspect that the rewards are not being delivered as promised.

If you recall from the set of qualities of an empath from chapter 4, the fifth quality is our big, open hearts and a desire to serve others, which makes us inclined toward careers focused on service as well as overgiving and putting ourselves last on the list. So, as empaths, we already come to this planet with a predisposition toward caring for others, amplified by the ability to feel their feelings and unconsciously take on their problems. Add to that the societal programming of sacrifice (which shows up a little differently for each gender), and we have a lot of resentful, discontented people with health, relationship, career, and financial problems who think they are doing exactly what is expected of them by their parents, their church, or society. And not just what is expected, but what they were told makes them a *good person*.

There are a lot of miserable people who have no idea that they are contributing to their own misery, let alone that they possess the power to change their circumstances. It is a compelling argument to say that putting others first makes you a good person. Who could refute that?

But if you look closer and investigate the origins of all the messages of sacrifice and other-centeredness, you will almost certainly find *denial of self* as the central axiom. Whether you currently identify with or practice any form of Christianity, our society—our country's very foundation—was built upon teachings of denial, sacrifice, original sin (from which many sects say we can never recover), denouncement, repression, inequality, suppression, and punishment, all of which come from the Church.

These beliefs still linger in the collective consciousness regardless of what type of spirituality you practice now, so almost certainly your upbringing was influenced in one way or another by at least some of these doctrinal misinterpretations. Fundamentalist messages sneak into the subtext of our values and expectations in the most insidious of ways. Most church leaders would have us believe that each day we are faced with evil temptations and have the opportunity to reenact the story of Adam and Eve in the Garden of Eden, except this time we better get it right. Of course, these expectations are derived from the same belief system that tells us that we are lost causes and nothing we do will ever rectify or atone for original sin. So, in essence, we screwed up and got what we deserved by getting kicked out of the garden, yet at the same time we better keep trying to make ourselves worthy, even though nothing we can do for the rest of eternity will restore us to our former divinity and expunge our original fall from grace.

Is the absurdity sinking in yet?

In 2016 I wrote an article for *Evolving Magazine* that expresses how this messaging and motivation has so deeply penetrated our society. Consider this excerpt:

In a recent moment of clarity, I realized the key to achieving the happiness I seek does not lie in pleasing some supreme authority or following a specific set of rules to the letter. It is not about putting our desires below God's. It is not about self-sacrifice or denying and suppressing our power, creative expression, or aspirations. It is not about doing enough. (Enough of what? And how much is enough anyway?)

There is no vindictive God sitting up in heaven with a clipboard and a stopwatch, observing us bumping around the maze, trying to figure out how to play a game to which we've never been given the rules—all along laughing his butt off as he continues to put checkmarks in the "she didn't get it right again" column.

God is not setting us up to fail, judging, and then punishing us because we made a wrong turn. I refuse to believe in a supreme being that would give us free will, set us up to fail, then condemn us for eternity because we didn't get it right.

But, oh boy, how that belief system has invaded the deepest corridors of our collective psyche. No matter how much my intellectual mind sees and rejects the glaring flaws in that system, I still shudder with incredulity as I observe my reaction to failure and disappointment. I act as if I have a debt to pay that I will never be able to settle—that I must be punished for my transgressions because, surely, I did not get what I wanted because I did not pray long enough and hard enough.

We are not being punished when our life doesn't go the way we want! But it is so easy for us to backslide in our enthusiasm and wallow in that place of self-flagellation and doubt at the slightest hiccup in our plans. Somehow our understanding of how we achieve our dreams got coupled with a very specific set of do's and don'ts.

Our guilt would have us believe that if things don't go the way we want, then it's our fault because we didn't (fill in the blank) correctly or long enough. Plus, we now have to pay penance in addition to the toll already being extracted by our self-blame and humiliation.

Here's the real truth: It isn't God who makes you feel flawed. We do it to ourselves.

I know it might seem odd to be harping on the failings of Christian doctrine when my next topic in the Evolutionary Empath Tool Kit is supposed to be about self-care, but they are significantly linked. This subject was substantial enough to blossom into a chapter all its own. These fallacious and misleading teachings are pervasive and insidious, and it takes diligent, dedicated inner work to extricate your truth from millennia of conditioning. Patriarchy and the Church have had a long and incestuous relationship throughout history, and it directly affects your belief about and your ability to engage in self-care (not to mention a whole host of other things that we won't go into here).

BEING A GOOD PERSON
DOES NOT EQUAL SELF-DENIAL

It is vitally important to understand the origin of the messages our culture gives us about caring for ourselves (and, consequently, caring for others). And it's not just because your grandparents grew up during the Depression. Understanding the pervasive and penetrating nature of our programming is critical in beginning to unravel the old dictates and replacing them with new values. If the fundamental message underlying the way we are expected to operate in the world is "You are a flawed, dirty sinner, and you must do everything possible to regain God's favor, including all manner of sacrifice, denial of self, and putting others first," then it is no wonder that we have an epidemic of depression, despair, greed, and narcissism (which is what happens when our needs are denied and banished to the realm of the shadow)!

The message to be a good person is convincing, but each one of us needs to do our work to unearth the specific motivation and implication underneath the behaviors we have adopted in our quest to be that good person. There are a thousand different ways to be a good person in the world, but being a good person shouldn't be about serving others to the detriment of your own well-being. If your version of "being a good person" is infused with undertones of "You are not as important as others" or "Your needs, desires, wants, and wishes are insignificant" or "God will reward you if you deny yourself" or "Others will favor you if you sacrifice yourself," then it is time to do some purging!

So let me be clear here. I'm not anti-Christian (though I do take issue with many of the interpretations of Christ and his teachings), and I'm not talking about putting yourself first at all costs. If a mother is forced to choose between feeding herself and feeding her child, is she going to feed her child first? You bet she is. But she would not be acting from a place of suppressing or devaluing her own needs. It would be from place of practicality and conscious choice. As an adult, she can manage without food much better than a child can.

It is important to recognize that there is a vast difference between victim mentality and conscious choice. Most people's ideas about sacrifice and putting others first are derived from decades of internalized messages that encourage victimization. People in this mind-set don't usually stop to realize that they have a choice and can adopt an entirely different set of values. In operating from this victim place, which is driven by self-sacrifice, they have bought into a benign-sounding social merit (being a "good person" or "taking care of others") that is actually counter to their own interests, happiness, and well-being.

On the other hand, sacrifice, when examined in the light of deliberate choice, becomes a weighing of priorities, a conscious forgoing, or a trade-off. It becomes a purposeful decision made from a place of personal power. In the light of consciousness and consideration for all involved, one does not make decisions that continually reinforce poor health, exhaustion, financial overcommitment, resentment, and self-denial. You can bet that healthy decisions are a vital component of good self-care.

SERVICE DOES NOT EQUAL SACRIFICE

If you recall from chapter 4, as empaths we have big, open hearts and a desire to serve others. It's one of the five qualities of an empath. But service does not imply *at all costs.*

There are multiple archetypes that come into play when we consider what it means to be of service. Archetypes are patterns of behavior that transcend culture. Borrowing from Caroline Myss's *Archetype Cards,* I want to look specifically at the patterns of the monk/nun, martyr, knight, warrior, servant, and slave.

The Monk/Nun Archetype

In addition to our predisposition to put everyone else first, we have millennia of religious programming to overcome. I know I have had past lives as a monk, nun, and other similar roles of religious service. In these scenarios, you were expected to give up all your worldly possessions, deny the flesh, and suffer through your existence hoping that God would take mercy on you at the end.

Though there are virtuous aspects to the archetype of monk or nun, the aspect that is most detrimental is sacrifice. In religious terms, sacrifice can mean slaughtering an animal or person to appease a god. It can mean giving away something valuable or important in service to something or someone that is considered more valuable or more important. Inherent in all of this is the belief that your will, desire, needs, and happiness must be subordinated. That your will, desire, needs, and happiness *cannot exist on an equal level* with those of another person. It is a form of denial. And it creates victimization.

It is critical to recognize the consequences that occur when we are not aware of our strong motivation to be of service to everyone but ourselves. In our efforts to create peace and harmony, we often allow ourselves to be a doormat, acquiescing to other people's preferences, doing whatever it takes to make the other person happy, and staying in patterns of abuse for way too long. We do a great job of rationalizing our behavior, making excuses, and enabling unhealthy situations. But really we are entrenching ourselves in a deep chasm of denial and resentment. We victimize ourselves.

What we feel, need, and desire is still true, *whether we acknowledge it or not.*

So when we deny something, it festers into seething resentment and anger, which we then project onto whoever is around us because we can't admit that it is our own. Spiritual bypass often accompanies the archetype of the monk/nun because attention is taken away from the flesh—away from human emotions and desires—and focused on denying the self in order to serve something greater. It doesn't have to be that way anymore. We must upgrade our definition of service to one where all are served, which ironically means caring for yourself first.

The Martyr Archetype

The idea that being of service equates to sacrifice is still coded in our cultural discourse and expectations. It says that you cannot meet your own needs and the needs of others, while honoring both yourself and the other as equals. It only "counts" if you are bled dry, if you have given everything. So another archetype that naturally follows is the martyr, and one of the synonyms for *martyr* is *willing victim.*

We are subject to enough victimization from external sources that we don't need to add to the weight of it by victimizing ourselves. Change starts from within. We have to learn to take responsibility for our own energy. That can be a tall order when it is certainly easier to keep playing the victim, blaming everyone else for our condition and lack of support, and maintaining the status quo.

The shadow martyr, according to Carolyn Myss, utilizes a combination of service and suffering for others as a means of controlling and manipulating them.[1] It is related to the victim archetype, which says that we often (subconsciously) like to play the role of the victim because of the positive feedback received in the form of sympathy or pity.

The unhealthy martyr gives not from a place of love, but from a place of racking up points. The self is denied, but the martyr will let you know how much he or she is giving up "for your good" or "for the cause." Have you encountered this type of person before? Or maybe you are this person? When you look at it from the point of view of energy, doesn't it feel yucky to receive from someone who is giving to you from a place of martyrdom? It doesn't feel clean. For me, I can clearly sense the unspoken expectations, the strings attached. This is not service. This is manipulation with a clear agenda.

The Knight and Warrior Archetypes

The archetype of the knight elicits thoughts of chivalry, loyalty, protection, service, and devotion. Taken to the extreme, the shadow knight will fall into self-neglect as he focuses single-mindedly on his mission. His motives are different from the martyr's. For the martyr, the end result isn't as important as getting noticed for the sacrifice. For the knight, honorable causes pursued with devotion are the motivation. Sometimes the knight's mission morphs into the rescuer or the warrior (other related archetypes). In any version, when the knight neglects himself, he cannot be fully available to give himself to his cause.

When your mission is to be of service to another, what, in reality, is the quality of the service you are providing when you are in deficit? Can you be fully present? Do you have reserves of energy you can call on when necessary? Can you show up with a loving heart, or are you hiding buried resentment? Are you telling yourself it's worth it for a noble cause, while in the meantime your health, finances, and relationships are all suffering? It doesn't matter how worthy your cause is if there's no life force left in you to contribute.

In this conversation, it is important to consider the plight of the warrior, as it is a similar energy to the knight. The warrior is a fighter, a soldier. If there's a battle to fight, the warrior is equipped—and eager—to do it. Something to defend? Call upon the warrior. Yet in modern day-to-day life, outside of actual military combat, the warrior is confused. He's standing ready to fight, but there are no clear battle lines and no clear enemy. Today's battlefield looks different, and it requires an adjustment in the way the warrior (and the knight) show up.

Instead of fighting *against* something, the new warrior energy asks us to advocate *for* something. The desire to fight, defend, and protect needs to be channeled into self-advocacy. And yes, it means advocating for others, too. But you cannot pour water from an empty cup. You cannot reach deep inside of you in those challenging and dark times for the strength, courage, and determination to stay the course if what you are reaching into is vacant. It is not selfish to tend to yourself first. But it flies directly in the face of the old knight and warrior mind-sets. The traditional knight or warrior will sacrifice himself until he is dead, knowing he died valiantly. The new knight and warrior need to recognize that they cannot be of true service to others until they first care for their own needs.

The Servant and Slave Archetypes

We can't talk about service without looking at the archetype of the servant. There are many ways in which "servant" has manifested throughout time: public servants, clergy, house help, social workers, indentured servants. But the shadow servants in all of them fail to also be of service to themselves and lose all focus on the value of their own lives. The altruistic mission of the servant is to be available to others for the benefit and enhancement of their lives.

But, once again, how much service are you able to render when there is nothing left to give? How much can your heart really be in what you are doing when underneath it boils with exhaustion and resentment? At what point does service become mechanical? A servant without a "you" inside is just a robot.

The shadow aspect of the slave archetype lacks the power of choice and self-authority. Slaves follow orders that violate their own integrity. For years, I said yes to things I didn't want to say yes to, said no to things I really wanted to say yes to, and pretended it was all okay. I honestly didn't know how to identify what I really wanted in so many instances. I was so removed from my core and had so few boundaries that I didn't recognize that I was violating my own integrity. Instead I listened to the influence of what I thought others wanted me to do or what I thought I had to do to be accepted, promoted, valued, or loved.

I had no concept of my own authority. How could I? I gave all my authority away for love. I had to get pushed really hard, with my back up against the wall, before I would ever consider pushing back. I talked a good game, but I was a pushover. I swallowed enough anger to power Los Angeles. And it was years before I could recognize that I was angry *when I was angry.* Oftentimes my anger would fester and seethe for weeks or months. Then something innocuous would happen, like stubbing my toe, and I would have an all-out cussing, screaming hissy fit on the floor. Clearly the reaction did not fit the incident!

I was so used to violating my own integrity that I couldn't recognize when it was happening in the moment, and my anger would finally come out months later. It was maddening because, that far removed from the original incident, it was difficult to trace the source of my anger. After running this pattern time after time, what I realized next was even harder to swallow: I was actually mad at *myself.* It was easy to throw my anger at anyone or anything that gave me an excuse to showcase those emotions and even sound righteous. It was hard to admit that I was really angry at myself for violating my own boundaries.

If we are to be of service to ourselves and to humankind, then service must shift its position on the arc of the pendulum. Instead of swinging to the extreme, it needs to hang steady in the balance between service to self and service to others.

A NEW DEFINITION OF SERVICE

In New Earth consciousness, we will need a new relationship to the concept of service, one that will carry us forward into the era of heart-centered awareness, where our own needs are just as important as another's. Not more or less, but equally significant. It will necessitate a balance that has not been previously present. This balance will require us to be more fully present, listening to and expressing our own truth. In the old paradigm, service was "easy" in that you simply denied your own needs and deferred to someone else's. New Earth service will require you to show up, do your inner work, have an opinion, and make the occasional hard choice.

This fresh relationship to service doesn't mean we are to live a self-absorbed, self-serving life, immune to the plight of others. Balance means weighing your needs against the needs of the other(s) *in each and every circumstance.* There is no one convenient decision you can make and apply to every scenario indiscriminately. Each time you are called upon to serve another, you must make your choice *based on your truth in that moment.* And what your truth is today may not be your truth tomorrow. It is a more painstaking and time-consuming practice because you have to show up in your body, be present, assess your state, tell yourself the truth, be vulnerable, and then risk how your answer will land for the other. But it is a more authentic way of being of service that honors the giver.

BECOME MORE LIKE THE MOTHER
AND LESS LIKE THE FATHER

If we are going to anchor heart chakra consciousness, the return of the divine feminine, and the new human blueprint on this earth plane, then we need to be up to the task physically, emotionally, mentally, and spiritually. And we can't do that when we are constantly depleted, overwhelmed, exhausted, and other-focused to the point that our physical, mental, and emotional health is in decline! Our work in holding these higher frequencies is sacred and crucial. Sadly, there just isn't room in the current paradigm to value this type of work and the amount of effort it involves. As conscious spiritual beings, we're here to help change that. And yes, that will require some swimming upstream for a while as well as enduring people calling us selfish, self-centered, and, heaven forbid, a bad person.

The patriarchy (which is essentially the unchecked masculine expressed to the extreme) makes no room for the feminine principle. And yes, Christianity—as well as most other world religions—is steeped in the patriarchy. Caring for yourself, being gentle or compassionate with yourself, crying, giving yourself downtime, nurturing yourself, honoring your body as a sacred temple, eating right, spending time in nature to rejuvenate, enjoying sexual pleasure, expressing and creating beauty through art, dance, or music . . . these are all considered luxuries or even foolish indulgences in our society. They are "nice to haves" that are sometimes deemed weaknesses or guilty pleasures, and they are the first things to get booted when it's time to buckle down.

Underneath the smile that says, "Sure, go ahead and take the day off" or "Yes, I'll watch the kids for you" or "No, I don't think you're too emotional," we often find questioning of our loyalty, dedication, mental stability, trustworthiness, competence, will, and drive.

When my father died in September 2013, I asked my employer for three days off (a Wednesday, Thursday, and Friday) so I could have five days to be with family out of state. At the end of my stay, I was still fragile, emotional, and not ready to return. I needed just a little more time. I called and asked him for one more day (which I don't think was an unreasonable request and which I was willing to take without pay). Instead of being supportive, he grudgingly gave me the additional day but balked at my request, questioning whether I really needed the extra time and saying to hurry back because "they needed me." Even though all of this was conveyed in a nice tone, I wanted to punch him in the face. How dare you make me feel bad for asking for one more day to be with family because my father died. How dare you even question what is in my best interest! But I know my story is not uncommon.

I titled the next chapter *"Radical* Self-Care" because for most of society, the idea of self-care as a daily practice is a radical decision. It requires a major shift in mind-set and values. It takes a reshuffling of priorities and commitments. And unless you live alone on an island, it is bound to piss off a few people in the process.

Consider what Andrew Harvey has to say in his book *The Hope* about service to yourself as an instrument of the divine:

> One of the great lessons that loving the Divine Feminine has begun to teach me is how to mother myself, how to make sure that the instrument I am using to try to do Her will in the world is treated with something of the Mother's tenderness and respect. This means looking after the soul through sacred practice, looking after the mind through constant inspiration, looking after the heart and its emotions by deep shadow work, and looking after the body by diet, exercise, and sufficient rest.
>
> For most Sacred Activists the greatest challenge is to look after the body. Many of us have inherited a belief that the body is inferior, something we have to compel to do the will of our heart and spirit. This is a great mistake. How can the Birth [referring to the birth of the divine human] take place in the body if we do not revere and cherish it? And how can we keep working with sacred energy and balance in the world if our bodies are under assault from our own body shame and our own careless habits? Try to eliminate everything in your life that compromises your body's health—poor eating habits, stressful situations, lack of sleep. You will find that being a mother to yourself in this way will bring a peace and joy into your life that acts as a perfect "ground" to receive the Divine Energy.[2]

Self-care, at its core, is a feminine principle. It is one of the reasons why embracing the divine feminine is so crucial to our evolution as a species. Mothering yourself, nurturing yourself, recognizing and acknowledging your own needs, deeply loving yourself—these are not luxuries! These are what await us when we can accept and integrate the influence of the divine feminine into our being. And it is a logical conclusion (I hope) that if we render ourselves as sacred and valuable, by extension we apply the same value to one another, our planet, the animals, and all sentient beings. Andrew Harvey goes on to say:

> Every human being is an incarnation of the Divine waiting to discover the truth of his or her real identity; by honoring and taking care of all aspects of your human self, you are honoring your creator, whose presence in you is your secret truth. Your human self is the living temple of your Divine Self; doesn't your Divine Self deserve its temple to be as strong and balanced as possible?[3]

If there is a part of you getting triggered as you read this chapter, it's okay. I understand. Our programming runs deep, and some would argue that I am advocating pure selfishness or that the level of self-care I recommend is impractical and unrealistic. If you are a person who strongly identifies with your ability to be there for others, to be reliable, to be the one that everyone else turns to, to take care of everyone's needs, to fix everyone else's problems, then I invite you to examine what underlies this drive. I can almost guarantee you that there is some way in which you are denying, suppressing, or diminishing the importance of your own needs. Is there possibly an archetype of martyr or rescuer being played out? An unspoken dialogue that says, "Look how great I am because of what I give up"? A concealed arrogance that believes you are superior because you sacrifice and deny? A hurt child who doesn't feel she deserves attention and love? A warped internalization of Christian teachings that believes your sacrifice will net you some unnamed reward?

I know these questions might sting, but your ability to love yourself depends on your ability to recognize and ask for what you need. Which means that you have to value yourself enough to believe that you deserve it. Which means that you need to understand what motivates you and what message lies at the core of your behavior. Otherwise, you won't ask for what you need. Or if you do ask, you won't do it when your need is at a two or three out of ten. Instead you'll wait, and then you'll blow up, making demands or accusations, and let your victim scream your inequities at the top of her lungs because now your need is an eight or nine out of ten, and it just can't be stifled any longer. This is what happens when we keep our needs locked away in the shadow. They don't come out as conscious requests. They erupt forth as explosive demands or accusations.

This is also what happens when we expect others to just intuit our needs without explicitly stating them. It goes back to the romantic relationship notion that our partner loves us so much that he or she will "just know" what we want and need without us ever saying anything. Frankly, it's an immature expectation. And it's not fair to the other person! We have been told for so long that it is annoying and weak to be needy. That we're "high maintenance." That we need to "shut up or I'll give you something to cry about." Or "Quit complaining. You don't have it nearly as bad as children in Africa." So we suppress our needs, banishing them to the shadow, where—if you remember—they don't go away. Anything we relegate to the realm of shadow will always be seeking expression. Except it will express itself in inappropriate ways at inappropriate times. Hence the tendency to blow up when the internal pressure becomes too intense.

Bringing our needs out of the shadow and into the light of consciousness is the first step in giving ourselves the self-love and self-care we are so desperately lacking. We know how to beat ourselves up. We know how to push ourselves beyond our limits. We know how to keep our needs to ourselves. We know how to run ourselves into the ground. We know how to deny and suppress. These are all highly masculine, driving energies. We have no idea how to just be, how to receive, how to rest, or how to surrender. Self-care is not for the faint of heart.

Your heart understands that you are no good to anyone if you are unable to function. You cannot show up, be 100 percent present, and give your best when you are running on fumes and have expended your reserves. And you certainly cannot be all things to all people. Though a commonly used illustration, the following elucidates the point perfectly: when you're on a plane and the cabin experiences a loss of air pressure, you are instructed to put your own oxygen mask on first and then aid those who need assistance.

You may not realize it, but you've been living a low-oxygen life for years. It's okay to put on your oxygen mask. Actually, it is more than okay. It is *essential* to your very well-being, your capacity to grow your energetic container, your ability to hold a higher frequency for yourself, and your journey toward wholeness. It's time to recognize and chuck the epic lie we've been told for centuries. There is no garden to get back into.

Radical Self-Care:
It's Okay to Be First!

As empaths, not only do we need regular self-care, we need it more frequently than the average human. With our sensitive nervous systems, it takes a much smaller dose of stimulus than it does for a "normal" person to overwhelm us and cast us into overload. Plus, our predisposition toward putting everyone else first means that we need to be doubly aware of our energetic state and energy "bank account."

I invite you to use the concept of an energetic bank account as you consider and establish your own personal self-care practice. If you think of the energy you expend on daily activities, relationships, children, work, chores, obligations, and so on, at some point you run out of energy—your account balance becomes critically low or even overdrawn. Self-care means keeping a daily account of your balance and prioritizing the activities that will feed—or increase—your account balance. The intention is to keep your energy bank account full, or as full as possible, at all times. Rumi sums it up perfectly: "Never give from the depths of your well but from your overflow."

Paige's Story

Paige is a kindhearted and compassionate nurse. In addition to her heavy workload, she has several friends who are actively dying and often spends the night at their home so they won't be alone. She is currently taking regular classes in herbalism and working toward certification. When she is asked to join a social gathering or go to a show or event, she has difficulty saying no. She takes charts home on a regular basis because she can't finish them at work. Paige is constantly exhausted, struggling with weight loss, sciatica, and constipation. She has very little time for herself.

Natasha's Story

Natasha is in nursing school taking more than a full load of coursework and working every weekend except one each month. Her husband is struggling with physical issues, and she manages the finances, cleans the house, cooks, and does the laundry. She is diabetic, overweight, and struggling with other physical issues as well. She is chronically exhausted and doesn't recognize when she needs to ask for help, how to ask for help, or how to take care of herself.

Irene's Story

Irene is a gifted massage therapist and huge-hearted person. Yet she has no self-love. She has lived on the streets, been an addict, and struggled to hold down a job or have consistent income. Her pattern in relationships is to hook up with men who are abusive and demeaning. She would give her life to pull anyone else off the street and get them on their feet, but she has no idea how to do that for herself. Her life has been one episode of self-sabotage after another because she doesn't believe she deserves any better.

Does any of this sound familiar?

Self-care isn't just a once-a-day indulgence. It is a multiple-times-a-day necessity. Gratefully, self-care is not as marginalized as it once was; it is starting to be recognized as a stress-relieving, longevity-enhancing, health-improving, mental-health-sustaining essential. You'll still have to deal with people who consider it an excuse to be lazy or selfish (including your own Inner Critic), but make no mistake, for empaths, self-care is an absolute requirement. We must have the courage to throw off everyone else's expectations and definitions of what we *should* do to care for ourselves. Bless them for being in our lives, but they don't know what's best for us!

So what exactly do I mean by "self-care"? In general, self-care includes activities that feed you, calm your nervous system, help you regain your center, cleanse and restore your energy field, reduce anxiety and stress, recoup from exhaustion, and make you smile and laugh.

The types of activities that self-care could comprise are many and often specific to the individual, but I have included the following list to give you an idea of the scope of activities that can be considered self-care. In the end, you know best what self-care is for you.

- Spending time in the bath, sauna, hot tub, or pool
- Being alone (walking in nature, going for a drive, escaping on a weekend getaway, or reading or journaling in your favorite nook)
- Performing conscious breathing exercises, even if it's just taking a deep breath to clear your energy field
- Using all manner of essential oils, homeopathic remedies, incense, sage, flower essences, tinctures, and supplements
- Drawing boundaries (see chapters 8 and 9 on drawing boundaries; both chapters could be included here!)
- Creating and immersing yourself in beauty of all kinds by decorating your home, dressing in a way that pleases you, putting flowers on the table, creating an altar, appreciating art, or enjoying nature
- Saying no
- Allowing yourself creative expression (dancing, singing, art, crafts, writing)
- Giving yourself enough sleep and downtime (without obligations)
- Acknowledging and releasing pent-up emotions through methods

like crying, screaming, journaling, seeing a therapist, exercising, or listening to music

- Asking for what you need and standing up for yourself
- Tending to the energy of your home, office, car, or other spaces to keep the energy clean, clear, and harmonious
- Giving yourself a break or taking the pressure off
- Practicing meditation, praying, journaling, or affirmations daily
- Participating in regular health practices such as yoga, colonics, energy therapies, massage, or floating
- Eating whole, organic, nutrient-dense foods
- Giving yourself time to consciously "check out" (I call this staring out the window and drooling)
- Doing your inner, shadow, and family-of-origin work, tending to your inner child, healing old wounds, forgiving, and releasing what no longer serves you
- Allowing instead of forcing, and recognizing that everything has its own natural timing
- Participating in sports and leisure activities that feed you

In chapter 6 I stated that practicing radical self-care involves listening to your body, developing trust, making adjustments to your physical environment and to your relationships, giving yourself plenty of downtime, honoring natural rhythms and cycles, drawing boundaries, and caring for your nervous system. Many of these are closely related to one another or are a natural outcome of each other, so they all won't necessarily have their own headline in this chapter, but they will all be addressed.

LISTENING TO YOUR BODY
AND TRUSTING YOUR INTUITION

When I worked at a local career school, the owner did not understand that I didn't want to be accessible every waking hour of the day. I was the campus operations director, and he wanted me to be available on my phone and through email even when I wasn't in the office. I wasn't given a work phone and was expected to use my own electronic devices to be reachable. He didn't seem to understand my philosophy, which basically states, "If I am so important that things won't work without me, then I haven't done my job of empowering the people around me to make decisions on their own."

When I go to the gym, I don't take my phone. When I go to the barn and ride, I don't bring my phone with me. When I go hiking, I don't have my phone on me. My phone is not an appendage. My boss never understood the separation that I needed to create for my own sanity and well-being. He interpreted it as a form of disloyalty and lack of commitment.

He was available all the time, even on vacation. He had a different relationship with boundaries. And while I understood that as the president and CEO, he needed to have an extra level of connection to his work, it still spoke to a patriarchal way of running a business. If I were in his shoes, I would give my people instructions about what to do when I'm on vacation and empower them to make decisions without me. I don't want to be interrupted on my vacation unless it is an emergency. When I get away from the office, I need to completely detach from it.

I offer this as an example of listening to yourself. So many times our intuition will tell us what we need and what is right for us, but we ignore it. Then we go into behaviors designed to please others or to fit in, and we lose ourselves once again. Our body is a highly tuned, highly accurate receiver, and if we listen to it, we will find the answer to every question inside of us.

If you're an empath, then I already know you're intuitive, so it's not my intention to give you pointers for developing your intuition. For us, it's more about "releasing the hounds." We've kept our intuition cooped up for years, ignoring it, having a love-hate relationship with it, and sometimes lamenting its very existence. Set it free, my friend. In this section of the book, as well as the chapters that deal with boundaries, clearing your energy field, and defining yourself, there are lots of tools that can help you begin to relate to your intuition as an asset and an ally. Your intuition is a huge gift and navigational tool, and it is meant to be used!

Our intuition—that inner knowing—gets our attention in many ways. It can be a knowingness that just drops in, a flash of a vision, a bell or some kind of signal that sounds in your head, a heavy sensation in your gut, a tightness in your chest, a flush of heat in your body, tingling, an animal that crosses your path, a sign on a billboard or license plate, cold chills, goosebumps, a momentary headache, a sick feeling in your stomach, or lightheadedness or a sense of floating.

Our bodies react in myriad ways to everything in our environment. I cannot overemphasize the importance of reestablishing a relationship with your physical and energetic bodies and paying attention to the subtle signals they give you. Your body and your entire energy field are communicating with you all the time.

Closely related to listening to your intuition is then *trusting* your intuition. For so long we have been invalidated and taught to deny what we have felt or sensed by those who thought they were teaching us good life skills. But being told that you are weird, wrong, hearing or seeing things, making things up, too sensitive or thin-skinned, selfish, emotional, or fragile completely decimates our trust in ourselves. Therefore, part of practicing good self-care is going to involve reestablishing trust in yourself and inviting a new relationship with your body and your intuition.

How do you do this? As with all of the practices I am advocating, it will take time. Awareness is 80 percent of the battle. When you become aware of how you have been rejecting your own needs, dismissing your instincts, and engaging in other damaging behaviors of denial, the healing immediately begins just in the acknowledgment. Setting intentions and giving yourself permission are also necessary steps in making change.

Please listen to track 4 of the audio tracks, "Meditation to Connect with Your Physical Body," for a guided meditation to help you connect with your body.

Another great tool for reconnecting to your intuition and the intelligence of your body and energetic system is journaling. I encourage you to journal regularly about what you feel and sense, how you perceive circumstances or conversations, or if something seems fishy to you and to dialogue with your body. Over time, as you look back at what you wrote, you can compare your intuitive "hits" to how things actually played out.

In your journaling I invite you to apply the following question to each circumstance you are considering changing or even to daily activities: "Does this feed me or does this drain me?" This question is highly revealing and can be applied to relationships, activities, food, television programs, music, careers, and more. Allow your body to speak its truth and listen to what it is telling you.

☼ Getting to Know Your Body

Set aside some private quiet time for this exercise. You can do it with your clothes on or off. Touch every body part and write down the first thing you sense: temperature, color, emotion, density. It doesn't have to make logical sense. Begin the dialogue and then do this often, especially if you know that you are disconnected from your physical body. You will most likely find that once your body knows that you are listening and making time to hear it, it will begin communicating more frequently with you.

Let me give you another example of listening to yourself. I love music of all kinds. If you looked at my iPod you would find rap, classical, country, big band, jazz, blues, alternative, electronic, heavy metal, ethereal, house music, and more. Yet what feeds me and what drains me can be different from hour to hour.

In the same car trip driving around town, I might start out listening to classic rock with the volume turned up as loud as it will go, shift to disco, then country, and by the end be listening to classical piano at a soft volume. If I was listening to the classic rock tune I started the trip with, it would be grating and draining on my energy. How do I know? Because I feel it in my body. At the beginning of this hypothetical trip my energy is in a place to enjoy and be fed by loud music, a great beat, and singing at the top of my lungs. At the end of this car trip, my energy is in a softer place, and I crave instrumental music. Our energy is shifting all the time, and self-care means we need to be constantly listening to our bodies.

It is also important to understand that listening to your body doesn't just mean obeying the common signals of "I'm hungry," "I'm tired," "This hurts," or "I need a break." Our bodies store old traumas, injuries, repressed emotions, anger, resentment, betrayal, rejection, violations, disappointment, and more. There are two levels of listening to your body that are essential to distinguish: listening to your body *in the moment* and listening to what is *stored in your body.*

Up to this point I have mainly been talking about listening to what your body has to say in the moment. But a deeper dive must occur if we are to understand, shift, and heal our patterns of coping, suppression, and chronic stress. There are different methods you can use to tune in to this hidden aspect of the body, but I find that a guided journey (where someone else is leading me through the process) is incredibly effective because I can drop into the space of deep listening and not have to bounce back and forth between being the facilitator and the facilitated. Toward that end, I have created a guided meditation (see below) that I highly encourage you to use more than once!

Please listen to track 5 of the audio tracks, "Meditation to Identify and Release Stored Emotions," which will help you identify and release any deeply buried pain, emotions, and trauma trapped in the cells of your body.

ADJUSTMENTS IN YOUR ENVIRONMENT

Because of our sensitivities, our environments are extremely influential in either helping or hurting our state of being. For me, my home is my womb space. I highly value peace and harmony and invest a great deal of time in keeping the energy of my home clean, clear, harmonious, calm, pleasing, and of a high frequency. This also includes my yard, office, and vehicles.

It is important to take into account that we live in a chronically overstimulating world. If you look back 100 years ago, there were no computers, cell phones, pagers, beepers, televisions, gaming stations, handheld radios, iPods, alarm clocks, microwaves, emails, texts, laptops, or internet. It was still uncommon for people to have telephones, refrigerators, washing machines, radios, or cars. Billboards were few and far between, and people were not bombarded twenty-four hours a day with news, advertisements, programming, facts and figures, lights of every color, someone constantly trying to communicate with them, or a barrage of beeps and clicks from a few dozen electronic or mechanical devices constantly vying for their attention.

Our nervous systems (and hence, often our adrenal systems) are overtaxed. And it is becoming harder and harder to find a place to go where you can get away from all of these sounds, influences, and expectations. This is another reason that self-care is critically important, and not just for empaths.

You may not be able to control what's going on in the outside world, but you can make a lot of adjustments inside your home. Significant aspects of your environment can include everything from how family members speak to one another to lighting, temperature, ambient sounds, aromas, placement of furniture and decorations, use of color, family TV time (and volume), natural sunlight and air, plants, blinds and curtains, and more. Give yourself full permission to adjust whatever you need to adjust. Your home doesn't have to look like or function like anyone else's!

Now, of course there are always the people you live with to consider, so I'm not advocating forcing change on your loved ones, dictator style. But it is important that you have a conversation with them so they understand your needs and can support you. This is part of creating a harmonious environment. When there is discord in the home, it is almost impossible for anyone (not just empaths) to relax, rejuvenate, and feel safe. Generate the courage to have these conversations. It is vital to your well-being. If not, hire a coach or therapist to facilitate the process.

Also, as sensitives, we can easily become overloaded from loud noises, large crowds or public places, violence (whether real or fake), other people's drama, and more, so it's important to remove or at least minimize harsh, loud, violent, overwhelming, and chaotic energies from your surroundings. Of course, what constitutes a supportive environment depends on the individual, and you'll need to make your own decisions about what changes are right for you, but I've provided some examples and suggestions below to give you an idea of where you might start:

- Stop watching loud, violent, or highly sensational TV programs or movies.
- Limit your exposure to large crowds (shop at different times of day, go to entertainment events off-hours, etc.).
- If there are people in your life who do not contribute to your positive growth and support your evolution, gently but firmly cut the cords and let them go.
- Be honest with yourself about your belief in drama and trauma as a way of learning your life lessons. Do you attract drama and trauma in your life? Do you attract people who have chaotic energy and are always surrounded by drama? Give yourself permission to learn with ease and grace and let go of drama and trauma.
- Remove or adjust any harsh or grating influences (don't have the TV or radio constantly on or sleep with your phone or other elec-

tronic devices nearby; assess the types of lighting you have in the home).

The flip side of the coin to disliking loud noises, chaos, violence, and so on is that we value harmony, peace, calm, serenity, and tranquility. So make whatever changes to your environment that you need in order to promote the energies that support you and keep your nervous system calm. Here are some suggestions:

- Clear your home space regularly. I offer this as part of my array of services, and I am very thorough. An average house clearing takes me about three hours. But you don't have to be this thorough each and every time! A simple ten-minute saging (burning sage) can do wonders. You can do the super-detailed version a few times a year.
- Enforce quiet times with the children (if applicable) or times during which your partner, parent, older child, or babysitter can watch or take the children to give you the quiet time you need.
- Change the lighting, curtains, or when and how light and air are let into the home.
- Allow yourself to "check out" from time to time (as mentioned, I call it staring out the window and drooling).
- Play soothing music when it feels supportive to do so.
- Bring nature indoors—get a few plants or a fountain, run an essential-oil diffuser, or bring in some rocks or crystals.
- Consider changing color schemes or creating one room in your house that is your "calm or meditation space."
- Shift the way you speak to other members in your household and ask that they do the same. Stop tolerating yelling, screaming, insults, et cetera, but be mindful that you don't become passive-aggressive in the process. This is often a deep-rooted behavior, so change in this area can take time and effort.

Give yourself plenty of outlets to allow energy to move. There are many psychological and physical conditions that result from energy flow being blocked or stagnant. When energy is blocked, slow, or stagnant, it can look like many things, including depression, lack of inspiration, anger, confusion, frustration, or the inability to come up with creative solutions to problems. To keep your energy "engine" running clean, give yourself multiple and regular creative and physical outlets. Here are some examples:

- Dancing
- Singing
- Playing an instrument
- Painting, drawing, sculpting, or other crafts
- Walking, running, biking, swimming, or other cardiovascular exercises
- Yoga
- Tantric practice
- Sports or strength training
- Writing, blogging, or journaling

Remember the law of conservation of energy: energy is neither created nor destroyed; it just changes form. So, when you feel bottled up, stuck, need to release but can't, or need some way to move your energy, use these suggestions to allow the energy to change form and move out of your body and energy field.

ADJUSTMENTS IN RELATIONSHIPS

This aspect of self-care is always challenging. It is hard to let go of relationships that no longer serve you. But that is exactly what I am talking about.

If you are in a relationship that is taking more than it is giving, then you have two choices as I see it: confront the issue in hopes of eliciting change, support, or understanding (whatever your need is) or cut off the relationship entirely.

Those of us who are extreme people pleasers can easily lose our nerve. And many of us go blank in the moment or drop unconsciously right into codependence to try to make everything okay for the other person. Confronting someone takes preparation!

There are several preparatory exercises I offer to my clients. Do one or all of them as they suit you. The first is to write out what you want to say. Not that you're going to read it to the other person (although you certainly could if you feel you needed to). The idea is to get everything you need to say out of you without the threat of being rejected or interrupted, going blank, losing your nerve, or running away. It is cathartic and will help you get clear about what you want and don't want in the relationship.

If you do choose to read it to the other person word for word, you can preface the conversation like this: "It is important to me that I share with you everything that is in my heart. However, I know I have trouble remembering what I want to say or getting it all out. I've written it down because I care about you enough that I want to make sure I don't miss anything so that we have an opportunity to address these issues and heal. If I don't get it out because I forget it or get scared and stuff it down, then we can't get past this." Use your own words, but you get the idea.

Another preparatory exercise would be to role play. Find a trusted friend, mentor, or coach who will hold space for you while you speak your truth. You can read what you wrote, or you can just speak from the heart. Before you do this, prep the other person by explaining what you're doing and why, and what you need from him or her. When I coach this exercise in groups, I ask the receivers to be in 100 percent receiving mode. This means that they are deeply listening and receiving the other person's words. They are not to make sounds, nod in agreement, pat them on the arm, or otherwise interact. They are there to look them in the eye and receive. After you get everything out of you that needs to be said, then you can ask your listener for a hug or feedback or whatever you might need. It is also perfectly fine to just ask the receiver to listen, period, and not do anything else.

Other options include variations of the above, such as making bullet points or notes to refer to or rehearsing important statements out loud to yourself or a mirror. Remember, it is okay to be nervous. One of my favorite definitions of courage is being afraid and doing it anyway.

HONORING NATURAL RHYTHMS AND CYCLES

In our modern world, you can turn on the light at 2:00 in the morning, eat watermelon in January, purchase anything you want online twenty-four hours a day, set machines to operate or perform a function in the middle of the night, or talk to someone halfway around the world in an instant. Through miracles of the industrial revolution and advances in medicine, agriculture, science, and electronics, you can have anything you want at any hour of the day, any day of the year. There are some pretty sweet conveniences we enjoy as an industrialized nation. And sadly, as an unintended consequence, it has created a state where we are completely disengaged from the natural rhythms and cycles in our world and in our bodies.

In the name of progress and evolution, we've learned that we can manipulate or force the system to produce the outcome we want. No more waiting. No more suffering.

And why wait anyway when you can just make it happen? Why sleep when you can just take a few stimulants and get the project done? Why take time off when you can keep working and make more money? Why put forth the effort to cook using fresh, organic, whole foods when you can simply throw a package in the microwave and eat in six minutes? Why have an important conversation face-to-face when you can just as easily text or instant message someone? Why fix or repair something when you can just throw it away and buy a new one? Why experience discomfort or pain when you can just take a pill? Why honor the innate rhythms and cycles of your body and of the natural world when you can just apply yourself with more voracity and force the outcome? I don't intend to go on a long rant here, nor do I have all of the solutions for restoring the balance that we have lost in our world and in our bodies. But I do have a few suggestions.

The Earth is our mother. And it is because of her existence, particular location in the solar system, and relationship with other celestial bodies that we experience the cycles every single day. From the seasons to day and night, weather patterns, tides, and the Great Year, we cannot escape cycles.

In our own bodies we have innate rhythms, too: the flow of cerebrospinal fluid, our heartbeat, biorhythms, circadian rhythms, menstrual cycle, blood pressure, and organ clock. (In Chinese medicine, energy—or *chi*—moves through the body's meridians and organs in a twenty-four-hour cycle; every two hours the energy is strongest within a particular organ and its functions within the body.)

Yet we have found innumerable ways to bypass the "inconvenience" of so many of these natural timings if they don't suit our purposes, and we consider ourselves more advanced because of it. We think we are too busy, too important, or too overloaded with responsibilities to deal with the nuisance of waiting. We have convinced ourselves that forcing things to occur at an unnatural time or pace or bypassing them altogether—when in reality they are truly necessary and incur a great cost when we interfere—is an evolved way of conducting our lives.

Our bodies are highly complex, sophisticated communication systems. When they are operating optimally, and we have a close enough relationship with them to hear what they are communicating to us, they will tell us everything we need to know. The answers are within. Simple yet critical functions such as when to eat (and when to stop eating), when to sleep and when to get up, or when to rest and when to work operate in natural cycles. Warning systems such as adrenaline and our heart rate, central nervous system, gut instincts, or "sixth" sense are all available to us if we listen. Emotional movement of energy comes in cycles, too. Our bodies, if allowed to operate without restriction, know when to grieve, when to get angry, when to cry or laugh, when to nurture, when to shake from fear, and when to protect.

You don't have to look far to recognize that many of the results of our "advanced" way of living are actually catapulting us backward. We are a nation that has seen an increase in obesity, stress, sleep disorders, depression, suicide, bankruptcy, anxiety, and just about every indicator of overall physical, mental, and emotional ill health.

When we lose touch with the natural rhythms and cycles of our bodies and the world around us, we lose our center. Some might say that we even lose our soul. We certainly lose our connection—our *grounding*—to the planet and to our own bodies. And we lose our sense of the sacred. Self-care, as I am recommending it, is a critical way to reestablish your connection to your own body and to nature and the natural world and to restore your sense of well-being.

BUCKING THE SYSTEM

In our society, we have so many judgments about what is acceptable or appropriate behavior. We let the church, our boss, the health care system, school, magazines—our very culture—dictate how we should live our lives. If what you need, what you need to express, or what your body is trying to communicate to you is not allowed or approved of, then you have to stuff it, hide it, make it go away, or pretend it's not there. Rest? Sorry, our firm requires you to work eighty hours a week to make partner. Grieve? Sorry your mom died, but if you're not back to work tomorrow, we'll give your job to someone else. Eat healthy? Sorry, but the food and agriculture industries have made it seductive, cheaper, and easier to purchase processed and fast foods. Screenings? Sorry, but your health insurance doesn't cover that procedure. Talk about your feelings or fears? Sorry, but our church doesn't acknowledge that kind of darkness.

As a result, we've completely lost touch with our priorities. And we've adopted other people's values because we're convinced that it's the only way to make a living, be successful, or get ahead.

Yet what's even more tragic is that what we are compromising in the process is *not obvious*. Physical, mental, and spiritual health decline is usually so gradual that we don't recognize the signs until we are in crisis. Well, let me wave the red flag—we are in crisis! Empath or not, our self-care as a society is abhorrent, and it's time to buck the system.

You're not supposed to walk around exhausted all the time. But in our culture, we wear it like a badge of honor. Just have some more coffee or a couple of Red Bulls. You're not supposed to have intestinal distress on a daily basis. But processed foods, too much sugar, ingestion of a multitude of chemicals, growing portion sizes, and a whole host of other food industry deceptions make it seem like what we eat, along with the subsequent intestinal distress, is normal. We're not supposed to run from one thing to the next and be chronically overcommitted. We're not supposed to be regularly depressed, stressed, and on the verge of blowing our stack.

Our lifestyle throws our nervous system into a constant state of fight or flight. Add to that the extreme sensitivity we possess as empaths, and it is a recipe for disaster. We replace natural with artificial, emphasize quantity over quality, and value the quick fix over long-term consequences and mass production over craftsmanship. It's easy to get sucked up in the whirlwind.

In all of this, it's important to forgive yourself for getting swept up. We trusted our parents. We trusted authority figures. We trusted what we were being taught. And why wouldn't we? It's how our human developmental system works. In the early stage of human evolution when we were all part of small tribes, trusting what you were told kept you alive and doing what others did ensured that you were not kicked out of the tribe. That wiring is still a part of our animal brain.

Precious few are naturally designed to question everything from a young age. I most certainly was not one of those questioning people. I was gullible, ignorant, naive, and trusting. I am still amazed at all of the deceits I bought into and expectations I took on as my own. I felt duped and taken advantage of. But now I know better and am doing my inner work to reclaim my power by asking questions and making conscious choices. Part of your inner work will be to make these determinations for yourself, do your own forgiveness work, and make new choices.

Reclaiming your mental, physical, emotional, and spiritual health will take time. Unraveling the influences of our society can take months and years, but it is worth the effort. And it will help you make the essential transition from being a victim to reclaiming your power through conscious choice. Be gentle with yourself. Treat yourself with love, respect, compassion, and understanding as you unearth and release old programming, beliefs, and expectations. That's what self-care is all about.

Becoming More Fully Embodied

What is embodiment? To reduce it to its essence, embodiment can be most simply compared to being fully present. And this might be a fairly accurate description of embodiment in the moment. However, embodiment over time is a much more complex undertaking and implies considerably more than just how present you are. Think of it as *presence over time.* When I discuss this topic, I like to preface it with a true story that illustrates the crux of what embodiment is about for me, and why it subsequently became a major focus of my sacred work in the world.

A few years ago I had an epiphany during a ceremonial gathering. It was an overnight event, and we were to rise early the next morning to do a ritual honoring at the exact time of a particular celestial event. As we were all discussing plans, the convener of the event got triggered, began to regress, and started getting defensive. She walked out in a bit of a huff and left the rest of us looking at each other quizzically, trying to mitigate the uncomfortable silence.

The next morning, as we were doing the ceremony, a revelation hit me like a bolt of lightning: *What is the point of all of this "spiritual practice" if we can't relate to the human standing next to us? If we can't have an honest conversation about how we feel? If we can't speak our truth and communicate clearly?*

This epiphany illuminated what immediately became a new

foundational pillar of my sacred work, and I knew I was to eventually bring teachings on embodiment to my clients and students. The significance of embodiment as it was being shown to me provided a critical link, highlighting connections between different aspects of the work I had already been doing. Over the next few years I developed an entire mystery school around embodiment, which also became the subject of my master's degree project. To me, embodiment is essential to our development as individuals and evolution as a species.

One of my favorite quotes is from French philosopher and priest Pierre Teilhard de Chardin: "We are not human beings having a spiritual experience; we are spiritual beings having a human experience." In the past, the poster child for spirituality was the mystic on a mountaintop, who achieved ecstatic states of bliss and oneness, eschewed money and possessions, and devoted all of his time to spiritual practices that transcended this limited and painful human existence. But those times are past, and that model is not relevant on a mass scale. And further, those mystics didn't have all the answers. Modern life asks us to strap on unresolved childhood issues, hunger, divorce, differing political views, a mortgage payment, three kids, ailing parents, lack of sleep, corporate greed, getting laid off, global warming, and all the others issues we confront on a daily basis, and then try to be spiritual in the midst of all of it. That is where the true work of being embodied lies . . . in the *human* experience.

One of the main reasons for incarnating in human form is to learn how to bring our connection with Spirit all the way down into our body and to fully inhabit our human selves—not to engage only in practices that would have our consciousness leave our body! The comprehensive human experience asks us to embody it all: the muck, the beauty, the fear, the love, the agony, the ecstasy, and everything in between. To *feel* our feelings. To ride the sublime roller coaster of the natural rhythms and cycles of our earthly existence. To embrace the exquisite joy and agony of our frailty and our magnificence. To be a human bridge between heaven and earth, Spirit and matter.

Embodiment is about being human *and* divine, not trying to avoid our humanness! If we are on this planet to evolve spiritually, to remember our true nature as creative beings and be that, then what is there to act as an anchor for this divine energy if we don't have a physical body? And not just a physical body, but one *that we are fully inhabiting?* We are conduits, and through us, divine and cosmic energies are anchored on this earth plane. We are the great alchemists, acting as receiver-transmitters of divine consciousness and sophisticated light codes through the complex organic machinery that is our physical body. And we need to be fully present inside of our bodies to experience our greatest potential and power as said alchemists and creators. This is both the miracle and the paradox of our human earthly experience. It might seem counterintuitive that the more "grounded" we are in our *human* form, the more divine consciousness and authentic, creative power we can channel, radiate, and wield, yet that is exactly what I am articulating.

THE MECHANICS OF EMBODIMENT

It is important to understand that learning to be fully embodied is a process that takes time. It is not a stationary feature. You don't set it like a clock and then walk away. It takes conscious effort and attention to be embodied. Our level of embodiment (like our energy field) is dynamic, nonconstant, and ever changing. And it evolves as we evolve.

Being embodied is a complex concept because it is affected by so many factors that are always in flux: our emotions, the solidity of our boundaries, the state of our energy field, our state of mind, our energetic physiology, how empowered or disempowered we feel, how we handle something that triggers us in the moment, how much of our inner work we have completed, how we talk to ourselves in our head, how much repressed pain and emotion we carry, and how adept we are at handling adversity, to name a few.

Though your level of embodiment at any given moment might vary, there are components we can point to that—taken together—give an indication of how embodied you are. To illustrate this concept, consider blood pressure. Our blood pressure changes depending on whether we are sitting, standing, lying down, exerting ourselves, meditating, sleeping, experiencing stress, and so on. But in general, it is a marker of overall cardiovascular health.

In a similar way, your adeptness at being embodied—and staying embodied—can be determined by how much (and how often) you are able to do the following:

- Fully inhabit yourself
- Remain present
- Stay grounded
- Remain centered in your authentic power
- Maintain a solid energy container
- Run your full life force, unimpeded
- Practice healthy boundaries
- Acknowledge and feel all of your feelings, good or bad
- Avoid unconscious addictive behaviors, escapism, codependence, or anything that serves as a crutch
- Allow yourself to be seen for who you are
- Do your inner work of healing trauma, pain, shadow, and woundings
- Speak your truth
- Allow yourself to feel the full extent of your highest highs and your lowest lows
- Exercise your powers of manifestation, bringing ideas and dreams fully into form
- Accept that you are a full-spectrum human being, meaning that you recognize and embrace the entire spectrum of human experience: pain, ecstasy, sorrow, joy, loneliness, elation, confusion, clarity, loss, grief, accomplishment—all of it
- Recognize and practice being a channel of spirit into matter and

matter into spirit and an active bridge, walking in both worlds simultaneously

As an empath, it is challenging for us to stay present and focused, especially if we are still living in an unconscious (not yet awakened) state. Our heightened sensitivities add to that challenge. Everything in the list above takes practice, dedication, effort, and a fair amount of undoing of old habits. And, empath or not, just about every person on this planet walks around only partially embodied.

THE DISEMBODIMENT EPIDEMIC

There are many reasons why one might not be fully embodied. A few are healthy or beneficial, but most are detrimental if sustained over time. For example, in a moment of acute trauma (such as a car accident) many people have had the experience of leaving their bodies, even witnessing themselves below as they float above themselves in a hospital room or at the scene of the accident. This is an example of leaving completely. It is actually a protective measure—a coping mechanism—that your psyche employs to keep you from experiencing the intensity and pain of a particular trauma.

It is also common for people to leave their bodies during times of abuse (physical, sexual, verbal) or intense fear (certain phobias, bullying, intimidation), when witnessing atrocities (war, hostage situation, acts of terrorism), or when experiencing certain psychological conditions such as PTSD, dissociative disorder, or multiple personalities. Leaving momentarily or for short periods of time is not bad. It is a protective measure naturally wired into our system that helps us cope with what is happening in the moment.

The issue develops when you stay disembodied, or only partially embodied, as a daily state of being. Unfortunately, most people walk through their lives completely unaware of how unembodied they really are. You might even think of it as a form of dissociation. When this disembodiment becomes chronic or permanent, it is essentially a form of soul loss.

For people who have a history of sustained trauma, abuse, or neglect, what was originally a coping mechanism (checking out or leaving their body) to deal with acute episodes turned into a permanent state of being. Being permanently out of your body can become dangerous, not to mention contribute to the following feelings, conditions, and states of mind:

- Feelings of depression
- Spaciness
- Feelings of being lost or an outsider
- Difficulty focusing
- Difficulty making decisions
- Exhaustion or fatigue
- Lack of motivation or desire
- Physical clumsiness or incoordination
- Difficulty connecting with others
- Inability to complete projects
- Frequent injuries or accidents
- Disillusionment
- Inability to manifest
- Aloofness in relationships
- Fear of intimacy
- Extreme mood swings (apathy when out of the body, intensity when in the body)
- Inability to commit to or stay long-term in a relationship, project, job, or home

Disembodiment is like being drunk at the wheel of car. Alcohol impairs your judgment, reaction time, and ability to discern what is real and what isn't. Being unconsciously half-embodied is a dangerous but also highly unfulfilling way to live life because you are applying only a portion of your full life force to your existence. The rest of your life force has retracted out of you and is floating around, disembodied, or leaking out into the ether.

I discovered through my work with clients and students that I have the ability to perceive people's energy patterns, specifically tuning in to their emotional and energetic bodies. What I find with most people I've encountered is that they are embodied to roughly about their chest (the heart or fourth chakra), meaning that life-force energy is descending and circulating through their body downward from the crown, but not making it all the way down their body and grounding into the earth. They aren't "completing the circuit." Another way of describing this is that their life-force energy has retracted, like roots of a plant being pulled up, so their consciousness operates mainly in the upper chakras instead of their entire being. There are a lot of other factors I consider when determining people's level of embodiment and the challenges they face, which I won't go into here. But as a general gauge, most people hang out in the upper chakras. And there's good reason for this.

The lower chakras are more dense and vibrate at a lower frequency. They are where most of the "earth difficulties" lie. It can be painful to completely inhabit the third, second, and first chakras because those are the chakras that hold the majority of our pain, traumas, repressed feelings, fears, insecurities, and everything we don't want to look at, acknowledge, or deal with. The lower chakras focus on the real-world, daily, practical, human experience. The first three chakras are "turned on" in sequence and develop from the time we are in utero up to approximately four years of age. They are the foundation upon which our more "sophisticated" development occurs. It is amazing how many lifelong patterns of behavior get set during this period of time.

Let's briefly look at each of the lower three chakras in this context. The first chakra, or root, is the home of everything practical and physical and is involved in maintaining survival and support of the body itself. It is our roots. It is oriented to our physical identity and is concerned with self-preservation and our most basic survival as a human. When energy is blocked, repressed, or not flowing properly through the first chakra, it can show up in the following disempowering behaviors or feelings:

- Difficulty bringing a goal into full manifestation
- Feeling stuck
- Being afraid to take action or move forward
- Being afraid to take risks
- Experiencing paralyzing fear/anxiety
- Being resistant to change
- Being run by old patterns and limiting beliefs
- Believing in lack and limitation (there isn't enough to go around)
- Having only enough to survive or just get by
- Believing that life is a struggle
- Not being able to forgive/holding on to core wounds
- Operating from a scarcity mind-set

The second chakra, or sacral chakra, is the place of our emotions and feelings of desire; it is the place where we recognize that we want something. The second chakra is oriented to self-gratification and is the home of our emotional identity. It is also related to sexuality and pleasure. This is the first level of information coming into the body that tells us which way to "move" (what decision to make). If it feels good, we tend to move toward it. If it feels bad, we tend to move away.

When energy is blocked, repressed, or not flowing properly through the second chakra, it can show up in the following disempowering behaviors or feelings:

- Feeling overwhelmed
- Denying your feelings/acting the martyr

- Getting into power struggles with others
- Feeling guilty because of what you want
- Judging others
- Feeling undeserving
- Taking life too seriously
- Being rigid and lacking the ability to go with the flow
- Experiencing sexual dysfunction
- Making poor decisions motivated out of instant gratification

The third chakra, or solar plexus, is the place of our will, our personal power, and our vitality. It is oriented to self-definition, also called the ego identity or concept of self. It takes will and effort to get through the challenging parts of life, and the third chakra is where we direct our fire into some kind of activity toward achieving our purpose and goals.

When energy is blocked, repressed, or not flowing properly through the third chakra, it can show up in the following disempowering behaviors or feelings:

- Feeling unworthy or inferior
- Fearing failure
- Fearing success
- Engaging in negative self-talk or criticism
- Feeling victimized
- Being unable to complete projects
- Lacking willpower or determination
- Feeling self-doubt and insecurity
- Being unable to enforce your boundaries
- Giving away your power to others
- Being a control freak

These lower chakras are also closest to the ground (the root chakra is our grounding chakra, where we connect in to the earth), which means that when we are fully in our body, fully inhabiting all of the chakras, then we are fully present and can acutely feel the "weight" of our human existence. In this instance, weight doesn't imply "bad" so much as it does gravity. Imagine that you haven't been fully living in your body, and then all of a sudden you have an experience of full embodiment—registering every sensation, feeling, and experience. It can feel heavy, overwhelming, awkward, dense, limiting, and taxing. And there is a certain amount of truth to that. It takes effort to be in human form! It takes determination and courage to accept and embrace the full human experience, especially the most difficult aspects like living with the unknown, taking risks, or experiencing injustice, abuse, neglect, betrayal, abandonment, inequality, greed, human frailty, and death.

It is much easier to hang out in the upper chakras because they are lighter, more expansive, less dense, and less limiting; they just feel better. The upper chakras are more conceptual, archetypal, intellectual, and abstract. There we can contemplate life, the cosmos, spirituality, creative expression, dreams, symbolism, and philosophy. The point of view of the uppermost chakras is about the collective, so from there we can see the bigger picture and contemplate humanity and the issues of the planet as a whole. If we stay in the upper chakras, we don't have to deal with the core woundings, stored traumas, unresolved issues, and the most personal and private aspects of our individual life experience.

However, our ability to be fully embodied rests squarely on the solidity of our base (the first three chakras). If we aren't circulating our life force essence through our entire being, it is difficult to live a life of full consciousness. That is why it is so crucial that we do the work to heal our wounds and stabilize our foundation, manage our energy, draw boundaries, ask for what we need, speak our truth, and move out of mere survivalism. If we don't, then it will be nearly impossible to *hold the space for our own bigness* and to be able to handle and manage the awesome potential that we have the privilege of accessing as creators.

In *Creating on Purpose,* Anodea Judith and Lion Goodman explain that for something to come into form, it must travel down the chakra system; it starts as source consciousness received at the crown chakra and completes the cycle as matter (physical form) in the root chakra.[1] Do you realize the significance of this? Nothing happens without you! Take a moment to let that really sink in . . . you are a bridge between the realms of the unmanifest and the manifest, and nothing in *your* life comes into form without *you*. You really are a magical, creative, powerful being. But you have to inhabit yourself to experience the magic.

As evolutionary empaths, we chose to embrace a significant mission, and our ability to be effective at anchoring heart-centered consciousness—first in our own lives and then in our families and communities—is directly proportional to our ability to be in our bodies. Let me be clear . . . I absolutely spend time in altered states, connecting with my Spirit guides, traveling different realms of consciousness, and expanding my visionary capacity. But I always follow up those practices by bringing the conceptual, abstract, intangible, and subtle into the realm of the practical. Said another way, I bring my visions, revelations, and experiences down into my body and anchor them in the 3-D plane of my physical body, physical day-to-day reality, and physical relationships.

AVOIDING SPIRITUAL BYPASS

So many ancient spiritual and religious beliefs as well as current-day practices advocate the upward directing of our energy and focus with practices of transcendence, such as prayer, meditation, and chanting, which are intended to connect us to the divine or experience bliss or to help us forget our pain and suffering.

What I consider misguided interpretations expect us to believe that experiences of the body are unclean, shameful, ignoble, and undesirable, cause suffering, and, in extreme points of view, are even immoral or sinful. Ideally these base human emotions and experiences are to be avoided and bypassed, and when we are able to do so, it is a sign of enlightenment. In this type of philosophy, the only way to reach enlightenment is to transcend the physical body and the physical experience. The human experience is to be endured, and the only way to endure it is to practice rituals that take our consciousness *out* of our body. Many religions tell us that these practices are often the only way we can make ourselves acceptable in the eyes of God, and the more we practice rituals that take us out of our body and out of the human experience, the more holy we are considered. And, if we do want to "indulge" in earthly pleasures like accumulating possessions, having sex, or feeling our feelings, there's plenty of guilt and punishment promised to dissuade us.

I have a problem with this point of view. If the purpose of being in human form is to eschew everything human and do our best to re-create our experience of being one with God through practices that take us *out* of our body, then what is the point of incarnating in the first place? We could just stay in spirit form.

Anodea Judith, an expert on the chakra system, has conducted a great amount of research on ancient spiritual practices, wisdom teachings, and spiritual traditions across the globe. In *Creating on Purpose,* she says:

> When you follow only the upward current, denying your body and the material world, you may become spiritually strong but physically weak or ineffective. Temporary withdrawal from the material world is important from time to time, as it offers the ability to gain wider perspectives. But eventually, you must come back down to earth to apply what you've learned to the real world and deal with the situations around you.[2]

Let me be clear: spiritual practices that focus on the upward direction of our energy are important and necessary. And it certainly feels better than slogging through childhood wounds, facing our demons, owning our projections, and overcoming the voice of the Inner Critic. Looking for the good in difficult circumstances, practicing gratitude, meditating, praying, having compassion, using affirmations, developing your relationship with Spirit, seeing the magic in all of creation—*these are all vital and valuable practices.* I do them all myself.

However, if we consider only the "happy" or "positive" emotions and experiences to be valid and acceptable, then we are denying half of our human existence. There are enough influences in the world that would have us suppress the distasteful parts of ourselves; we don't need to add to that judgment and censorship with our own denial and repression!

Anger exists. Rage exists. Feelings of betrayal, abandonment, disillusionment, and worthlessness exist. Our Inner Critic exists. Depression exists. The ugly thoughts we have about hurting another person don't go away because we pretend the thoughts aren't there. Denying and suppressing something doesn't make it go away. In fact, denial causes us to revert to addictions and false personalities to maintain the illusion. Thinking you can avoid something only means you have to go into an addiction to suppress it.

I believe that one of our greatest spiritual challenges is to fully live a human life. Being embodied—and staying embodied—takes immense courage. This earth school is a unique opportunity for us to navigate and experience the full spectrum of human design. Transcendent spiritual practices are part of this experience, but I think too much emphasis has been placed on them, while not enough has been placed on the balance. One of our missions as humans is to weave the polarities of spirit and matter, mind and body, masculine and feminine, heaven and earth. This is what I mean by saying that we are a bridge, a conduit between Spirit and matter. We are at the point in our evolution where we are ready to take the leap from duality consciousness to unity consciousness. It is not about one or the other. It is about *both.* Can you hold the space inside yourself for the resolution of these "opposites"?

In her book *Wheels of Life,* Anodea Judith shares:

Most interpretations of the chakras focused on transcending our physical reality, portraying it as inferior or degenerate. Life is suffering, we are told, and the transcendent planes are its antidote. If life is suffering and transcendence the antidote, the logic of this equation implies that transcendence is counter to life itself. . . .

I do not believe that we need to sacrifice our zest for life and its enjoyment in order to advance spiritually. Nor do I see spirituality as antithetical to worldly existence, or that spiritual growth requires intense domination and control of our innate biological natures, hence of life itself. I belief this is part of a control paradigm, appropriate to a former age but inappropriate to the current challenges of our time. These challenges require models of integration rather than domination.[3]

We are full-spectrum humans. Said another way, we are all saints, and we are all murderers. (And if you believe in reincarnation and have lived enough lives, then quite literally you have probably been a saint and a murderer.) We must acknowledge that every possible expression of human behavior is within us. Pretending it isn't there doesn't make it go away. The point of being in a body isn't to escape or deny; it's to learn how to be both human *and* divine.

Our true power and strength come from inhabiting all of ourselves. And our greatest power? It lies hidden within our shadow. When we can face our fears, love the parts of us that we believe are unlovable, confront the stuff that scares us the most, and own every bit of who we are—good, bad, and ugly—then we multiply exponentially our ability to walk through this world fully grounded, present, and hiding from no one. And we can begin to own our empathic gifts and love ourselves for our uniqueness and courage.

Spiritual bypass is a term that means essentially living in the upper chakras and denying, avoiding, or bypassing the more base and distasteful human experiences and emotions. What does this look like in everyday life? It tends to show up in people who say, "I don't want to hear that negativity" when you need someone to talk to because your boss didn't put you in for an award for the massive project you just completed brilliantly, and your inner child is screaming. These are the fake, happy people who think all of life's problems can be fixed with a few simple affirmations: "God will provide"; "Everything happens for a reason"; "It will all work out." These are the therapists who cannot engage with you to any level of depth because they haven't gone to those depths within themselves! These are the disconnected clergy members who recite the same abstract, ineffectual, and impractical bible verses at funerals, marriage counseling sessions, and weddings because they have no idea what real human life feels like. These are the churches that only want to focus on the "light" and don't talk about things like the shadow, anger, or sexuality. These are the spiritual support groups that do "lite" spirituality and don't acknowledge real issues or offer any teachings or experiences of substance. These are the places and people with whom you don't feel you can be authentic or tell your truth. These energies make us feel like we have to pretend to be happy and that everything is just fine.

Please understand that I am not trying to lambaste these people or imply that I am somehow better than they are. I have been in bypass myself. We all have to some degree! We are all human and we all struggle to be present and do the right thing. But it is important to be able to understand and identify what spiritual bypass looks like, in both yourself and others. A big part of that discernment will be in how you feel. How do you feel when you are with that person, at that church, or in that social group?

Spiritual bypass is seductive, and it may seem like the person employing it is enlightened and has it all figured out. But ultimately it gets us nowhere. In his book *Spiritual Bypassing*, Robert Augustus Masters says, "Spiritual bypassing is the use of spiritual beliefs to unconsciously *avoid dealing with* painful feelings, unresolved wounds, and developmental needs. It's so pervasive, and largely goes unnoticed, and such actions often do more harm than good."[4]

Masters goes on to say that spiritual bypass is a very persistent shadow aspect of spirituality, manifesting in the following mind states or behaviors:

- Exaggerated detachment
- Emotional numbing and repression
- Overemphasis on the positive
- Anger-phobia
- Blind or overly tolerant compassion
- Weak or too porous boundaries
- Lopsided development (cognitive intelligence often being far ahead of emotional and moral intelligence)
- Debilitating judgment about one's negativity or shadow elements
- Devaluation of the personal relative to the spiritual
- Delusions of having arrived at a higher level of being[5]

So being a full-spectrum, embodied human being doesn't mean acting on every childish, narcissistic, self-indulgent, or enraged impulse we have. It simply means acknowledging the whole package and showing up fully in who we are, valuing all positions on the spectrum equally. As Linda Star Wolf says, "The light, the dark, no difference."[6] She is a fierce advocate of doing your shadow work.

Our history is replete with philosophies, religions, and systems of government that encourage and foster the split between mind and body, specifically with emphasis on the mind and deemphasis on the body. Recalling the discussion from chapter 10 on the masculine and feminine, this can be said another way. Remember that the masculine is associated with the head or intellect, and the feminine is associated with the heart, which includes feelings and experiences of the body. The subtext underneath all of the patriarchal teachings and especially spiritual traditions influenced by the patriarchy is, once again, that the masculine is of greater importance and value than the feminine.

As an empath, we have our work cut out for us because oftentimes our go-to moves include checking out, leaving our bodies, or dissociating in some way just to cope with all of the overwhelm and overstimulation. As with all of the practices in this book, baby steps are important.

IS IT REALLY THAT IMPORTANT TO BE EMBODIED?

It is easy to say, "Well, I've been doing fine up to this point and didn't even know embodiment was a thing. Why is it something I should put time and effort into?"

To that I would reply, "Have you really been doing fine?"

It is difficult to illustrate the critical nature of this topic because it is like so many medical diseases and conditions: the degradation is so slow or long-standing that it is almost impossible to have a clear comparison or memory that illustrates the difference between health and disease.

You might have heard of the boiling frog parable. Sorry if this is a bit morbid, but it illustrates the point. The premise is that if a frog is put suddenly into boiling water, it will jump out because it clearly registers the change in temperature and that the water is hot and life-threatening. However, if the frog is put in tepid water that is then brought to a slow boil, it will not perceive the danger because the temperature change occurs slowly enough that the frog will adapt. In this way the frog's system cannot register that the change in temperature is detrimental and therefore the frog will cook to death.

In the onset of many diseases and conditions, the decline in particular markers of health occurs so slowly that you don't recognize how degraded your quality of life is until something acute happens. You tire a little more quickly, you have occasional trouble remembering things, you have indigestion a little more than you used to, and your joints ache more frequently. These are all symptoms that are easy to dismiss or trivialize and conclude that they don't really point to any particular condition.

It is similar with the subject of embodiment. Refer back to the list of disembodiment symptoms from the "Disembodiment Epidemic" section of this chapter. Can you identify with any of these qualities?

As empaths, we signed up for a momentous job on a cosmic level. Only you can decide how important it is to pursue fuller embodiment. But I can almost guarantee you that you will be less effectual in every aspect of your existence—from the mundane to the profound, and especially in the area of soul purpose—if you do not learn to fully inhabit yourself and run all of your life-force energy.

To illustrate this, consider the importance of oxygen to human life. The oxygen carried in the blood is usually referenced as a percentage of the maximum amount of oxygen the blood can carry. Normal oxygen saturation levels range from 95 to 100 percent. Simply put, oxygen levels under 90 percent are considered low. This is a condition known as hypoxemia. So if your oxygen level drops a mere 10 percent, you can experience devastating effects such as shortness of breath, skin discoloration, confusion, rapid breathing, rapid heart rate, wheezing, sweating, and coughing. That 10 percent makes all the difference in the quality of life.

The concept of embodiment is similar. You may have grown so accustomed to disembodiment's version of hypoxemia that you don't even realize there is something amiss.

BEING PRESENT WITH
YOUR BODY AND EMOTIONS

Being fully embodied requires a diligent self-check-in practice. As I spoke about in chapter 7 when addressing how to manage your energy field, checking in with yourself multiple times a day is crucial in determining your state of being, the status of your energy container, what you've taken on that isn't yours or whom you've let into your field that doesn't need to be there, the amount of stress you're carrying in your physical body, and more. Now you can add gauging your level of embodiment to that check-in process.

If you can endeavor to be present and grounded, many other issues of disembodiment will resolve themselves naturally. If you refer back to the symptoms of disembodiment from the "Disembodiment Epidemic" section, you'll see that there is an intuitive connection between being present and grounded in your body and the resolution of many of the symptoms. If you are present and grounded, then your life-force energy is fully present and circulating through your entire body. It means that you are in the moment, focused on what is occurring, and being with whatever is present with you. When you are present, you are not lost in the past or the future. Your attention, energy, and consciousness are all gathered in the present moment.

Remember, embodiment can be most simply compared to being fully present, which is a suitable description of embodiment *in the moment*. But when you contemplate what embodiment means as a greater concept, you can think of it as *presence over time*. The practice of being present with your body and emotions is a moment-by-moment practice. Over time, you will be able to string together those moments into longer periods of embodiment. As this occurs, you'll most likely begin to realize that you can no longer ignore the unresolved issues, traumas, and woundings that are lingering in your field. A direct result of focusing on embodiment is doing your inner healing work. A direct result of doing your inner healing work is greater embodiment.

In addition to your check-in process, guided meditations are a great way to do a deep assessment of what is present in your body and emotions, especially if you are not adept at tuning in to yourself yet.

Please listen to track 6 of the audio tracks, "Meditation to Assess Your Physical and Emotional State," for a guided meditation to help you check in at any time with what is present in your physical and emotional bodies.

Reclaiming Your Identity: Living from Your Own Center

Growing up as an empath, I had no one in my young world who could identify or who valued my empathic nature, my sensitive nervous system, my wide-open heart, or my perceptions of energy and the unseen realms. I had no one to show me how to manage my energy or even help me understand what I was experiencing and why. It was not done deliberately or with malice; it was just that nobody in my sphere of influence knew what tools to teach me that would permit me to express these unique qualities yet still feel safe in the world. These priceless tools could have allowed me to keep hearing my own voice and stay in my center.

Instead, it was easier—and I really had no other choice—to abandon my empathic self wholesale in favor of practicality and fitting in. After years of getting emotionally and energetically decimated, I learned to shove it all underground and constructed elaborate, yet still inadequate, armor. Except armor is not a substitute for boundaries or self-care, neither of which I had.

In my earlier years I was not known for my ability to listen to Spirit's subtle (and not so subtle) attempts to get my attention. I completely ignored the whisper, the tap on the leg, the nudge on the arm, the elbow in the ribs, and even the slap on the back. It took a 2×4 to the forehead to get my attention. Spirit obliged.

The seeds of my spiritual initiation were planted in 2000 when I experienced a mild depression. I saw a counselor, simplified my life, tried (and immediately rejected) medication, and made a few profound discoveries about myself and my patterns that allowed me to relax and gain a new perspective on how to move forward. After about nine months or so, life seemed to be back on track. I now call these events the "prequake tremors."

I left the Air Force in 2002, after over a year of preparation for my new business as a financial advisor. I fully expected that this would be my career for the next five or ten or even fifteen years. My soul had other plans, and I quit after five and a half months because I hated it. My full-on, no-holds-barred spiritual awakening had begun in earnest, and I could no longer hold back the floodgates of change.

Carefully laid plans and expectations were destroyed. Everything began to fall apart. Everything was dying at once. In addition to embarking on (and then disembarking from) my new career, my marriage began to fall apart. My financial stability began to crumble. It felt like everything that I valued or counted on as solid somehow betrayed me. What I thought was "truth" was a facade or an illusion. I began to be stripped of everything I thought I knew. I had no idea who I was, what I wanted, or what to do next.

As I traveled through the experiences of my own awakening, I can tell you that I never thought I'd make it to the other side—I couldn't even imagine what the other side looked like! I cried, I screamed, I wallowed in despair and doubt, I shouted at God, and I was sure that I would never figure out how to control my emotions. For the first five years I was on an intensely accelerated path of transformation. I often describe that period of time as living a hundred years in the space of five.

In those five years, the physical losses were overwhelming. I lost $25,000 from quitting my financial planning business "too soon," I cashed in all of my investments, borrowed thousands from family, used up all my savings, got divorced, moved four times, was let go from two different jobs, was on unemployment twice, had garage sale after garage sale, took four loans against the cash value of my insurance policies, made my footprint smaller and smaller, lowered my standard of living, squeezed every ounce of money out of all the possessions I could spare, and relied heavily on my current husband for financial support.

The emotional and mental "damages" are much more difficult to quantify.

But what I can say is that this transformation required everything of me short of the "ultimate sacrifice." And though I didn't die in the flesh, I lived through the death of my former self. When I finally made it to the other side, nothing in my world looked the same. Home. Relationships. Marriage. Finances. Job. Self-image. Possessions. City. State. Nothing. As one of my friends said to me recently, "You don't do initiations lightly!"

So much of me—my identity, beliefs, values, patterns, dreams, expectations—got burned off in the molting. The fires of Kali, the Hindu goddess of death and destruction, were ruthless, yet surgically discriminate. Anything that was excess baggage, didn't serve me, or held me back got consumed. There wasn't much that survived the furnace, but what did survive was alchemically transformed into a new substance.

When my awakening began, I had no sense of my own self. Yet, when I finally stumbled out of the spiritual crucible, for the first time I had an inkling of who I was. The parts of my psyche, personality, and will that withstood and persisted after this massive shamanic death gave me a renewed sense of identity, purpose, and confidence. It's from this process that I was inspired to create my spiritual business and be of service to others on a similar path.

Though hard-won, I had, at long last, located my precious center.

THE ROAD TO WHOLENESS

My story is not uncommon. As humans, we don't do such a good job of listening to ourselves, our intuition, or the messages from Spirit when they first appear. We can be pretty bullheaded and arrogant. So it often takes a devastating upheaval to get our attention. Over time we learn to listen to ourselves sooner and don't require so much chaos and drama to motivate us toward change. However, in the beginning it can feel like the forces of the Universe are stacked against us. I suspect that you can relate. As empaths, it's even more challenging. Getting to know who we are and learning to stay in our center can seem like almost impossible undertakings.

While I would love to tell you that returning to wholeness and living life using your own compass will be easy and here's the ten-step process to follow in precise order, I can't. Because it's not the truth. There is no one formula, and it doesn't happen within a prescribed time frame, and it is not a linear process. Reclaiming your identity and living from your center will take time, effort, and commitment. It will be confusing, demanding, exasperating, agonizing, heartbreaking, baffling, and laborious. There will be casualties. And it will be totally worth every second, every setback, and every scar.

As a collective—remember the empathic "big bang" I spoke of?—our current path as evolutionary empaths is like storming the beaches of Normandy on D-Day. We are the first wave. There's likely to be a huge amount of attrition, but our stalwart souls knew we could do it. There is a bigger purpose being served, and it is our time. It may be the hardest undertaking of your life, but I promise you, you *can* discover who you are and reclaim your sense of self. You *can* learn to trust yourself and lead with your heart. You *can* be—and *are*—a pioneer. You came here for a *big* mission. When the strength of your body fails you, lean on the strength of your soul. Your soul knows. It has the blueprint.

You were built for these times. Your soul chose to come here in the precise configuration that makes you, you. Showing up as anything less than you—even 99 percent of you—is not enough. Coming back to yourself and standing in your absolute authentic self is the most important undertaking of your life. The world cannot benefit from your brilliance when you are not inhabiting yourself. You must come home to yourself.

Do your inner work. Reclaim your shadow. Acknowledge your masculine and feminine. Embody yourself fully. Embrace your humanity and your divinity. Add tools to your toolbox. Heal your wounds. Make amends. Raise your awareness. Trust your heart. This is the work of returning to wholeness. It is the unspoken subtitle of this book.

EXTERNAL VS. INTERNAL VALIDATION: MOVING FROM YOU DEFINE ME TO I DEFINE ME

It is normal in early developmental stages to seek external validation. We need to know that we are loved by our parents and that our basic needs will be attended to. We need touch, affection, reassurance, and constant care in the beginning. Yet part of healthy childhood development includes increasing phases of autonomy.

Especially in Western society, the messages we receive about our own personal authority are conflicting and undermining. Anodea Judith speaks of it as fighting a legacy from previous generations that believed in the ultimate authority of God over man, man over woman, and parent over child.[1] This means that we don't enter the world with a level playing field. The deck is stacked against us from the beginning. There are very few influences that advocate for personal authority, so we must do the difficult work of cultivating it for ourselves in the face of so many influences that would tell us we are wrong. Or going to hell.

As empaths, we have even more to overcome because we are wired to be "other" centered. Remember, our nature is to blend and merge. While this can be a valuable tool in specific circumstances, it can no longer be our modus operandi. The job of learning to live from our center requires that we move our locus of experience from outside of us to inside of us. We need to learn to be centered on self, not centered on others. We need to learn to validate ourselves, not rely on validation from others.

In *Eastern Body, Western Mind*, Anodea Judith says:

> Without relationship to the self, reflective consciousness is impossible. We are cut adrift, disconnected from our ground, lost and lonely and end up seeking our ground through another. They become our reality, and the weight we impose upon them—the weight of our own self-denial—usually drives them away. We then lose all the energy we have invested in them, including pieces of ourselves. . . . When we give everything, we bankrupt ourselves. We lack a center to which others can be attracted because, quite simply, no one is home. There is no one inside us to love because we have given ourselves away.[2]

Ouch. For me personally, this describes perfectly the first thirty or so years of my life. I didn't know who I was and didn't feel I was "enough" on my own. My value, my worth, was defined by everything outside of me. As I moved into adulthood and my authentic self was met with more and more disapproval, I abandoned myself and learned to drop my anchor in another person. That person became my center, and I would lose myself in that person. I didn't know how to inhabit myself. My core was vacant.

Learning to define yourself will take time and effort. Later in this chapter I provide tools and exercises for exploring your inner landscape and discovering your preferences, desires, likes, dislikes, values, and more. But it's important to recognize that the big shift is moving from looking for validation outside of yourself to seeking validation inside. You validate you. What does this mean? At the most basic level, it means that you accept yourself, love yourself, are compassionate with yourself, trust yourself, and believe in yourself. You decide what is right and wrong for you.

Deservedness and worthiness issues often get triggered when learning to validate yourself. As empaths, we don't usually have a strong sense of self, and our self-worth has been unconsciously defined by how good we are at tending to others' needs. There might be some serious work for you to do to learn to *believe* that you are enough—that you are worthy of advocating for yourself, that you deserve it, that your needs matter. You may not even know what your needs are in the first place. This is all part of the journey. As I said before, transformation and change occur in a nonlinear, spiral path, and when you work on one aspect of yourself, it will affect others. When you do the work of learning to validate yourself, you will become more adept at recognizing and asking for what you need. As you do the work to recognize and ask for what you need, you will become more adept at validating yourself. It is the same with all of these tools.

RECLAIMING YOUR IDENTITY: THE EXERCISES

By practicing pieces from each of the chapters in part 2 of this book—tools in your Evolutionary Empath Tool Kit—you will begin to recover aspects of your personality and inhabit yourself more fully. It bears repeating that this is a journey and not a destination, so be sure to address your own expectations in the process. Give yourself permission for it to unfold however it needs to, and understand that as you shift, your external world will most likely shift in some way as a consequence. Most of us have more experience living as an unconscious empath than as a conscious one. Reclaiming your identity and living from your center will be a lifelong pursuit, but the benefits begin immediately.

The exercises I have included in this section provide opportunities to get to know yourself at a deeper level, to remember parts of yourself that you might have forgotten, and to begin to define yourself separately from your parents. Use whichever ones call to you.

Before I dive in, allow me to make a quick qualification. There are many ways to approach the topic of "who am I?" In this discussion, I assume the spiritual identity piece—we are all one, we are all individuations of Spirit with equal abilities as creators, and we are all spiritual beings having a human experience—yet, at the same time, we chose to be in a body. This section is about exploring the *human aspect* of who you are.

☼ Personality Assessment Systems

There are all manner of personality tests and other systems available, if you resonate with this type of tool. Here are several for your consideration:

- **Myers-Briggs Type Indicator, or MBTI.** Based on the ideas of Carl Jung, this assessment shows whether you are an introvert or an extrovert and to what degree you understand the world through sensation, intuition, feeling, and thinking. (A variety of websites offer this test for free, including the HumanMetrics website and the Truity: Scientific Personality and Career Tests Online website.)

- **DiSC Assessment.** This test evaluates behavior by focusing on the traits of dominance, inducement, submission, and compliance. (The test can be taken for free at the Discprofile website or the 123test website.)

- **The Winslow Personality Profile.** This assessment measures career success and happiness by evaluating twenty-four personality traits to help you find your strengths. (The test can be taken for free at the Winslow Assessment website.)

- **The Enneagram.** This is a model of nine personality types: reformers, helpers, achievers, individualists, investigators, loyalists, enthusiasts, challengers, and peacemakers. (The test can be taken for free at the Enneagram Institute website.)

♥ **Shamanic Astrology.** Shamanic astrology, as sourced by Daniel Giamario and my friend and colleague Cayelin Castell, is different from traditional astrology in that it does not emphasize sun signs but rather operates through an archetypal and mythical framework that is anchored in the "as above, so below" mysteries. You are welcome to use any school of astrology that speaks to you, as they all provide slightly different perspectives.

☼ Three Characteristics

In this exercise, you'll go back to the checklist in the "Are You An Empath?" section in chapter 4. From that list, select three characteristics or traits that have been the biggest struggle or biggest source of pain, frustration, or confusion in your life. In your journal or notebook, write the qualities down and then answer the following two questions for each quality:

1. What have I learned from this characteristic or experience; what is its *gift* to me?
2. What do I know about myself as a result of this characteristic or experience?

Before you begin writing, close your eyes, call upon your higher self, and connect to that wisdom and greater perspective. Allow yourself to be a channel for your highest wisdom. Go deep within, allow the wisdom to flow through your pen, and write from the perspective of this higher consciousness. If you've ever done automatic writing, this is similar. You are meant to be conscious and connected to the experience while it's happening, so if you leave your body or detach when you do automatic writing, then intend that you will stay fully present and allow higher wisdom to inform you.

You can do this exercise with as many qualities from the list as you like. Exploring too many qualities at one time can be overwhelming, which is why I suggest starting with three. Come back to this exercise as often as needed.

☼ One Hundred Things

When I assigned this exercise to one of my clients, you'd have thought I asked her to climb Mount Everest. This was one of the hardest things she had ever done because she was so used to defining herself through others that she was clueless about who she was.

The exercise is simple. Make a list of one hundred things you know about yourself. Here are some examples from my own list:

1. I don't like roller coasters because they make my body hurt.
2. Whenever something bad happens, I always blame myself first.
3. I need a fair amount of regular time by myself.
4. I love horses. When I'm with them, I don't care about the heat, cold, or being hungry; I don't think about anything else but being in the moment.
5. I am the princess in "The Princess and the Pea" when it comes to sleeping: I can't sleep on hard surfaces, and I am very sensitive to noises and new places.
6. I like living in a climate with four seasons. I enjoy the change in weather and temperature.

☼ How Does Your Body Communicate with You?

Our bodies contain a highly developed system of sensors and receptors that provide foolproof ways of telling us how we feel about something. For whatever reason, you might have turned your sensors off. If so, I encourage you to give your body, your feelings, and your internal communication system *permission* to transmit to you and to receive the messages. Your body will *always* have the answer. Our reactions to everything always register in the body; we just have to learn to identify them again. Often, people will feel something in their gut, chest, or heart space. Maybe you get flushed or have shivers.

Here are a couple of examples from my body. When I experience something as being the truth for me (such an aha moment, somebody giving an accurate perspective of an event, reading an oracle card), I will momentarily tear up or choke up. Another way my body talks to me is that when I get tired and I'm pushing myself too hard and need to rest, I will get sick to my stomach and very cranky. My solar plexus (third chakra, place of personal power) will get hard and knotted, as if I am literally trying to gut through instead of rest, or force things instead of being in a place of receiving.

Over time you will begin to recognize what happens physiologically when you encounter something that resonates as truth, or when you encounter something that your system does not want. This can apply to anything, from the food you want to eat to a decision you need to make to your impression of a person you've just met. Keep a journal and note the ways your body communicates with you.

☼ Explore Your Parents' Values

The idea behind this exercise is to externalize your internal dialogue, values, expectations, and beliefs. When something's in our own head, it can be difficult to determine if it's really our truth or not. If you see the quality outside of you, it is easier to have a clearer reaction to it. So many of the rules we live our life by, especially in our first few decades, are overwhelmingly influenced by our parents. By exploring your parents' values by writing them on paper, you can begin to analyze them objectively. This will allow you to see patterns and have a more honest reaction to them. You might realize, "Wow! I do that exact same thing, but it really isn't my belief or my value or my behavior; it was my mother's."

On a piece of paper, make a column for each of the major

influences in your childhood through age sixteen, such as parent(s), step-parent(s), or grandparent(s). Write their name at the top of each column.

Now, write down as many things as you can remember about each person when you were growing up. Here are some to consider:

- What did they value? What was important to them?
- What sayings did they always say when you were growing up?
- How did they react to adversity? To unexpected abundance or gifts?
- What were their common behaviors?
- What were their favorite hobbies or pastimes?
- What was their prevailing mood?
- How did they react to their children?
- What was their view of parenting?
- What were their priorities?
- What did they complain about?
- What made them the most angry?
- What did they try to "hammer into you?"
- What was their view of religion/spirituality?
- What were they afraid of?
- How did they react when things didn't go their way?
- What did they do to vent or release frustration?

Now go through the list and begin to distinguish between what you were exposed to and absorbed growing up and what is truly your own belief or value. This can be a time-consuming process, so do it in stages if that helps you work through it without overwhelm. Begin to consider each entry and clearly decide if that belief or value really resonates with you or not. If it doesn't, give yourself permission to let it go. It doesn't make you wrong, and it doesn't make your parents wrong. This is an exercise in getting clear about who you are (and who you aren't).

☼ *Take an Energy Inventory*

It is easy to be influenced by what other people want or expect from us. Because of this, it can be immensely confusing to figure out what is authentically our truth (or passion, desire, need, goal, dream, etc.) among countless external energies and influences. Add to that our propensity to give until we have nothing left and to put everyone else ahead of ourselves, and we can become drained, unfulfilled, and resentful before we realize what has happened.

It is helpful from time to time (once a quarter or a couple of times a year) to take an energy inventory. This means making a list of everything that's in your life, everything that you have chosen to invest energy into, and then asking yourself, "Does this feed me or does this drain me?"

What you're considering is if they are authentic expressions of you or things you are engaging in to try to give yourself meaning, purpose, status, favor, acceptance, et cetera. Things that are an authentic and true expression of yourself almost always feed you and do not drain you.

When you do this exercise, make sure that your list includes the following categories:

- Relationships
- Hobbies/recreational activities
- Family obligations/responsibilities/children
- Job/work
- Workouts or physical activities
- Church and community
- Household chores
- Education or personal enrichment

Be as thorough as possible. This list is just a place to start, so feel free to add as many additional categories as necessary. Consider keeping the list where you· can access it in three or six months to check in on your energy inventory in the future.

☼ What Makes You Feel Light and Expansive?

This exercise is one you can use anytime, during any situation, to assess if something is in alignment with your truth. Almost universally, if something is in alignment with your truth, it will cause you to feel light and expansive. If you'd like to use this as an exploratory exercise, you could make a list of activities, decisions, relationships, or other items of question and feel into your answer with each one, asking yourself, "Does this make me feel light and expansive or heavy and contracted?"

Since we as empaths are so good at sensing subtle energies, it should be pretty easy for us to determine when something feels heavy, dense, and contractive versus light and expansive. This is a way to discern if something rings true for you, Is something you're attracted to, or is something that resonates with you. What is beneficial and in alignment with your authentic self will feel light and expansive. For some people it might even feel like a sense of relief. What is not beneficial or out of alignment with your authentic self will feel heavy, dense, and contractive.

Before you do this exercise, though, there is one critical distinction to make. Resistance can sometimes read as heaviness. Sometimes our reaction to something might *feel* heavy, but it's because we are experiencing resistance. Resistance is not necessarily a clear and immediate indication of "no." It is something to be explored. It means you just got triggered. Resistance is a flag that tells us there's an opportunity to learn more about ourselves and possibly heal a wound or fear. Once we have explored it, the final answer might be a yes or it might be a no. So you will need to be very honest with yourself and learn to discern the difference between your internal solid no and an initial resistance that shows up out of fear.

☼ Make Decisions with Your Heart

Making decisions with your heart is all about remembering how to use your feelings as a navigation system. Your body and your feelings will tell you the truth every time. You just have to remember how to listen to the signals. Several years ago I recorded *How to Make Decisions with Your Heart: A Guided Meditation,* which leads you through a powerful visualization process you can use over and over to get a clear and accurate reading from your heart and emotions.

In most Western-style societies, and for many centuries, more value has been placed on the masculine qualities than on the feminine qualities. Making decisions with your head (i.e., masculine principles of logic, reason, what can be proven, etc.) has been valued over making decisions using your heart, emotions, intuition, or feelings. The way back home—the way back to your center—is through the heart. Said another way: lose your mind and come to your senses!

Using this meditation can help you develop "muscle memory" so that, over time, you can gauge your reaction to any situation accurately and instantly. This meditation is available for purchase at www.bluestartemple.org/meditations.

☼ Who Were You as a Child?

Exploring who you were as a child before the world began to unduly influence your behaviors and decisions can be a fantastic way to help you remember who you are and to regain your center. *Disclaimer: This may or may not be helpful depending on your childhood experiences. Some people have very few memories of childhood. Some people have repressed much of their childhood. You might choose to ask one or both of your parents, if it's possible, to gain perspective on your likes, dislikes, and inclinations as a child. If you don't feel this exercise would be helpful, don't use it.*

For this exercise, you will simply write in your journal about yourself as a child. How did you play? What activities were you attracted to? How did you respond to people around you? What did you spend time imagining? What were your "prized" possessions? What did you want to be when you grew up?

Here are some themes for me that were very present as a child that are core pieces of me now: Native American spirituality, horses, love of natural elements (rocks, stones, trees, fur, etc.), fantasizing about magical objects, being in nature, being physically active, climbing trees, exploring, and being sensitive to others' emotions.

☼ Ask Other People

I'm sure that asking other people might sound counterintuitive when we've talked so much about trying to extricate ourselves from everyone else's ideas, desires, emotions, habits, and so on. But here's what I mean: Sometimes we can't see ourselves at all, and it helps to have a trusted friend or relative to reflect ourselves back to us. I imagine that there are at least a couple of people in your life who have known you for a very long time, maybe since you were a child and who have seen you at your best and your worst. This should be someone you trust implicitly, someone you know will tell you the truth.

For this exercise, simply ask them how they see you. You can conduct this as a conversation, or you can ask them to write things down and send them to you. Ask them what words they would use to describe you and to give you examples of things you did or said that they would describe as "so you." Ask them about the qualities they think of when they think of you. Ask them about common reactions, habits, or preferences they have observed in you. Be sure to give them a little context, so they understand why you're asking and what purpose this exercise is serving.

Please listen to track 7 of the audio tracks, "Meditation to Stay in Your Center," for a meditation to help you stay in your center.

FROM LIABILITY TO ASSET

The ability to view being an empath as a gift doesn't happen at the wave of a magic wand. However, embracing your empathic nature is a natural outcome of doing all of the inner work and practices recommended in this book. Ultimately, viewing your abilities as a gift is a *choice*, and it's your choice. But that choice comes at a price.

The price of viewing your empathic abilities as a gift is that you don't get to claim to be the victim anymore. When you make the choice to see your abilities as gifts, that is the precise moment that you take full and complete responsibility for yourself. When you do that, being a victim can no longer exist in the same space.

Viewing your empathic abilities as a gift also allows you to own your uniqueness and the individual expression of your empathic abilities. Viewing them as a gift marks a major shift in your perspective; your empathic nature is no longer an aspect of yourself that you do battle with or wish you didn't have but a set of characteristics that you recognize as having great value in the world. You begin to "use your powers for good." You come to a state of peace and acceptance with this part of yourself. You begin to acknowledge that all of the experiences you have had in life have led you to this point. They have shaped who you are today in this moment.

Embracing your empathic gifts means that you no longer disown or keep in the shadow this major part of yourself. When you own the contribution that you are, you are then fully in "the light," unafraid to see and be seen by others. Our greatest source of pain and conflict is always our most powerful medicine. Your conscious walk as an evolutionary empath will radically change how you show up in the world. You can use the following exercise and meditation to explore this in more depth.

☼ My Empathic Gifts and the Value They Provide

Draw a vertical line down the middle of a piece of paper to make two columns. Label the left column "My Empathic Gifts" and label the right column "The Value They Bring to the World." If you don't know where to begin, you might choose to look at the checklist in the "Are You an Empath?" section in chapter 4 to give you ideas to populate the left column.

After you complete the above step, circle three of the gifts that you consider to be your most powerful or that have the potential to be your "strongest medicine." For each of these three, journal about what you can do to further develop or apply the gift. Think about times this gift helped you or helped others. Creating this list will aid you in forging a new relationship with your empathic qualities and, hopefully, your acceptance of the cosmic role you are here to play.

Please listen to track 8 of the audio tracks, "Meditations to Connect with Your Gifts," for a meditation that will connect to your gifts.

Self-acceptance is a soothing and much-needed balm for empaths and is really the outcome of viewing your gifts as an asset instead of liability. After a lifetime of rejection, denial, confusion, overwhelm, internal conflict, and all of the other traveling companions of the unconscious empath, self-acceptance is our much-deserved prize at the end of the race. Self-acceptance brings with it self-love, confidence, focus, passion, authenticity, clarity, courage, discernment, and so many other wonderful gifts. Allow yourself to deliver and receive the love, validation, support, and acceptance you have longed for.

YOU ARE THE EMERGING EVOLUTIONARY EMPATH

You chose to be an empath. Your intrepid soul made the decision to come into this existence with a special set of qualities uniquely designed to evolve human consciousness toward a heart-centered existence as we move along our path of ascension. You are part of the first wave of stalwart spirits designed to break apart the old paradigms and establish an entirely new way of relating to all of life. You chose to come here at this specific point in the turning of the age and in the cycle of the Great Year. Do not underestimate the significance of your life experience or your contribution to the cosmos.

Step into your soul's mission! Start from wherever you are. The "outer trappings" (your job, house, city, etc.) don't have to change for you to embrace your deeper purpose, and they don't decide the extent of your contribution to the planet. Be who you are, wherever you are. Doingness comes from beingness! Be you in your relationships. Be you at the grocery store and gas station. Be you at the movie theater and at parties. Be you at home alone and in a crowd of people. Be you with the kids and with strangers. Don't undervalue the difference you can make "just" by being your authentic self.

You are an evolutionary empath. The morphic field of the empath has been established, and you can draw strength from it and contribute strength to it. You are here to raise the collective vibration of humanity and the planet. Your conscious awareness holds a vibratory field that invites others to join in and is magnified by every other person moving into higher consciousness. As one person, you make a difference. Trust your heart. Use your tools. You were made for these times.

I leave you with the words of Walt Whitman . . .

O Me! O Life!

O Me! O life! of the questions of these recurring;
Of the endless trains of the faithless, of cities fill'd with
the foolish;
Of myself forever reproaching myself, (for who more
foolish than I, and who more faithless?)
Of eyes that vainly crave the light, of the objects mean—
of the struggle ever renew'd;

Of the poor results of all, of the plodding and sordid
*   crowds I see around me;*
Of the empty and useless years of the rest, with the rest
*   me intertwined;*
The question, O me! so sad, recurring, What good amid
*   these, O me, O life?*

Answer.
That you are here—that life exists, and identity,
That the powerful play goes on, and you will contribute
*   a verse.*

How to Use the *Evolutionary Empath* Audio Tracks

When introduced to any new subject matter, engaging with the material in multiple ways helps me anchor the concepts and principles in my physical reality and move them from the conceptual realm to the visceral realm. Especially when the topic is nonphysical, intangible, or subtle—such as energy, emotions, feelings, patterns, thought processes, spirituality—it is vital that you develop your own relationship with and felt understanding of the concepts. The eight audio tracks that accompany this book are designed to give you a direct experience with your body, energy field, a variety of archetypes, and your unique empathic qualities. In this way you can begin to embody the knowledge as *body wisdom* instead of just "knowing about them."

Because the audio tracks are guided meditations, they should be played when you have the appropriate setting available. This includes a quiet space where you will not be interrupted and time to be present with the journey, instead of cramming it in before rushing off to another obligation. Take your time and be open to each experience. I encourage you to have a journal nearby and to write about any notable aspects after you finish each track.

It is not critical that you listen to every single guided meditation. If the subject of a particular track doesn't appeal to you, trust your intuition. You may choose to listen to the tracks in the order in which they are mentioned in the book, or you are welcome to listen to them in your own preferred order. However, I do recommend you at least read the chapter that the audio track is contained within so you have a greater context for the guided journey. Also, feel free to listen to a track as many times as you desire, as some are designed to build a skill or awareness. The audio tracks can be downloaded at

audio.innertraditions.com/evoemp

1. "Where Are My Edges?" (chapter 7)
2. "Meditation to Connect with Your Inner Masculine" (chapter 10)
3. "Meditation to Connect with Your Inner Feminine" (chapter 10)
4. "Meditation to Connect with Your Physical Body" (chapter 12)
5. "Meditation to Identify and Release Stored Emotions" (chapter 12)
6. "Meditation to Assess Your Physical and Emotional State" (chapter 13)
7. "Meditation to Stay in Your Center" (chapter 14)
8. "Meditation to Connect with Your Gifts" (chapter 14)

Notes

INTRODUCTION:
A WISH, A MISSION, AND
A HUNDRED MONKEYS

1. Martin, "Morphic Field and Morphic Resonance."

CHAPTER 2. THE GREAT YEAR
AND CURRENT CYCLE OF ASCENSION

1. Cruttenden, *Lost Star,* 106.
2. Cruttenden, *Lost Star,* 111.
3. NASA's Chandra X-Ray Observatory website, quoted in Cruttenden, *Lost Star,* 111.
4. Cruttenden, *Lost Star,* 178.
5. Cruttenden, *Lost Star,* 179.
6. Hunt, *Infinite Mind,* 30.
7. Hunt, *Infinite Mind,* 31.
8. Hunt, *Infinite Mind,* 31.
9. Hunt, *Infinite Mind,* 31–32.
10. Hunt, *Infinite Mind,* 32–33.
11. Cruttenden, *Lost Star,* 184.
12. Cruttenden, *Lost Star,* 52.
13. Cruttenden, *Lost Star,* 71.
14. Cruttenden, *Lost Star,* 73.

15. Ruby Falconer, personal communication with the author.

16. Ascension Symptoms website, "Ascension Signs and Symptoms."

17. Alleyne, "Welcome to the Information Age."

CHAPTER 3.
EVOLUTION OF THE EMPATH

1. Judith, *Eastern Body, Western Mind,* 10–11.

2. Judith, *Global Heart,* 23.

3. Judith, *Global Heart,* 27.

4. Judith, *Global Heart,* 3.

5. Berman, *Dark Ages America,* 245.

6. Roser, "Child Mortality."

CHAPTER 6. NO MORE DENIAL:
WE ARE THE NEW HUMAN BLUEPRINT

1. Miro-Quesada, "Pachakuti Mesa Tradition Quechua Terminology," 2.

2. Wolf, *Shamanic Breathwork,* 81.

3. Wolf, *Shamanic Breathwork,* 80.

PART 2.
THE EVOLUTIONARY EMPATH TOOL KIT:
THE PRACTICE OF BEING HUMAN AND DIVINE

1. Cruttenden, *Lost Star,* 73.

CHAPTER 8. BOUNDARIES:
YOU AND I ARE ONE, BUT WE ARE NOT THE SAME

1. Taylor, *My Stroke of Insight,* 143.

CHAPTER 9. BOUNDARIES: THE 3-D APPLICATION

1. Ury, *The Power of a Positive No,* 10.

CHAPTER 10. EMBRACING THE
DIVINE MASCULINE AND FEMININE
AS CONSCIOUS EQUAL PARTNERS

1. Sharma, *The Monk Who Sold His Ferrari,* 51.
2. Giamario with Castell, *Shamanic Astrology Handbook,* 162.

CHAPTER 11.
STOP TRYING TO GET
BACK INTO THE GARDEN

1. Myss, *Archetype Cards,* 70.
2. Harvey, *The Hope,* 120.
3. Harvey, *The Hope,* 121.

CHAPTER 13.
BECOMING MORE FULLY EMBODIED

1. Judith and Goodman, *Creating on Purpose,* 11.
2. Judith and Goodman, *Creating on Purpose,* 16.
3. Judith, *Wheels of Life,* xiv.
4. Masters, "Spiritual Bypassing."
5. Masters, "Spiritual Bypassing."
6. Linda Star Wolf often makes this statement in her workshops, podcasts, and online posts.

CHAPTER 14.
RECLAIMING YOUR IDENTITY:
LIVING FROM YOUR OWN CENTER

1. Judith, *Eastern Body, Western Mind,* 191.
2. Judith, *Eastern Body, Western Mind,* 255.

Bibliography

Alleyne, Richard. "Welcome to the Information Age—174 Newspapers a Day." *Telegraph,* February 11, 2011.

Aron, Elaine. *The Highly Sensitive Person.* New York: Three Rivers Press, 2001.

Ascension Symptoms website. "Ascension Signs and Symptoms." Accessed August 21, 2018.

Berman, Morris. *Dark Ages America. The Final Phase of Empire.* New York: W. W. Norton, 2006.

Cruttenden, Walter. *Lost Star of Myth and Time.* Pittsburgh, Pa.: St. Lynn's Press, 2006.

Giamario, Daniel, with Cayelin K. Castell. *The Shamanic Astrology Handbook.* Instantpublisher.com, 2012.

Harvey, Andrew. *The Hope: A Guide to Sacred Activism.* Carlsbad, Calif.: Hay House, 2009.

Hawkins, David R. *Power vs. Force.* Carlsbad, Calif.: Hay House, Inc., 2002.

Hunt, Valerie. *Infinite Mind: Science of the Human Vibrations of Consciousness.* Malibu, Calif.: Malibu Publishing, 1996.

Judith, Anodea. *Eastern Body, Western Mind: Psychology and the Chakra System as a Path to the Self.* New York: Celestial Arts, 2004.

———. *The Global Heart Awakens.* San Rafael, Calif.: Shift Books, 2013.

———. *Wheels of Life.* Woodbury, Minn.: Llewellyn Publications, 2015.

Judith, Anodea, and Lion Goodman. *Creating on Purpose.* Boulder, Colo.: Sounds True, 2012.

Martin, Yolanda Zigarmi. "Morphic Field and Morphic Resonance." Spiritual Resources website, posted September 2013.

Masters, Robert Augustus. "Spiritual Bypassing: When Spirituality Disconnects Us from What Really Matters." Robert Masters website.

Miro-Quesada, Oscar. "Pachakuti Mesa Tradition Quechua Terminology." Handout from the Path of the Universal Shaman Advanced Intensive. Copyright 2014.

Myss, Carolyn. *Archetype Cards*. Carlsbad, Calif.: Hay House, 2003.

Roser, Max. "Child Mortality." Published online in 2019 by Our World in Data website.

Sharma, Robin. *The Monk Who Sold His Ferrari: A Fable About Fulfilling Your Dreams and Reaching Your Destiny*. San Francisco: HarperSanFrancisco, 1999.

Taylor, Jill Bolte. *My Stroke of Insight: A Brain Scientist's Personal Journey*. New York: Penguin Group, 2006.

Tolle, Eckhart. *A New Earth: Awakening to Your Life's Purpose*. New York: Plume, 2006.

Ury, William. *The Power of a Positive No: Save the Deal, Save the Relationship— and Still Say No*. New York: Bantam Dell, 2007.

Wolf, Linda Star. *Shamanic Breathwork: Journeying beyond the Limits of the Self*. Rochester, Vt.: Bear & Company, 2009.

Index

BOOKS OF RELATED INTEREST

Soul Whispering
The Art of Awakening Shamanic Consciousness
by Linda Star Wolf, Ph.D., and Nita Gage, DSPS, MA
Foreword By Richard Rudd

Shamanic Breathwork
Journeying beyond the Limits of the Self
by Linda Star Wolf, Ph.D.
Foreword by Nicki Scully

Womb Awakening
Initiatory Wisdom from the Creatrix of All Life
by Azra Bertrand, M.D., and Seren Bertrand

Unlocking the 7 Secret Powers of the Heart
A Practical Guide to Living in Trust and Love
by Shai Tubali

Power Animal Meditations
Shamanic Journeys with Your Spirit Allies
by Nicki Scully

Dancing with Raven and Bear
A Book of Earth Medicine and Animal Magic
by Sonja Grace

Ancestral Healing for Your Spiritual and Genetic Families
by Jeanne Ruland and Shantidevi

INNER TRADITIONS • BEAR & COMPANY
P.O. Box 388
Rochester, VT 05767
1-800-246-8648
www.InnerTraditions.com

Or contact your local bookseller